URBAN SORES

Urban Sores
On the interaction between segregation, urban decay and deprived neighbourhoods

HANS SKIFTER ANDERSEN
Danish Building and Urban Research Institute

LONDON AND NEW YORK

First published 2003 by Ashgate Publishing

Reissued 2018 by Routledge
2 Park Square, Milton Park, Abingdon, Oxon OX14 4RN
711 Third Avenue, New York, NY 10017, USA

Routledge is an imprint of the Taylor & Francis Group, an informa business

Copyright © Hans Skifter Andersen, 2003

The author has asserted his moral right under the Copyright, Designs and Patents Act, 1988, to be identified as the author of this work.

All rights reserved. No part of this book may be reprinted or reproduced or utilised in any form or by any electronic, mechanical, or other means, now known or hereafter invented, including photocopying and recording, or in any information storage or retrieval system, without permission in writing from the publishers.

Notice:
Product or corporate names may be trademarks or registered trademarks, and are used only for identification and explanation without intent to infringe.

Publisher's Note
The publisher has gone to great lengths to ensure the quality of this reprint but points out that some imperfections in the original copies may be apparent.

Disclaimer
The publisher has made every effort to trace copyright holders and welcomes correspondence from those they have been unable to contact.

A Library of Congress record exists under LC control number: 2002027922

ISBN 13: 978-1-138-72523-2 (hbk)
ISBN 13: 978-1-138-72521-8 (pbk)
ISBN 13: 978-1-315-19198-0 (ebk)

Contents

List of Figures vi
List of Tables viii

1 Introduction 1

2 Social Segregation in Cities 13

3 The Appearance of Urban Decay and Deprivation in Western Cities 46

4 Explanations of Decay in the Urban Housing Market 55

5 Processes of Social and Physical Decay in Deprived Urban Neighbourhoods 98

6 Understanding Deprived Neighbourhoods – the Connection between Segregation and Neighbourhood Decay 125

7 Efforts to Combat Urban Decay 130

Bibliography 184
Index 197

List of Figures

2.1	The interaction between changes in social and spatial differentiation in cities	23
2.2	Greater Copenhagen divided into ring zones and sectors	26
2.3	Families with children as a proportion of all households, and elderly more than 65 years old as a proportion of the whole population, in different parts of Greater Copenhagen 1996	27
2.4	Average personal income and family fortune in different parts of Greater Copenhagen 1996	30
2.5	Proportion of people of working age (18 to 65 years) who are marginalised from the labour market, and the proportion of self-employed residents, leaders and professionals in service trades, Greater Copenhagen 1996	32
2.6	Proportion of immigrants – residents who are citizens of countries outside Western Europe, Canada, the United States, Australia and New Zealand, or who were born in developing countries, Greater Copenhagen 1996	34
2.7	The composition of the housing market in different parts of Greater Copenhagen 1996	37
3.1	Proportion of dwellings without bathrooms	50
4.1	Maintenance costs in DKK per square metre in social housing in Denmark 1990	58
4.2	The process of succession and decay	63
4.3	The final succession and decay process	63
4.4	The process of gentrification and renewal	65
4.5	Public intervention in the housing market that impedes urban decay in Europe	69
5.1	Model of processes of deprivation in Danish social housing estates	100
5.2	The tested model of processes of deprivation	108
6.1	Model of the connection between segregation and deprived neighbourhoods	127
7.1	Percentage of residents in 1990, before renovation started, who had moved out before 1996	145

List of Figures vii

7.2	Percentage of original residents living in the properties in 1986, before renewal, and still resident in 1990 after renewal, who moved away in the period 1990–96	150
7.3	Changes in the proportion of different social groups among residents in 1990–96	151
7.4	Model of the expected relations between Urban Committee efforts and changes in conditions on the estates	165
7.5	Proportion of estates (dwellings) that had serious problems in 1994 before the initiatives started, and the proportion of these where the situation became better or worse 1995–97	167
7.6	Moving frequencies for all residents and for residents in employment in the two periods 1994–95 and 1996–97, proportion of newcomers who were employed or immigrants, the relative decrease in the proportion of residents who were employed and the increase in the proportion of immigrants in the two periods	169

List of Tables

2.1	Average personal income for residents aged 18 or older, and average family fortune, Greater Copenhagen 1996	28
2.2	The proportion of the population aged 18 to 65 who are more or less permanently marginalised from the labour market and the size of the group of 'service professionals' – self-employed residents and professionals in service trades, Greater Copenhagen 1996	31
2.3	Proportion of residents in different tenures marginalised from the labour market, over-representation in and segregation between zones and sectors, Greater Copenhagen 1996	39
2.4	Total segregation of marginalised people among ring zones and sectors, divided into segregation caused by differences in the housing market and residual segregation due to other factors, Greater Copenhagen 1996	41
2.5	Proportion of residents in different tenures that are immigrants, over-representation in and segregation among zones and sectors, Greater Copenhagen 1996	43
2.6	Total segregation of immigrants between ring zones and sectors divided into segregation caused by differences in housing markets and residual segregation due to other factors, Greater Copenhagen 1996	44
4.1	Types of private landlords and their motives for investing and running rental properties	83
4.2	Statistical definitions of different types of landlords	84
4.3	Average investments per year in housing rehabilitation in 1991–92 in Danish blocks of flats built before 1950	86
4.4	Reasons for housing rehabilitation in 1991–92 among Danish landlords in blocks of flats built before 1950	89
4.5	The opinions of landlords on barriers for further rehabilitation in blocks of flats built before 1950	92
5.1	Results from two statistical models (logistic regression) explaining the extent of social activities and active residents on the estates (R-statistic * 100)	113
5.2	Results from a multivariable regression explaining social problems, measured by a combined index	115

List of Tables

5.3	Results from a statistical model (logistic regression) explaining problems with integration of immigrants (R-statistic * 100)	116
5.4	Results from a logistic regression explaining when estates had bad reputations (R-statistic * 100)	118
5.5	Results from four multivariable regressions explaining moving frequencies for different groups (standardised beta coefficients * 100)	120
5.6	Results from two multivariable regressions explaining how large a proportion of newcomers were employed or high-resource groups (beta coefficients * 100)	121
7.1	Variables in general logistic regression explaining mobility in poor housing in older blocks of flats	147
7.2	Main results of the best logistic regression explaining mobility in poor housing in older blocks of flats 1990–96	148
7.3	Variables characterising renewal work	148
7.4	Significant renewal variables explaining mobility in renewed dwellings 1990–96	149
7.5	Significant variables explaining gentrification in renewed dwellings 1990–96 (independent variable is 'newcomers employed with medium-high income or not')	153
7.6	Results from two logistic regressions explaining causes for increasing activity levels among tenants and an increasing number of social activities (R-statistic * 100)	171
7.7	Results of a linear regression explaining the causes of reduced social problems (Beta coefficient * 100)	172
7.8	Results of a logistic regression explaining causes for decreasing problems with integration of immigrants	173
7.9	Results of a logistic regression explaining why people move out of the estates	174
7.10	Results of logistic regression explaining when newcomers were in employment	177
7.11	Relative changes on estates with and without rent reductions in the number of residents in employment, immigrants and marginalised from the labour market, respectively	178
7.12	Results of logistic regression explaining causes for improved reputation	179

Chapter 1

Introduction

Most European countries have experienced special problems that have emerged in certain more or less well-defined parts of cities called deprived or depressed urban neighbourhoods. These problems were initially found in the oldest urban areas with the lowest quality housing. Since the beginning of the 1980s, however, in Europe they have also emerged in newer social housing estates outside city centres.

These neighbourhoods display visible physical and social problems that can disfigure the perhaps otherwise attractive urban landscape. In severe cases they could even be termed *sores on the face of the city*. They are often perceived by the public as places that are not inhabited or frequented by decent people – they are seen as *'places of exclusion'*.

The purpose of this book is to contribute to a deeper understanding of why such neighbourhoods come to exist and the impacts they have on cities. Urban decay is a result of the interaction between social, economic and physical changes in cities, but one of my main views is that deprived neighbourhoods also constitute a very important element of and contribution to this interaction. These areas are not just a simple result of social inequality and segregational forces, as they also create new segregation and inequality. In these neighbourhoods, strong self-perpetuating processes have been started involving complicated mechanisms that draw the areas into a downward spiral from which they rarely recover unaided. Such forces also impact the rest of the city. The deprived areas act as magnetic poles that attract poverty and social problems, and repel people and economic resources in a way that influences other parts of the city. They are the visible signs that cities are subject to special socio-spatial forces that create social and physical inequality, unstable conditions and sometimes destruction – most clearly observed in slums in large American cities.

For this study, I have drawn on research from three main but different fields:

1 research on segregation and its causes, carried out mainly by geographers and sociologists;

2 research, mostly economic, on causes and mechanisms of urban decay, and studies of public policies against it;
3 studies of deprived neighbourhoods and efforts to help them.

These three lines of research have followed their own separate courses and have rarely been combined. Studies of segregation have considered mainly spatial separation of different groups exclusively as a consequence of social inequality and cultural and racial differentiation, while characteristics of and changes in the urban structure have been less important. In contrast, economists, mainly Americans, have understood urban decay as a result of different households demanding different kinds of dwellings and surroundings that are located in different parts of cities. Finally, research on deprived neighbourhoods in Europe has either taken a very narrow look at the specific problems and circumstances in the studied areas or has seen this phenomenon as a general manifestation of what is called social exclusion in cities. Here, too, more profound analyses of the connection between the development of these neighbourhoods and the rest of the city are often missing.

However, comparing research from these different fields can provide a more thorough understanding of the interaction between spatial and social processes that lead to segregation, urban decay and deprived neighbourhoods. Much of the empirical material used in this book to illustrate analyses and qualify conclusions stems from my own research on Danish conditions during the last 10 years.

Exclusion of Places – the Interaction between Segregation and Urban Decay

Spatial segregation means that different social or cultural groups are separated in space and have settled in different parts of cities. In the literature, segregation is most often seen as a direct consequence of social inequality and cultural differences, as people from different social strata congregate or try to escape places of lower social status.

Some factors of importance to segregation are linked to public regulation of the central and local level of housing markets and of the location of housing. General housing policies and spatial planning implemented by local governments are of great importance. For example, it has been shown that two-thirds of the segregation in marginalised groups among sectors of Greater

Copenhagen can be attributed to the localisation of different tenures in the housing market (see p. 41).

It has been a common notion that urban decay and the creation of deprived neighbourhoods can be understood as a more or less simple consequence of segregation. However, this book proposes the theory that the relationship between these phenomena is more complex and that to some extent the relationship is two-way in the sense that urban decay creates segregation.

An important basis for understanding urban decay and deprived neighbourhoods is the idea that cities develop due to the interaction between social and physical changes. The socio-spatial dialectic (Soja, 1980), as it has been termed, is a continuous two-way process in which people create and modify urban spaces while at the same time being conditioned in various ways by these changes.

The distribution of people in space is a product of both social differentiation and of the fact that cities consist of many different places that have very different qualities. This spatial differentiation is a product of the social, physical and functional structure of the city, a structure that is continuously changed by economic investments and disinvestments as a consequence of people and functions being redistributed in space. This results in cities that are divided into identifiable areas that can be relatively homogeneous but exhibit distinctive characteristics that are very different from other neighbourhoods. The preferences for living in different kinds of neighbourhoods can vary between households with different needs and lifestyles, but people will always share some common values that result in some neighbourhoods being seen as more attractive than others.

My main point here is that *segregation is not a simple consequence of social inequality, but is a product of both social and spatial differentiation.* Segregation, therefore, is influenced largely by the development of spatial differentiation in cities, and this is possibly more important than the development in social inequality and social exclusion. Segregation and increasing spatial inequality are mutually self-perpetuating processes because the status and cultural identity of urban areas are determined by the composition of the people living there. Spatial differentiation leads to segregation while segregation creates spatial differences.

Urban decay is a name for some of the most important processes that produce increased spatial inequality. In both Europe and North America, certain parts of cities have been observed to decline in quality, and some places have deteriorated to the extent that buildings have been abandoned.

Different explanations on a micro level have been offered; for example that buildings have a limited lifetime or – especially in Europe – that public regulations have ruined incentives for maintenance. But empirical evidence does not always support these assumptions, or indicate that they are important causes of urban decay. Studies define no clear, isolated technical-financial reasons for the deterioration of buildings and most modern rent control systems appear to have only a limited effect on maintenance. More crucially, perhaps, are the norms, motives and behaviour of property owners, especially private landlords, as shown in a Danish study described later in this book.

In the mostly economic research on the development of American city centres, urban decay is most often attributed to changes in the demand for housing and location (Grigsby et al., 1987; Rothenburg et al., 1991). As the demand for single family homes in the suburbs grew and housing in city centres became obsolete, the American middle class moved away from city centres and was succeeded by low-income groups with lower housing demands who were unable to pay for high-quality housing (downward succession). In response, property owners were expected to reduce maintenance, and deterioration and slums appeared. In short, urban decay has been explained as a consequence of economic inequality and spatial market processes that create segregation.

However, more detailed studies of the economy and behaviour of property owners, residents and other actors in American slum areas (see p. 59) raise serious doubts about this theory's basic assumptions. They reveal that neighbourhood decay in the US cannot be explained simply as a result of segregation and succession. On the contrary, they indicate that succession is largely caused by urban decay. It is more appropriate to understand succession and decay as independent forces that interact and support each other.

Complex processes take place in American neighbourhoods in decay where three main factors interact: residents' changing social composition; physical deterioration of buildings and open spaces; and falling property values and economic losses for many property owners. As the character of a neighbourhood gradually changes and physical signs of decay become apparent, middle class residents leave and are replaced by low income and excluded groups who cannot afford high-quality housing and neighbourhoods. As a consequence, property values decline, investments cease and the neighbourhood decays further. When the process has passed a certain point, crime and insecurity become common, and emigration speeds up. Dwellings and buildings become derelict and finally whole areas can be abandoned. These have been left as open wounds in the middle of the city that cannot be healed or cured. Urban decay in American city centres has therefore become the single most important urban problem in the US. The term 'edge cities' has been coined, which reflects that all growth is taking place in the suburbs while centres decline and collapse.

These processes of decay have appeared to be very strong and difficult to stop. As early as the 1930s, a theory was proposed about a 'neighbourhood life-cycle' (Babcock, 1932) that explained how residential neighbourhoods inevitably, over the course of time, develop into 'poor blighted, or decadent districts'. This perception dominated American official thinking until the 1970s (Metzger, 2000). When gentrification began to occur in American cities at the beginning of the 1980s it became obvious, however, that the life-cycle theory of neighbourhoods was not a law of nature. Research on gentrification (see p. 65) has also revealed the crucial importance of the image of neighbourhoods and of expectations concerning their future social, economic and physical development. An 'iron law' of self-fulfilling negative expectations seems to have been a main factor behind the process of decay in American neighbourhoods, expectations that have been very difficult to change except in a few gentrified areas.

Better welfare systems and more extensive housing and urban policies in Europe have reduced the risk of hard-core slums, but problems have appeared in both older and newer urban areas. In the older areas, these problems have traditionally been attributed to the dominance of old and obsolete housing, while the appearance of problems on deprived social housing estates in suburbs has raised questions that demand new answers. Judging from the research literature, views seem to differ concerning the core problems of deprived neighbourhoods in Europe and vary even more concerning the main reasons for their occurrence.

Mainstream European research on deprived urban areas seems to be dominated by the view that the existence of slums is linked directly to and explained by general processes of segregation and social exclusion and impoverisation in cities. Deprived or depressed urban areas are seen mainly as *'pockets of poverty'* – spatial concentrations of poor and excluded people (see Lee and Murie, 1999; Madanipour, 1998; Cars et al., 1998; Social Exclusion Unit, 1998). In this sense, the main reason that problem areas develop is the general processes that create inequality and poverty in cities, namely global and local economic restructuring processes and defective welfare policies (Musterd et al., 1999; Parkinson, 1998). Deprived urban areas are understood as just another aspect of deprivation stemming from the general *exclusion of people* in globalised cities.

In this theoretical context, the crucial question is whether the spatial concentration of poor people in itself results in an increase in the poverty and social exclusion of residents – the so-called social neighbourhood effects. If these effects are substantial, there are good reasons for considering spatial pockets of poverty as a special problem that should be countered through public measures. If social neighbourhood effects are small, however, it is difficult to argue in favour of special area-based initiatives. Instead, other more general measures should be used that generally reduce poverty and social exclusion.

Some researchers in this field (Friedrichs, 1997; Musterd and Ostendorf, 1998) conclude that some neighbourhood effects can be found, but that they tend to be smaller in Europe than in American. Musterd et al. (1999) therefore conclude that 'in a European context, there are good reasons not to identify automatically social spatial inequality as such with "problems"'. Not surprisingly, these researchers are critical of area-based approaches used in many countries to solve problems in deprived neighbourhoods. Van Kempen and Priemus (1999), for example, conclude that:

> The battle against segregation and concentration is fought on the basis of ideas that are questionable in the Dutch situation, and probably in other European countries as well (van Kempen and Priemus, 1999, p. 655).

Research based on this theory often concentrates on the connection between deprivation of neighbourhoods and general trends in Western societies that tend to increase economic and social polarisation. A lot of literature in recent years has discussed the spatial consequences of globalisation and changes in the labour market and tried to connect this with deprived housing.[1] However, it has been difficult to identify a clear connection between these phenomena, and the literature has often been quite speculative.

Signs that segregation in general and deprivation of certain places are not just explained by globalisation and social exclusion include the fact that no direct connection seems to have been found between these phenomena and general social and economic changes at a national or regional level. Plenty of evidence shows that segregation and deprivation of neighbourhoods continue in situations where the national or local economy is booming and social inequality is decreasing.

In a national context, Denmark and Finland are examples of countries experiencing increasing employment and decreasing social inequality while segregation is increasing and new problem estates are appearing (Skifter Andersen and Ærø, 1997; Andersen, 1999; Hjarnø, 1996; Kortteinen and

Vaatovaara, 1999). Experience from the United States shows that slum growth in major cities has been most extensive in periods with the fastest growth in employment and incomes (Skifter Andersen, 1995b).

At a regional and local level, Mumford and Lupton (1999) conclude from their mapping of low demand for housing on problem estates in England: 'there is no straightforward link between city and neighbourhood fortunes ... Leeds has one of the fastest growing economies in Britain, but its poorest wards have not stopped declining'. Gibb et al. (1999) point out that:

> explanations for low demand do not all lie in issues of population loss, income and employment ... in regions with buoyant economies, low demand will remain a problem of particular property types and particular neighbourhoods.

Hall (1997) stresses that 'external factors cannot explain why particular estates are impacted upon more severely than others'.

Urban decay is linked to social segregation, which tends to concentrate the poor in the least attractive parts of cities. But it is not always obvious why some neighbourhoods have initiated a process of decline and others have not. There is a higher probability of deprivation and decay for neighbourhoods dominated by certain types of tenures and buildings in poorer cities in economic decline. But some of these areas have thrived while other types of neighbourhoods have had problems.

In this book, I have introduced a concept called 'exclusion of places' to clarify why neighbourhoods with the same starting point can have different fates. The processes linked to this concept involve the character of neighbourhoods gradually changing in a direction that makes them less attractive and more unacceptable as residential areas for people that have a choice in the housing market.

Evidence from specific studies has revealed that processes of decay similar to the ones found in American slum areas, often named 'vicious circles', are at work in deprived European housing estates. But the very different context in Europe – such as welfare policies, housing markets and tenure forms – means that they have another character and have rarely declined to the extent seen in the US.

I distinguish between interior and exterior processes of exclusion. The interior processes concern changes in the conditions inside the neighbourhoods, where negative social, physical, organisational and financial changes interact and reinforce each other. Some of the main processes concern the interaction between:

1. norms for using the area and physical decay;
2. social fragmentation and conflict spirals;
3. increasing insecurity and withdrawal as consequences of crime and conflicts resulting in reduced social cohesion and participation;
4. reduced or deteriorated private and public services;
5. internal stigmatisation and reduced self-esteem among residents;
6. external stigmatisation leading to difficulties in getting jobs, insurance and bank credits, and social isolation.

As a result of these processes, the physical environment becomes run down, social problems increase and social activity and employment among residents decline. The areas become gradually more and more difficult to manage and their reputations suffer.

The exterior processes of decay relate to the interconnection between the neighbourhoods and the rest of the city and the way this is expressed through people's movements in and out of the areas. As in American neighbourhoods in decay, the areas' images and reputations and expectations concerning their futures are of crucial importance. As shown in a Danish study of 500 neighbourhoods described in this book (p. 118), social problems and visible signs of decay lead to emigration of residents with social and financial resources. They are replaced by people on public support, often with their own problems, which accelerates the internal processes of deprivation. Sometimes nobody wishes to move into vacant property, local estates become empty and financial problems flourish.

These processes concerning exclusion of places can be seen as independent forces that create spatial inequality and segregation. They can occur quickly or slowly, but when they have reached a certain point, they tend to speed up regardless of the general development in the city concerning economic growth and social inequality. As a result, the areas in question become increasingly stigmatised and are perceived as diverging from the rest of the city. This has a marked influence on where people choose to live. The exclusion of places therefore leads to further segregation.

Public Policies against Urban Decay

Policies against urban decay in the US have, except for a few success stories, been quite unsuccessful (Kaplan, 1991; Adams et al., 1991). It seems as if most slum areas in major city centres have been declared beyond hope. Instead, programmes have been introduced that help people escape from these areas (Galster and Zobel, 1998).

In Europe, government programmes for urban renewal and housing rehabilitation in the older parts of the cities have been more successful. In most countries, especially northern Europe, slums in older housing built in the late 1800s and at the beginning of the 1900s have been removed. However, a great variety of instruments have been used, ranging from heavy, expensive public intervention to lighter regulations of and economic support for market processes of renewal. Comparative research on urban renewal policies (Skifter Andersen and Leather, 1999; Priemus and Metselaar, 1992) has not only shown major differences in the instruments used, but has also revealed that objectives and motives for these policies have differed very much from country to country. This variation can be explained only to some extent by differences in the national and urban context of the countries in question. One plausible explanation is that there has been a lack of thorough understanding of processes of urban decay, of why market forces were not always able to renew dwellings and urban areas, and of how public intervention could remove or prevent decay most efficiently. It seems as if urban renewal programmes have been somewhat ad hoc policies directed at solving physical problems that have been observed but not understood in parts of the cities.

This variation in policies is reflected in the results achieved. The best results seem to be achieved in countries that have used an arsenal of many different instruments adapted to solving specific problems in specific neighbourhoods with certain tenures and people.

In some countries, extensive general programmes have been very expensive and resulted in 'overkill' in a few selected neighbourhoods that by mere physical measures have been transformed into high-quality areas. At the same time, other neighbourhoods have deteriorated because of lack of effort and because low-income residents from the renewed areas have been displaced to these neighbourhoods.

In the most successful policies, economic support has been limited to what is necessary to remove market barriers for renewal, has targeted people in need of support and has involved many dwellings and areas. Sometimes these programmes have suffered because they have been directed more towards individual dwellings than areas, so that neighbourhood processes of decay have been difficult to stop. Programmes with combined support for buildings and for areas have therefore been most efficient.

The social consequences of urban renewal have been discussed, especially in countries with extensive programmes resulting in profound changes in neighbourhoods. The question is: should urban renewal promote gentrification to encourage economic growth and improved tax bases in municipalities or should it benefit existing residents more directly? Some researchers claim that gentrification and displacement of low-income residents indirectly promote decay in other parts of the cities (see p. 140). However, a study described in this book concludes that even the extensive urban renewal projects in Denmark have not resulted in much displacement of residents. Instead, it is concluded that the social composition of the areas has changed too little and this could cause future decay.

Area-based Initiatives on Deprived Housing Estates

Many European governments have initiated programmes featuring area-based initiatives in the fight against problems in deprived urban areas. However, the research literature contains many contradictions and disagreements on the effects of these programmes. Some researchers believe the purposes of such initiatives are questionable and the effects doubtful. One of the main reasons for this disagreement is that there have been different conceptions of the programme objectives and of the urban problems they aim to solve.

Many different strategies have been employed in area-based initiatives. The earliest were based mainly on physical improvement and embellishment. Later, mobilisation of residents, social support for weak groups and job training have been central. In recent years, more specialised efforts have been used, such as improvements of management and services, special actions against crime, marketing against bad reputations and changes of tenure. But there rarely seems to have been a clear and formulated strategy for these programmes and for the kind of problems they aim to solve.

Some research evaluations of the programmes have drawn quite negative conclusions regarding the efficiency of area-based initiatives and some more positive, depending somewhat on the effects expected. General conclusions suggest that efforts that are too short-term or narrow in their scope could do more harm than good in deprived areas because they lead to a public focus on the problems of the areas without having noticeable positive effects. Also isolated initiatives such as physical improvements or job training alone are unsustainable – in the latter case because people move away when they get jobs if the area does not improve. What are needed are long-term initiatives using a 'patchwork approach' that includes physical, organisational, financial and social aspects.

These conclusions are supported by the experience gained from a large Danish programme on deprived social housing estates described in this book (see p. 164). The programme included a combination of physical, economic, social and organisational measures on 500 social housing estates. The evaluation of the programme, two years after it began, showed that the negative social development on the estates had been stopped. Especially economic measures in the form of rent reductions proved to have an important impact on social stability and the composition of newcomers. However, the greatest effect was achieved where several types of measures were combined.

It is a main assertion in this book that one of the main reasons for the disagreement among researchers on the effects of area-based initiatives has been an inadequate understanding of the nature of deprived urban areas. As described above, in much of the literature, deprived neighbourhoods have been interpreted as 'pockets of poverty' – a spatial concentration of poor people in urban areas, caused by social inequality and segregation. This kind of understanding has meant that potential objectives of area-based efforts have been regarded as limited and their effects have been misinterpreted to some extent. An alternative understanding is proposed in this book that sees segregation as a product of both social and spatial inequality. Deprived urban areas are understood as 'excluded places', which themselves contribute to spatial inequality and segregation.

On this understanding, I have shown that area-based initiatives could have two different objectives:

1 to stop or reverse the exclusion of neighbourhoods;
2 to combat social exclusion at a neighbourhood level.

The last objective could be motivated by area deprivation creating special problems for people living in these areas and by local resources that could perhaps be mobilised to supplement public resources. However, I believe the first objective stated above to be the most important.

Danish efforts to revitalise 500 social housing estates suit the above understanding of how to combat urban decay. The Danish initiatives were based on four core strategies:

1 to strengthen social networks and reduce social problems in the areas (combat social exclusion);
2 to improve the ability of the estates to compete in the housing market (combat exclusion of place);

3 to reduce segregation in general;
4 to reduce other consequences of deprived neighbourhoods that would affect local authorities.

The Danish case therefore confirms the conclusion reached by Power (1997) and others – that area-based initiatives have a purpose and that they can also be effective. But we are 'swimming against the tide' (Power and Tunstall. 1995) and the initiatives must last long enough, extend far enough and also combine physical, organisational, financial and social aspects. It is a costly affair, but the alternative is to let the areas decline to the point at which they are abandoned and ultimately demolished.

Note

1 Examples are Sassen, 1994, Hamnet, 1994, Jargowsky, 1997, Wacquant, 1997 and Allen, 1998.

Chapter 2

Social Segregation in Cities

Social spatial segregation means that different people are located in different parts of cities. Segregation has been a rather ambiguous concept used in many different contexts. Sometimes it has been used to characterise general differences in the social composition of residents in different urban areas – synonymous with a term such as the social geography of cities. In other contexts, it refers to a spatial concentration of certain social or ethnic groups.

More precisely, segregation can be defined as the interaction between social differentiation and spatial distance (Olsson Hort, 1992; Saltman, 1991; Boal, 1997; Park, 1952). Spatial separation of groups of people should therefore be seen only as segregation if these groups differ in important social (or ethnic) respects. Most research on segregation has focused on how it affects the quality of life and social conditions of the groups that are separated. Both positive and negative consequences have been identified – often depending on the extent to which segregation has been voluntary or enforced (van Kempen and Özükren, 1998).

A further condition for using the term 'spatial social differentiation' for segregation may be if it prompts increasing inequality between the separated groups. A more precise definition of social segregation could then be that *segregation is a spatial separation of ethnic or socially different groups leading to increasing social or cultural differences between these groups.*

In this book, segregation is looked at from a special angle. What we are concerned about is the interaction between the economic/physical development of different parts of cities and the distribution of people in space. It could also be called the connection between people and places. More precisely, we focus on how segregation and urban decay affect each other.

We are therefore not going to discuss the social problems of segregation directly, though some of the consequences of living in deprived urban neighbourhoods are touched on in Chapters 3 and 5. The purpose of this chapter is to understand and examine the forces that lead to segregation and therefore indirectly influence processes of deprivation and decay in urban neighbourhoods.

The Socio-spatial Dialectic of Cities

The following sections consider the kinds of social differentiation of crucial importance to segregation, and cover some of the fundamental causes of segregation. I will argue that segregation is not a simple result of social inequality, but of the interaction between social and spatial processes that simultaneously create both social and spatial inequality.

Social Differentiation and Segregation

Few studies have distinguished between the general social geography of cities and segregation as defined above. Most have focused on how different social and ethnic groups have been distributed in space, often without explicitly noting the implications for urban social inequality.

Early studies generally began by describing the social and ethnic division of space in cities. This was done with the help of factorial analyses that measure the spatial variation of many different social variables. From the start, these 'social area analyses' (Shevky and Bell, 1955) indicated three main factors that explain spatial variation:

1 socioeconomic status;
2 family status;
3 ethnicity.

Such a three-dimensional model for the social structure of cities has also been supported by subsequent American studies (Herbert and Johnston, 1978). These studies have, however, rightly been criticised for lacking a theoretical basis (Dangschat, 1991), even though some authors have tried to explain the structure as a product of different developments in society.

Others have criticised the somewhat arbitrary choice of spatial division in the studies and the problems intrinsic to the method. For example, it is difficult to interpret the results of the factorial analyses (Herbert and Johnston, 1978).

Most studies of urban segregation have considered the locations of specific ethnic or social groups in cities. Early American studies were concerned with where different groups of European immigrants settled. These studies (reviewed in Peach, 1996) showed a process of gradual spatial integration. The first immigrants took up residence in ghettos near city centres – so-called zones of transition. A certain dissemination and assimilation occurred with second-generation immigrants that continued in the third generation.

However, this model of gradual integration has not occurred in the Afro-American population and only partly for Hispanics (Taeuber and Taeuber, 1964). The black population, especially, has remained in genuine ghettos and this concentration has increased over time towards an extreme black majority in some neighbourhoods – which has been called 'hyper-segregation' (Massey, 1994). This concentration of black people has been seen as a serious social problem in American cities, which is why American research on segregation has been directed almost exclusively against racial segregation (Huttman, 1992). With the exception of more general studies on social geography, American research over the past 30 years has not been overly concerned with segregation among white Americans from different social classes. This means that American theories on segregation have race relations as their main point of reference and therefore have limited validity in a European context (Dangschat, 1991).

In Europe, especially in the last 15 years, there has been some research on segregation of ethnic groups: refugees and immigrants (Huttman, Blauw and Saltman, 1992; Peach, 1997; Musterd and Ostendorf, 1998; van Kempen and Özükren, 1998). The point of departure has been cultural differences rather than race. There has also been an increased focus on segregation of socioeconomic and demographic groups. Studies were made of earlier segregation of different 'classes' in society, defined in terms such as blue-collar and white-collar workers and self-employed factory owners.

In the 1980s, segregation studies focused less on traditional class divisions in society, measured as differences in income, education and occupation, and looked at other kinds of social differentiation. One reason is that traditional socioeconomic variables are acknowledged to explain only partly how people choose where to live. In some earlier Danish studies (Møllgaard, 1984), the social division of cities is seen as a result of groups with different lifestyles and 'life forms' choosing different domains. The 'life form' concept that was developed (Groth and Møllgaard, 1982; Højrup, 1983) implied a general division into three social groups called the independent life form, the career life form and the wage-earner life form, respectively.

A more general criticism of the use of traditional class divisions has been based on the theories of Pierre Bourdieu, which ascribe importance to cultural aspects that have an essential influence on social stratification in society (Dangshat, 1991). This leads to the conclusion that differences in lifestyle and cultural values should be more relevant in studies of the social divisions of cities (Helbrecht and Pohl, 1995). This implies more than just a focus on where different ethnic groups are located.

However, another, more important, reason for changes in the focus of segregation studies can be found in new opinions on how to understand the nature of fundamental social inequalities in society. The former class concept has disintegrated as large parts of the working class have joined a new middle class. Instead, other social dividing lines have attracted attention – especially the barriers between the part of the population that is fully included in society and the labour market, and groups who have been called 'marginalised', 'socially excluded' or 'the underclass'.

The uses of these concepts have often been diffuse and inconsistent. In a Danish context, marginalisation has often been used in connection with the labour market. Marginalised groups have been synonymous with people of working age without work. Others (Goul Andersen, 1996) have used the term in a broader sense to include lack of participation in social activities and networks and lack of political influence.

The term 'social exclusion' originated in France and has been used a great deal in the European Union (European Commission, 1997). A lot of research literature has appeared in recent years based on this concept (Madanipour et al., 1998; Marsh and Mullins, 1998; Sommerville, 1998). It is seldom well defined and suffers from a lack of clarity. Social exclusion is seen mainly as the opposite of social integration, especially integration in the labour market, but it is often confused with poverty or a general lack of resources.

Finally, the concept of 'the new urban underclass' has been used in the United States and United Kingdom. In the USA, this concept has been used to cover what could be called voluntary marginalised people, i.e. groups who have other norms concerning family and work, and who do not wish to participate in society (Auletta, 1982; Murray, 1990). Other writers have seen 'the underclass' as socially excluded people who have developed other norms as a condition for survival (Wilson, 1987).

The new focus on marginalised groups in society has influenced segregation studies, especially those dealing with the spatial concentration of poverty and deprivation. Many studies have had trouble identifying marginalised groups effectively. In several studies, unemployment is the only variable (Power and Tunstall, 1995); others have used early pension, welfare payments or illness as criteria (Biterman, 1994; Hummelgård et al., 1997). Some studies use the number of single parents as an indicator – especially if this is seen as a symptom of missing family values (Murray, 1990).

The Emergence of the Segregated City

The historical background From the middle of the eighteenth century, old medieval city boundaries were broken up and the upper classes started to move out and occupy the most attractive parts of the surrounding country that had most natural attributes such as lakes, hills, forests or access to open land.

Olsson Hort (1992) for example, described the development of segregation in Swedish cities using three phases:

1 at the end of the nineteenth century, industrialisation resulted in a concentration of workers and the bourgeoisie around factories located mainly near city centres;
2 in the 1930s, the upper classes more consciously began to form domains in the surrounding country, from which the working class was excluded;
3 after World War II and especially from the 1960s, the middle class and top ranks of workers had the opportunity to move up in the hierarchy of domains in the suburbs. As a result, the traditional segregation of the classes among cities and suburbs has decreased considerably since 1940.

After World War II, large housing estates with blocks of flats were built in the suburbs of European cities – mostly as social housing. New segregational patterns arose in different parts of the suburbs as some of the poorest people moved out to the new estates. In the USA, the trend has been quite different, as very little housing has been built in the suburbs for low-income groups and the poor have been left behind in city centres.

Ecological explanations of segregation In the classical 'ecological theories' on social differentiation in cities, a redistribution of the initial distribution in space was explained mainly by the notion that different groups compete and try to dominate different spatial areas. The social structure of a city gradually changes as some groups 'invade' new territories and occupy empty space or displace groups that were once dominant (invasion). This allows other groups to take over the neighbourhoods they have left (succession).

The first ecological theories (Burgess, 1924 and 1925) postulated that social division results in a ring structure, with the wealthiest groups settling furthest away from the city centre and poor people nearer the centre. In the 1930s, a new theory suggested that the social division of cities developed in sectors (Hoyt, 1939). This structure was explained by different social groups expanding their territory in the same direction from the centre outwards into surrounding areas. Later theories talk about 'multi-centre' structures (Harris and Ullman, 1945) that have a more random distribution of territories.

The ecological theories of segregation were not without their merits. But they have been criticised for not defining the roles of economic development, public policies and public institutions (van Kempen and Özükren, 1998).

Economic theories of location Initially, people settled near industries and workplaces. This had a lasting influence on the structure of cities even though means of transport became more technically developed and residential areas spread.

In the traditional, predominantly American, theories of the localisation of people and functions in space, individual choices have been explained by the price levels in the land and property markets, which again have been dominated by the distance to city centres. According to the theory (Alonso, 1964; Mills, 1967), land prices decline with increasing distance from the centre and this has resulted in the decrease in plot ratio and increase in the size and standard of dwellings. This provides a social division of urban space in which low-income groups are settled in high-density areas near city centres, while incomes and housing consumption increase with the distance from city centres. Such a distribution has been found around American cities (Muth, 1969). However, later it was shown that some of the theory's basic assumptions were not valid (Wheaton, 1978). Instead, the actual distribution can be largely explained by the historical development of the cities, with the oldest and worst dwellings located near the centre and the newest and best housing furthest away.

Demographic explanations There is also a demographic aspect to this issue. Segregation in the housing market takes place as a consequence of residential mobility. A large number of mobility studies (see, for example, Rossi, 1955; Pickwance, 1973; Kending, 1984; Skifter Andersen and Bonke, 1980) show that large differences exist between the mobility of different life-cycle groups. Young people are very mobile, while families with children are less mobile. The elderly, especially, rarely move. This is not only because housing needs and demands change fast in the younger years. It is also because over the course of time, people get used to their present dwelling and neighbourhood (Hurtig, 1995) and feel a sense of loss if they have to move away. During the first phases of their lifetime, people establish more permanent habitation and tend to stay there for a long period of their life unless dramatic changes occur in their work or family situation. As a consequence, a certain sluggishness exists in the socio-spatial structure of cities. This is mirrored in the demographic differences between older and newer parts of cities. The older suburbs are often dominated by elderly people who have lived there for a long period, while young families with children dominate newer suburbs. This is a structure that can also be found in Greater Copenhagen, as will be illustrated in a section below.

Another important reason why the socio-spatial structure changes slowly involves the strong bonds that many people still have with certain places. Recent research in Denmark (Ærø, 2001) shows that many people still want to stay or return to the same urban neighbourhoods where they grew up or where they have family and friends. This seems to be especially important for immigrants (Børresen, 2000).

The effects of housing policies and physical planning In Europe, the social geography of cities has taken other forms than in the United States. This is due to the more egalitarian framework in Europe, more active state intervention in the housing market and more extensive regulation of land use provided by the state and implemented by local authorities.

Partly as a consequence of public regulation, the housing market has been divided into different tenures with different economic and legal conditions – more in some countries and fewer in others. These differences result in some tenures being more advantageous for certain social groups while other groups prefer or are restricted to other kinds of housing. In this way, the different groups have been separated according to certain tenures. This separation has been called 'segmentation of the housing market' (Lindberg and Lindèn, 1989; Olsson Hort, 1992). The concept has also been used in American literature to indicate a division of the housing market into sub-markets that are demanded by different social groups (Schnare and Struyk, 1976; Rothenburg et al., 1991).

The concept of housing market segmentation can be seen as parallel to segregation and concerns the division of groups into tenures instead of spatial separation. Segmentation can, however, lead to segregation if different tenures are separated in space. This has been the case in many European countries, for several reasons. The historical development shows that private renting was dominant in the oldest and densest parts of the cities with blocks of flats dating back to the beginning of industrialisation. In the suburbs, owner-occupied single-family housing has been most common, but social housing, mainly blocks of flats, has also been built. The localisation of these tenures has resulted to some extent from market demand. Social housing has been built in the least attractive tracts where land prices have been lower, while high-quality owner-occupied housing has been located in the most attractive environments.

The localisation of tenures has not, however, been a simple result of market demand. Land use has – to different extents in different countries – been controlled by local authorities. Physical planning has enabled the control of what kind of buildings and sometimes also tenures should be located in a municipality. Local authorities have therefore exerted considerable influence on the location of various tenures. Some Danish local authorities have therefore chosen to almost preclude certain tenures (Skifter Andersen and Als, 1986; Skifter Andersen and Ærø, 1997).

In this way, spatial separation of tenures can be seen as a result of a political/ institutional process. When a specific social group has attained political dominance in a municipality, they will try to use their political power to maintain this dominance. An effective way of doing this is to control the production of new housing (Saltman, 1991; Hjärne, 1991, Olsson Hort, 1992). In Denmark, there has been a clear connection between the political affiliation of the political majority in local governments and the tenure composition of new housing (Skifter Andersen and Als, 1987). Conservative dominated municipalities have built relatively little social housing – especially in parts of Greater Copenhagen (as illustrated below). In municipalities dominated by social democrats, during some periods, social housing has sometimes constituted three quarters of all new housing. There are interesting examples of what has happened in municipalities where the political majority has shifted. Sometimes this has led to a radical change in physical plans for the development of housing (Skifter Andersen and Als, 1986).

There are also examples of local authorities facilitating the building of social housing in urban areas with higher land prices. In these cases, local authorities have acted against the segregational forces coming from the market and promoted a blend of tenures. There has been a clear focus on such policies in Sweden for some years (Arnell-Gustafsson, 1983) and recently also in Britain, Holland and Denmark (Elsinga, 1996; Cole and Shayer, 1998; Kintrea and Atkinson, 1998; Ministry of Housing and Urban Affairs in Denmark, 2000).

In recent years other motives for controlling new housing have been important for Danish local governments. The budgets of local authorities have come under strong pressure because of a combination of demands from the state for limitations on tax increases and for increasing social expenditure. In this situation, more local governments have been concerned about the *fiscal* consequences for the local authority of building different kinds of new housing. There has been more focus on the increased expenses for social and housing benefits and the reduced tax base (Denmark has local income taxes) stemming from poor people in social housing. This has led to a reduction of social housing in the least wealthy municipalities, among them the City of Copenhagen, which published a new strategic plan for housing in 2000.

Discrimination in the housing market In the USA there has been a clear focus on how institutions that control the distribution of dwellings to applicants, create segregation through discrimination, especially against black people (Galster, 1992; Massey, 1994). It has been demonstrated that banks and real estate agents contribute towards keeping black and coloured house hunters away from white neighbourhoods by refusing them credit or referring them to other places. In spite of a lot of legal effort to change these practices, it has been estimated that this is the cause of between 25 and 50 per cent of racial segregation in the US (Galster, 1992).

In Europe, there has been less focus on discrimination as a cause of housing market segmentation and spatial segregation. Examples include reduced credit possibilities for immigrants belonging to certain ethnic groups or higher demands concerning deposits and down payments. In some countries (Great Britain, France) there has sometimes been a tradition for referring immigrants to the least attractive neighbourhoods (Huttman, Blauw and Saltman, 1992). In some cases, housing associations simply refuse to accept immigrants or set quotas so that they accept them only when other foreign ethnic households leave (van Kempen and Özükren, 1998). In Austria, foreigners have no access to social housing and no right to some forms of household-related allowances (Giffinger and Reeger, 1997). In Denmark and other countries, there has also been some discrimination against immigrants by private landlords, who prefer not to offer vacancies to immigrants (van Kempen an Özükren, 1998).

Systems for allocating social housing Even where no conscious discrimination takes place, systems for allocating social housing could lead to segregation. This has been seen in Denmark. Dwellings are allocated based on a waiting list and the housing associations cannot decide alone who is to move into a vacant flat. The waiting lists are, however, often long, so people who are able to solve their acute housing needs in other ways do not wait for their turn. Often, only the poor have no other possibilities and are forced to wait – and many are immigrants. Moreover, local authorities have a right to allocate up to 25 per cent of vacant dwellings to people with social problems. As vacant dwellings most often appear in the less attractive estates with high mobility rates, there is a tendency for local authorities to add more social problems to these estates and increase the concentration of poor people.

Segregation as Interaction between Social and Spatial Inequality

The development of cities has occurred as interaction between social and physical changes. It has been called a socio-spatial dialectic (Soja, 1980), a continuous two-way process in which people create and modify urban spaces while at the same time being conditioned in various ways by these changes. Areas in which people prefer to live and work, or have access to, continuously change. However, people's economic resources and preferences for and affiliation to places are also changing simultaneously. As a result, the social and physical structures of cities have undergone pronounced changes over the years. The growth of every town can be seen as a 'twin process of outward extension and internal reorganisation' (Knox, 1995). While cities have been extended by new estates on the suburban fringe, existing urban areas have been subject to functional and physical changes; they have sometimes been converted to accommodate new uses. In some, existing physical structures have become obsolete and have deteriorated.

Figure 2.1 illustrates how these changes occur in cities. The figure shows that the distribution of people in space is a product of both social differentiation and what I have called spatial differentiation. This spatial differentiation is a product of the social, physical and functional structure of the city, a structure that is continuously changing due to economic investments and disinvestments as people and functions are redistributed in space. Cities become divided into identifiable areas that can be relatively homogeneous, but exhibit distinctive characteristics that are very different from other neighbourhoods. Such areas differ not only by virtue of different physical qualities, such as housing stock, architecture, natural attractions, and access to transport facilities and service supply but also by less tangible qualities such as social image, status and security. For example, one study (Pacione, 1982) showed that the most important factors for residents' perceptions of their neighbourhoods were: traffic problems, street cleanliness and maintenance, accessibility to open spaces, frequency of antisocial activity (vandalism, violence etc.), accessibility within the city as a whole, social interaction and landscaping. Preferences for living in various neighbourhoods can vary between households with different needs and lifestyles, but there will always be some common values among people that result in some neighbourhoods being appreciated more highly by the majority, while others are seen as very unattractive.

The main point I would like to stress is that *segregation is not a simple consequence of social inequality, but is a product of both social and spatial differentiation*. Segregation, therefore, is greatly influenced by the development

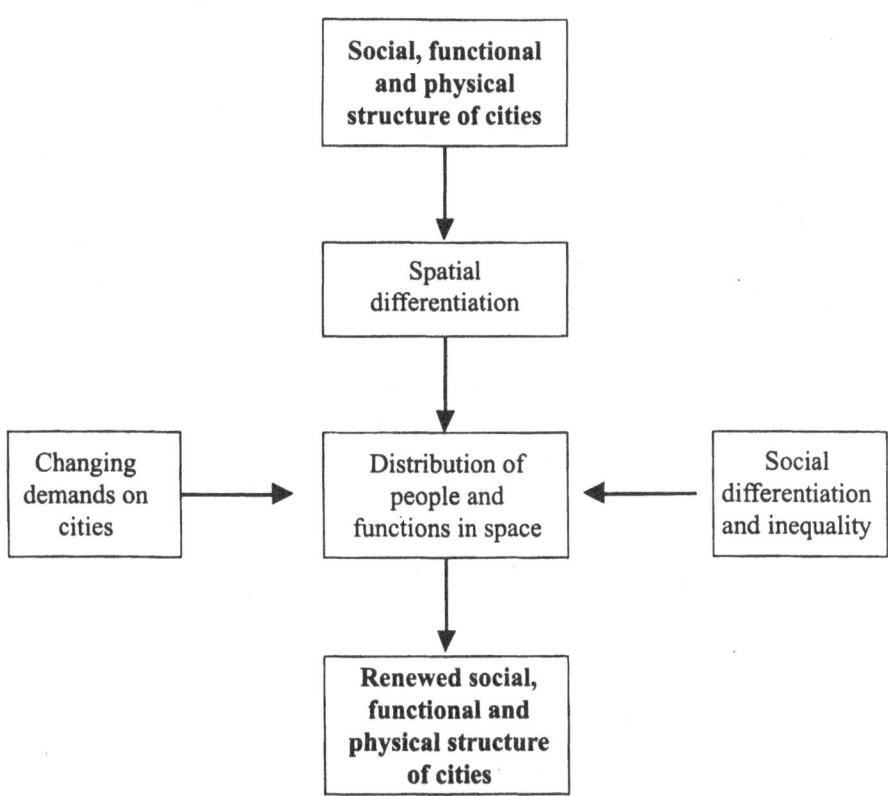

Figure 2.1 The interaction between changes in social and spatial differentiation in cities

of spatial differentiation in cities, and this is perhaps more important than the development in social inequality and social exclusion. Segregation and increasing spatial inequality are mutually self-perpetuating processes because the status and cultural identity of individual urban areas are determined by the composition of residents. Spatial differentiation leads to segregation, while segregation creates spatial differences.

Housing Market Segmentation as a Cause of Segregation – the Case of Copenhagen

This section illustrates the above analyses of causes of segregation by looking at the patterns of segregation in Greater Copenhagen. The analysis distinguishes between three main causes of spatial segregation in Copenhagen as the result of different kinds of processes that have taken place during the last 50 to 100 years. There is a distinction between 'basic socioeconomic causes of segregation', 'demographic causes of segregation' and 'segregation caused by housing policy and physical planning'.

The term 'basic socioeconomic causes of segregation' is used to mean processes by which, in the course of time, the most attractive parts of the area are invaded by the wealthier citizens. Increasing land and property prices in such areas are one reason why people with lower incomes move to less expensive parts of the city.

Demographic segregation is due to the chronological order in which Copenhagen has been extended over the past 100 years. As the city expanded, its new residential areas were populated mostly by young people and families. Many of these families have subsequently stayed in their dwellings or in the local area. As a consequence, the various parts of the city reflect the differences in age and family structure. The demographic component also influences the general pattern of socioeconomic segregation, as income and household composition vary with age. People aged 40 to 60 generally have higher incomes than younger people and the elderly. Zones dominated by middle-aged residents therefore tend to have greater average incomes than inner-city areas with many youngsters and elderly people.

The third factor analysed involves housing policies at both a national and local level. The national housing policy is a decisive factor in making the housing market more segmented i.e. some tenures are more attractive to high-income groups and less affordable for people with low incomes. Consequently, other tenures available for low-income groups become very unattractive to the wealthier part of the population. If the housing market is highly segmented, the location of different tenures in the urban space is of essential importance to segregation. And if housing policies and physical planning performed by local governments lead to a separation of tenures, widespread socioeconomic segregation will result.

In Denmark, local governments have had a considerable influence on the composition of local housing markets – first of all because they can prevent social housing by denying housing associations permission to build new housing. Secondly, they can use physical planning measures to control building type and size of sites for all new housing. Local governments in Greater Copenhagen have used these powers to create local housing markets that are extremely different. In some municipalities, social housing is the dominant tenure while it is practically nonexistent in others. This has contributed significantly to segregation among municipalities. We will refer to this as 'segregation caused by housing policies'.

Segregation in Greater Copenhagen

This section describes social segregation in Greater Copenhagen based on data from registers in the Statistical Office of Denmark adopted by the Danish Building Research Institute (Skifter Andersen and Ærø, 1997). The data is limited to a municipal level despite its more complex character.

The analyses are based on a division of the region into different ring zones and transverse sectors as shown in Figure 2.2. The ring zones consist of the centre (the City of Copenhagen and Frederiksberg Municipality) and three 'concentric' rings of municipalities called ring zones 2, 3 and 4. The area outside the centre is further divided into six transverse sectors called north, northwest, west, southwest, south and southeast, respectively. We will look at the demographic segregation first and then consider socioeconomic segregation.

Demographic segregation This section covers the proportion of households comprising families with children and the proportion of the population who are elderly (more than 65 years old) in different parts of the region.

Since urbanisation took place in the last century, a simple zone pattern has prevailed: the further from the city centre, the younger the population. Every year new dwellings were constructed at the edge of the existing city that were occupied by younger residents entering the housing market. This has now changed as the central part of the city has a decreasing proportion of pensioners and an increasing proportion of residents aged 15 to 34 (see Figure 2.3). Like a wave moving outwards from the city centre, the population is older in the second zone (the older suburbs constructed in the 1950s and early 1960s) and then becomes younger as you move outwards. It must be assumed that the next ring zones (zones 3 and 4) will replace zone 2 within, say, 20 years in terms of having most elderly residents. This process is completely in accordance with the classic model proposed by the Chicago School.

Figure 2.3 shows how the composition of households and age of people in each sector changes from the city centre to the outer rings of the region. The picture is similar in all the sectors. The frequency of families with children increases with distance from the centre in all sectors. Differences between sectors appear especially in zone 4 where the share of families with children is highest in the northwestern and western sectors, and lowest in the northern and the southwestern sectors.

26 *Urban Sores*

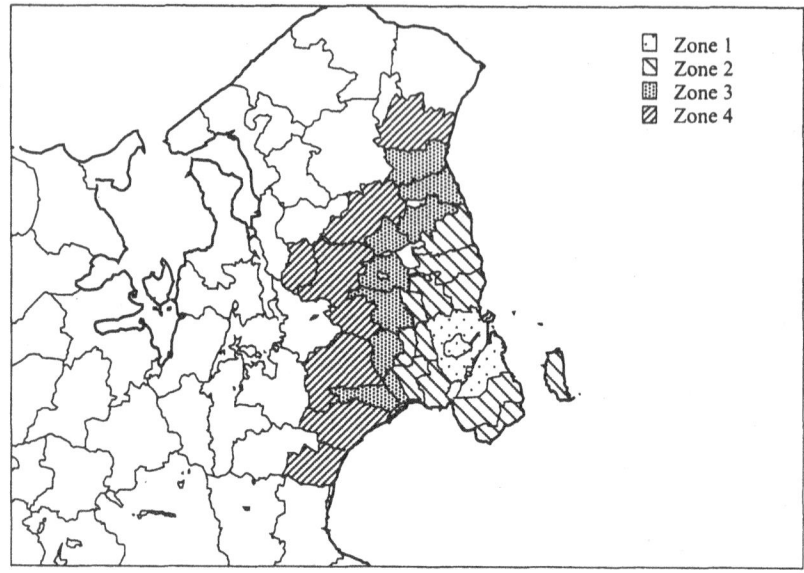

Ring zones

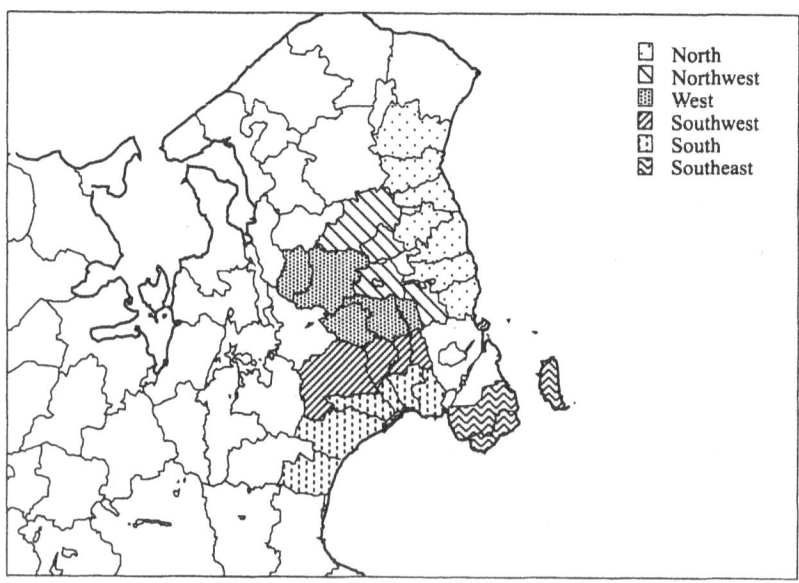

Sectors

Figure 2.2 Greater Copenhagen divided into ring zones and sectors

Social Segregation in Cities 27

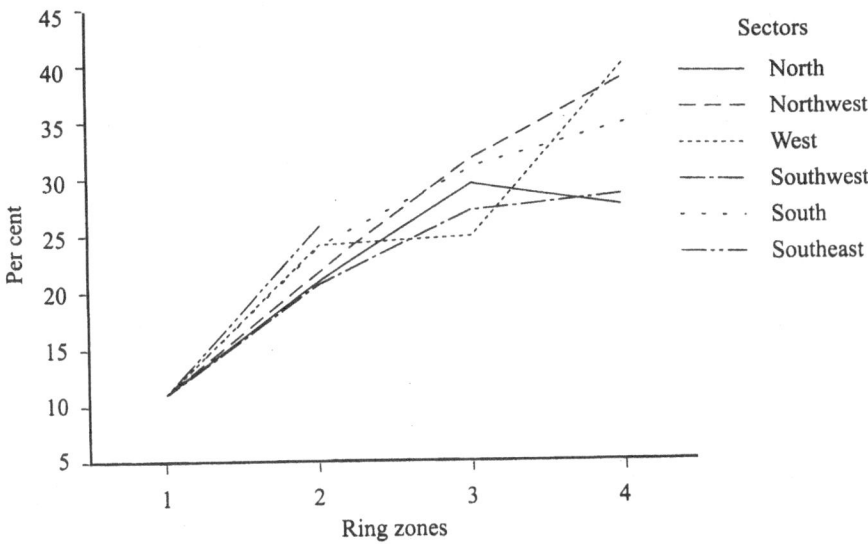

Families with children in different parts of Greater Copenhagen

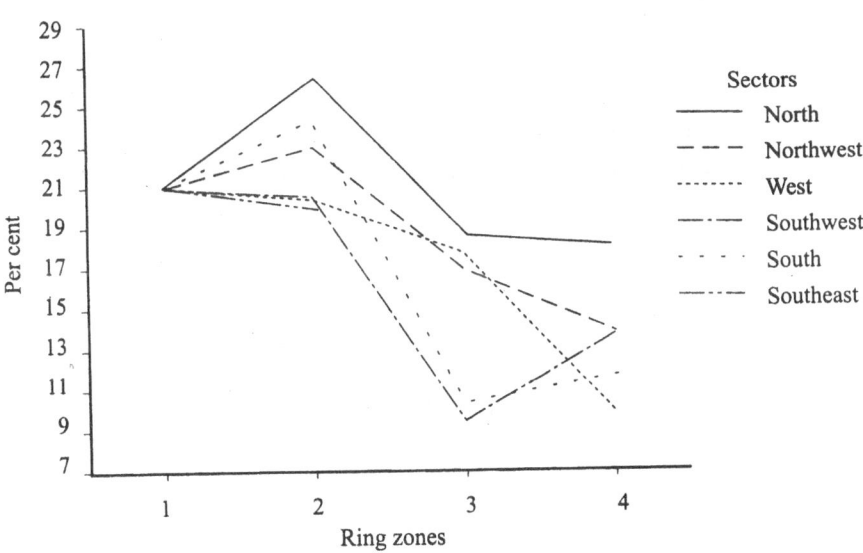

Elderly share of population in different parts of Greater Copenhagen

Figure 2.3 Families with children as a proportion of all households, and elderly more than 65 years old as a proportion of the whole population, in different parts of Greater Copenhagen 1996

At present, the proportion of elderly is highest in zone 2 (older suburbs) and decreases, with a few exceptions, in the outer rings, with the highest difference between rings 2 and 3. In the southwestern and southern sectors, however, there are more elderly people in zone 4 than in zone 3. On average, most elderly people live in the northern sector and fewest in the western and southern sectors.

The diagrams clearly confirm the theory that the demographic composition of residents in the region primarily reflects the historic urban development. There seems to be a difference in age and family structure across the zones of the city. This structure in principle has the same appearance inside the 6 sectors but some differences exist that can be explained mainly by differences in the chronological development of the sectors.

Segregation in relation to income and family fortune In general, Denmark, with its Gini coefficient of below 0.40, is a country with relatively similar incomes compared with many other countries. Even if segregation of different income groups is high, the incomes in different areas vary only a little. However, Table 2.1 shows considerable differences in income and fortune among residents in the sectors of the Copenhagen region. The average income in the wealthiest sector (north) is more than 30 per cent higher than in the poorest sector (southwest). Family fortunes in the region are much less evenly distributed, with a considerable difference between the northern and other sectors. The picture is the same elsewhere, with the least wealthy families living in the southwestern sector and fortunes and incomes increasing as you move either north or east from there.

Table 2.1 Average personal income for residents aged 18 or older, and average family fortune, Greater Copenhagen 1996

Sectors/zones	Income (DKK 1,000)	Fortune (DKK 1,000)
North	246	853
Northwest	205	372
West	194	274
Southwest	182	227
South	190	272
Southeast	195	337
Ring zone 1	162	168
Ring zone 2	205	510
Ring zone 3	212	401
Ring zone 4	208	362

It is clear from the table that zone 1, the urban centre – the municipalities of Copenhagen and Frederiksberg – comprises the poorest part of the whole region, with an average income of more than 20 per cent below the average for the suburbs, and family fortunes that are 60 per cent lower.

Figure 2.4 also shows that the pattern of income differences from zone to zone only to some extent fits the model formulated by Burgess (1925) and Hoyt (1939), which in general assumes increasing incomes with distance from the centre. This is the case only in some sectors and harmonises more with the pattern found in Toronto by Murdie (1976). On average, the highest incomes are found in zone 3, while the greatest fortunes are concentrated in zone 2. This can be partly explained by the demographic differences between the zones, where zone 2 has more elderly people with lower incomes but higher family fortunes.

It appears from Figure 2.4 that wealthier people especially are concentrated in the part of the northern sector that belongs to zone 2 and that it is only in this sector that zone 2 has higher incomes and fortunes than in the outer rings. In the northwestern sector, incomes and fortunes are highest in zone 3 and in the remaining sectors in zone 4. Fortunes are especially small in the municipalities in the southwestern sector located in zone 3.

This picture is confirmed if you look at the incomes in each of the municipalities, but some deviations can also be observed. Some municipalities in the northern part of the region have medium incomes and some of the southern municipalities have relative high incomes. We will try to explain these exceptions later by looking at the differences in housing policies and housing markets in the various municipalities.

Segregation of groups with different relations to the labour market Like most other European countries, Denmark has developed high polarisation regarding the scope for various groups to obtain employment and income through work. The majority of the population of working age are permanently employed, some people have occasional occupations and others are more or less permanently marginalised.

In this study, those who are permanently marginalised are defined as people aged between 18 and 65 who have:

1 taken early retirement;
2 social security or sickness benefits as their main income in the year 1995;
3 unemployment benefit and have been unemployed for more than 75 per cent of the last three years.

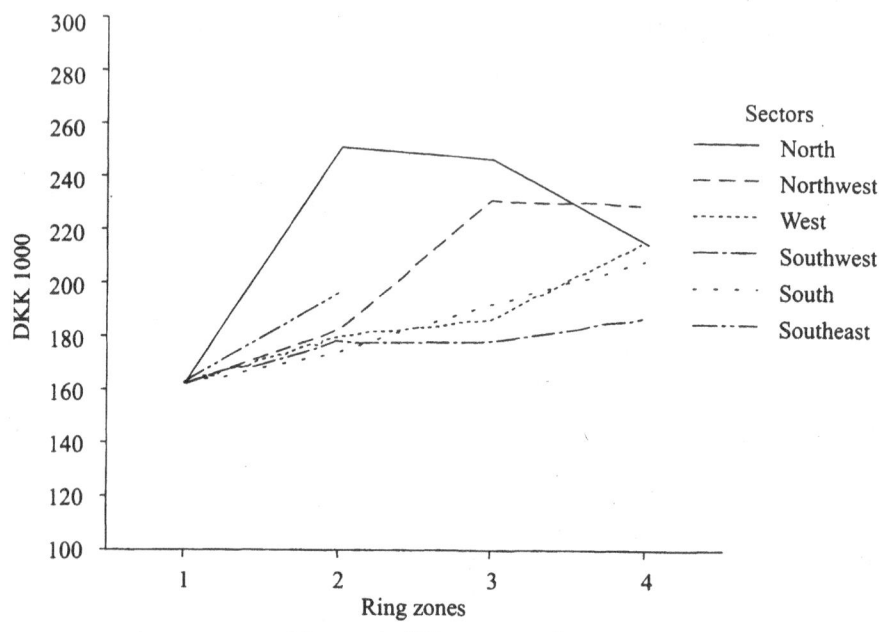

Average personal income in different parts of Greater Copenhagen

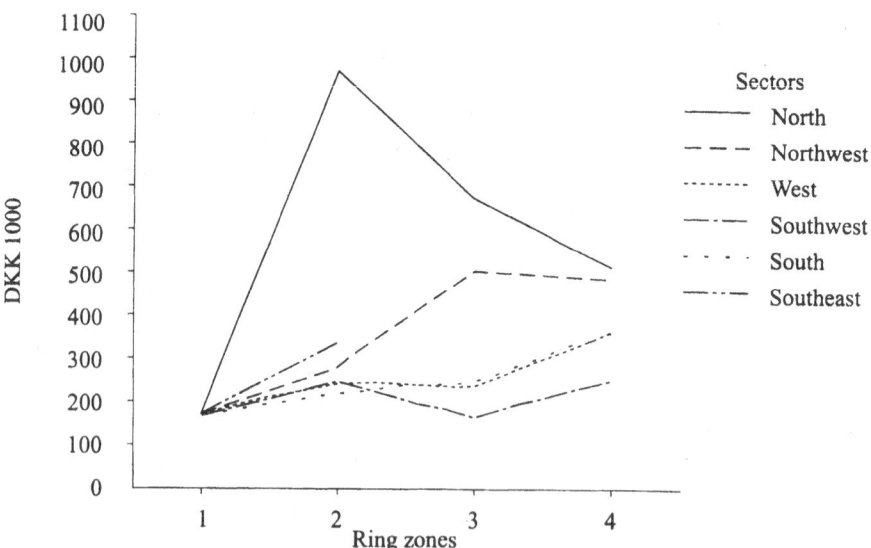

Average family fortune in different parts of Greater Copenhagen

Figure 2.4 Average personal income and family fortune in different parts of Greater Copenhagen 1996

On average, in 1996 this group constituted about 21 per cent of all people aged 18 to 65 years in Greater Copenhagen.

Table 2.2 shows that the segregation of people marginalised from the labour market follows the same pattern as the segregation of income groups. The highest concentration exists in the centre and in the southern and southwestern sectors, and the lowest is in the northern sector and in the outermost ring zone. However, a considerable proportion of the population in the most affluent parts of the region are still marginalised.

Table 2.2 The proportion of the population aged 18 to 65 who are more or less permanently marginalised from the labour market and the size of the group of 'service professionals' – self-employed residents and professionals in service trades, Greater Copenhagen 1996

Sectors/zones	Marginalised (%)	Service professionals*
North	14	9.2
Northwest	17	5.8
West	17	3.6
Southwest	21	3.0
South	20	3.3
Southeast	16	3.0
Ring zone 1	26	3.7
Ring zone 2	18	5.4
Ring zone 3	18	5.4
Ring zone 4	15	4.6

* Self-employed residents, leaders and other professionals occupied in service trades other than the retail trade.

It appears from Figure 2.5 that the segregational pattern is more complex than is shown in the table. The marginalised groups are absent especially in parts of the northern sector and in the outer rings of the northwestern and western sectors, but differences also exist between municipalities within these areas. The highest frequency of marginalised residents outside the centre is found in the southwestern sector in zone 3 and the southern sector, zone 2.

We will not explore the analysis in any more detail here, but segregation indices for the marginalised groups will be used in a later section to explore the effects of housing policies and housing markets on segregation.

32 *Urban Sores*

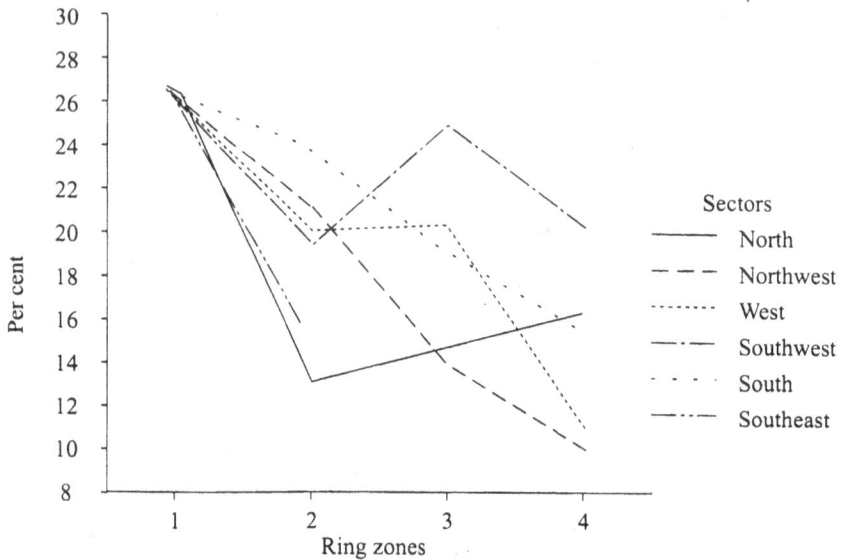

Marginalised from job market in different parts of Greater Copenhagen

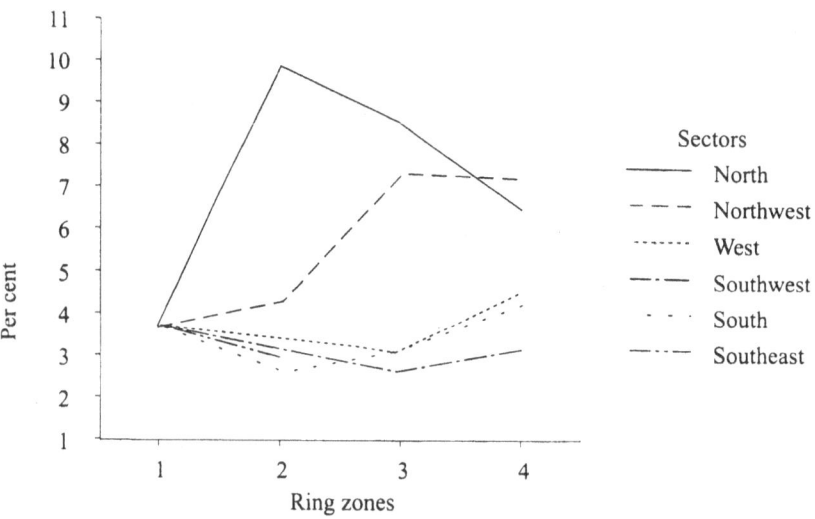

Leaders and professionsals in service in different parts of Greater Copenhagen

Figure 2.5 Proportion of people of working age (18 to 65 years) who are marginalised from the labour market, and the proportion of self-employed residents, leaders and professionals in service trades, Greater Copenhagen 1996

At the other end of the occupational spectrum, we have defined a group called professionals in service trades – a group that in much of the literature on the development of cities is expected to be an increasingly important and expanding group. In this study, we define them as self-employed residents, leaders and other professionals occupied in service trades other than the retail trade. On average, the group constitutes 4.5 per cent of the population aged between 18 and 65.

Table 2.2 indicates that service professionals are highly concentrated in the northern sector of the city while very few live in the sectors south of northwest and in the centre. Figure 2.5 shows that the inner parts of the northern sector especially and to some extent the outer rings of the northern and northwestern sectors have attracted service professionals, although there are relatively few in all other parts of the region.

Segregation of immigrants In the 1960s, Denmark employed many foreign workers, especially from Turkey and Pakistan, whose families followed later. We have also recently received many refugees from various countries.

In this study, immigrants are defined as all persons who are citizens of countries outside Western Europe, Canada, the United States, Australia and New Zealand, or who were born in developing countries. On average, they constitute 6.7 per cent of the total population in the region. Immigrants are a very segregated group, as seen in Figure 2.6. In general, the highest concentrations of immigrants are found in the southwestern and southern sectors – the lowest in the northern and southeastern sectors. There are, however, considerable differences within the sectors. Except for the centre of the region, there are most immigrants in ring zone 3. As will be seen in the following section, this is due to the chronological order in which the ring zones were developed, with immigrants especially tending to settle in social housing built from 1965 to 1980.

This pattern also appears inside the sectors, as show in Figure 2.6. The highest representation of immigrants is found in the parts of the southwestern and southern sectors that belong to ring 3, followed by the part of the southern sector in ring 2 and the southwestern sector in ring 4. These four areas vary considerably from the rest of the region. Some of the municipalities in these areas have a very high proportion of immigrants concentrated on social housing estates.

Fewest immigrants are found in the southeastern sector and in the part of the northern and northwestern sectors belonging to ring 2. Parts of ring 4 in the northern, northwestern and western sectors are also inhabited by quite a

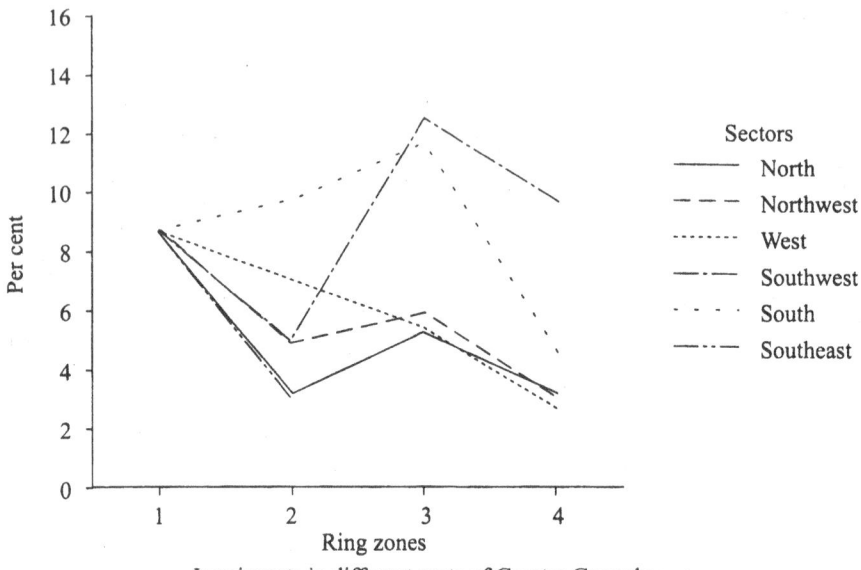

Immigrants in different parts of Greater Copenhagen

Figure 2.6 **Proportion of immigrants – residents who are citizens of countries outside Western Europe, Canada, the United States, Australia and New Zealand, or who were born in developing countries, Greater Copenhagen 1996**

large number of immigrants. As will be seen in a later section, this can be explained largely by the distribution of social housing in Greater Copenhagen.

Housing Policies in Denmark and their Consequences for Segregation

In the section above, we have shown some segregational patterns in Greater Copenhagen. In this section, we will discuss the extent to which this segregation is caused by housing policies or by more fundamental forces of segregation in cities.

The Danish housing market and housing policies The three main sectors of the Danish housing market consist of owner-occupied housing (53 per cent of the stock), social housing (19 per cent) and private rented property, etc. (28 per cent). The latter includes some cooperative dwellings (5 per cent) and dwellings owned by local authorities (3 per cent).

In all three sectors residents have received some kind of public support. Owner-occupiers have received indirect subsidies through the tax system, social housing has been subsidised directly through lower payments on loans, and in the private rented sector, strong rent control has kept rents at a level of about 40 per cent below the market level (Lejelovskommissionen, 1997). Elderly owners with lower incomes and all those renting property are eligible for receive housing benefits.

The Danish tax rules, housing subsidies and regulations for the housing market have resulted in a strong distortion of the demand for housing among different groups of the population. Households with higher incomes and tax payments have had much greater incentives and scope for buying a home than low-income groups. International comparisons have shown that the Danish tax subsidies for owner-occupiers have been at a higher level than in most other European countries (see Haffner, 1993). On the other hand, the housing benefit system encourages people with low incomes to settle in rented dwellings. The situation is made worse by the fact that parts of the social sector have quite high rents, which make them even more unattractive to people who do not receive housing benefits, while older and cheaper dwellings are very difficult to find. This benefit system, combined with the rent structure, tends to concentrate marginalised groups, e.g. people on welfare, people who have taken early retirement and those with low incomes, in the newer parts of the social sector while people in employment try to avoid them.

That is why over the past 20 years Denmark has experienced increasing social segmentation in the housing market – especially in cities. The employed, more affluent part of the population has increasingly settled in owner-occupied detached housing, while marginalised groups, etc. have been concentrated in newer social housing and in the least well-maintained private rented accommodation (Skifter Andersen and Ærø, 1997). That is why the location of housing with different tenures has a significant influence on segregation in the cities.

The influence of local authorities on housing supply in municipalities In Denmark, local governments have had a considerable influence on the composition of local housing markets. Firstly, they can use physical planning measures to control the type and size of sites for all new housing. By laying out most of the urban space for one storey and detached housing and putting higher demands on the minimum size of plots of land, local authorities can restrict new housing to expensive owner-occupied dwellings.

Social housing in Denmark is built and owned by independent nonprofit housing associations that decide in principle where and when to build. But in reality, local governments are in complete control because they grant permission and provide some of the funding. By denying this, they can prevent social housing from being built in certain municipalities.

These powers have been used by local governments in Greater Copenhagen to create local housing markets that are extremely different. Especially in the period before 1980 when private housebuilding was booming, some local governments chose not to accept any new social housing. In this same period, housebuilding in other municipalities was heavily dominated by social housing. There was a strong link between the type of political party that dominated local governments and the kind of housing built. A study in 1986 (Skifter Andersen, 1987), showed that in municipalities led by social-democratic mayors in the beginning of the 1980s, more than 40 per cent of new dwellings built in the period 1970–83 comprised rented housing. In other municipalities, the average was only about half of this figure and several municipalities built no social housing at all in that period.

After 1980, when private housebuilding activity ceased, there was a general increase in the construction of social housing. Even some conservative-dominated local governments have accepted the concept (Skifter Andersen and Als, 1986). Therefore, new social housing has been more equally spread in recent years.

Overall, however, tremendous differences exist in the composition of the housing market in different municipalities in Greater Copenhagen. This has also resulted in differences between the different sectors and ring zones in the region. Figure 2.7 shows the composition of the housing market in ring zones and sectors. The chronological development of the city has resulted in pronounced differences between the different rings. The centre is dominated by private renting (65 per cent), which constitutes less than 20 per cent of suburban dwellings. On the other hand, owner-occupied housing is most common in the outermost ring zone. Few are found in the centre and the majority of these are small owner-occupied flats. Social housing is most common in zone 3, where most of the larger problem estates built in the 1960s and 1970s are located. Social housing in zone 2 and in the centre is older.

It could be argued from the figure that the composition of housing supply in the different municipalities largely follows the general segregational pattern of the region. It could also be argued that this shows that housing supply is just a simple response to demand from households wishing to take up residence in different locations. People with higher incomes demand owner-occupied housing and that is why the majority of dwellings in the most attractive parts of the region are owner-occupied. In other municipalities, demand from low-income groups creates more social housing.

Social Segregation in Cities 37

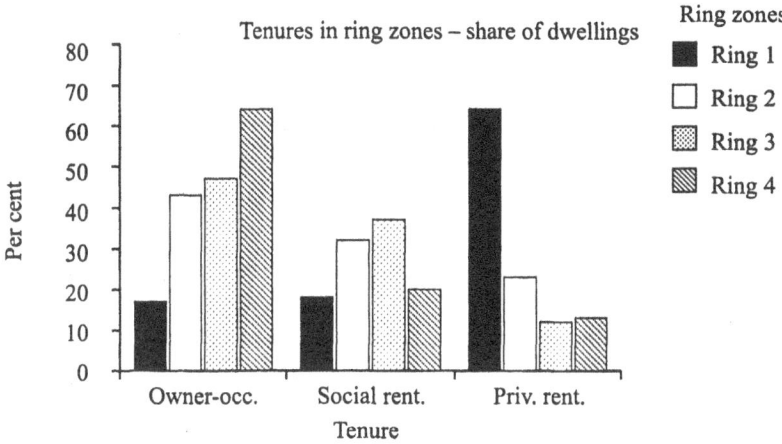

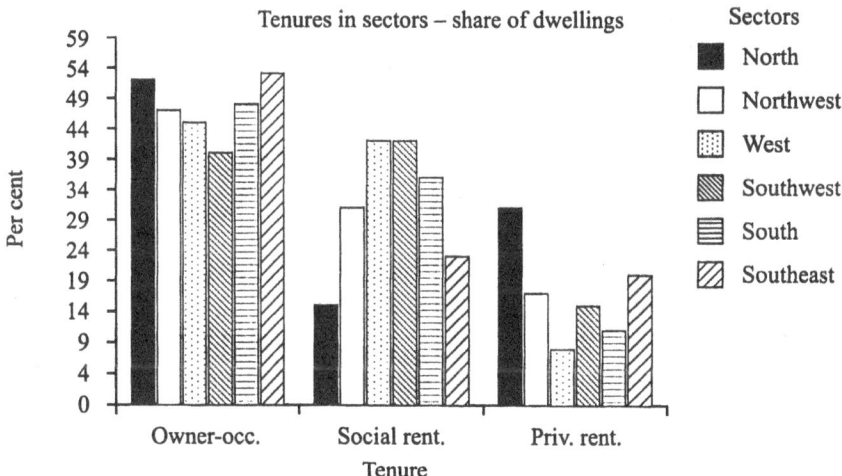

Figure 2.7 **The composition of the housing market in different parts of Greater Copenhagen 1996**

In a Danish context, things are not that simple. As mentioned, the housing market is highly regulated. The location of different kinds of new housing is very much a political decision made by local governments and local demand is of minor importance only. Moreover, all municipalities are part of a common housing market that comprises the whole region. It is therefore possible for local governments to attract people with higher incomes using a housing policy that promotes the construction of new owner-occupied housing. At the same time, they can force low-income groups to leave the municipality by not allowing or supporting social housing.

The fact that some municipalities have only very few social dwellings is therefore more a result of political processes than of market processes. Municipalities with many high-income households tend to be dominated by conservative or liberal political parties who are generally opposed to social housing. Moreover, the politically dominant groups often have a clear interest in trying to keep out groups of the population who cannot pay taxes (Danish municipalities are financed by income taxes), who need expensive social services and who do not fit into the high social status of the local area.

The composition of the housing market in the municipalities cannot therefore be simply a response to demand for location from different groups because there are large differences between municipalities inside the same sectors of the region – municipalities with almost the same location. In five municipalities, social housing forms less than 10 per cent of the stock. They are not – as one might expect – concentrated in the northern part of the region. On the contrary, they are scattered throughout different zones and sectors. One is in the centre (the municipality of Frederiksberg), one is in the northern sector, and two are to the west and one to the south. In five other municipalities, more than half of the dwellings are social housing. They are, however, all located in the western, southwestern and southern sectors.

Comparing two pairs of neighbouring municipalities with almost equal locations in the region is of special interest. The first pair comprises the municipalities of Karlebo and Horsholm, each located in zone 3 of the northern sector, and Ishøj and Vallensbæk located in zone 3 of the southern sector. In the north, Horsholm has only 16 per cent social dwellings, while Karlebo has 34 per cent. In the south, Vallensbæk has just 3 per cent, while Ishøj has 51 per cent. It is difficult to argue that these differences are purely a result of market forces.

The Effect of Housing Location on Segregation

As concluded above, the location of housing supply must be seen as a result both of a) general segregational forces in the city that make different groups demand different kinds of housing in different parts of the region and b) political processes that influence the location of housing supply in ways that can support or counteract general segregation. The location of housing supply is therefore not a simple response to general segregation, but has a separate importance for the spatial location of the population. In this section we will look at indices of segregation for people marginalised from the labour market and for immigrants, respectively, and will try to calculate the extent to which this segregation is caused by differences in the composition of the housing market in different parts of Greater Copenhagen.

Segregation of People Marginalised from the Labour Market

As shown in Table 2.3, marginalised people constitute nearly 40 per cent of the residents of working age in social housing in the region whereas only 8 per cent in owner-occupied housing are marginalised. A large part of the latter group are people living in owner-occupied flats in the centre of the region.

Table 2.3   Proportion of residents in different tenures marginalised from the labour market, over-representation in and segregation between zones and sectors, Greater Copenhagen 1996

	All dwellings	Owner-occupied	Social rented	Private rented
Proportion of residents (%)	21	8	37	26
Ring zone		*Over-representation, %*		
Ring 1	25	23	18	6
Ring 2	-15	-5	-10	-17
Ring 3	-15	-10	-10	-27
Ring 4	-28	-5	11	-9
Index of segregation	10.5	4.9	6.2	4.2
Index of dissimilarity	13.3	5.3	9.9	5.7
Proportion of residents (rings 2–4)	17	8	34	22
Sector		*Over-representation, %*		
North	-20	-13	-2	-8
Northwest	-3	-10	-4	0
West	-2	1	-12	-12
Southwest	21	9	6	-2
South	14	9	8	25
Southeast	-9	25	-14	10
Index of segregation	6.7	5.3	3.6	4.6
Index of dissimilarity	8.1	5.7	5.4	5.9

As shown earlier, compared with the average for the region, the group of marginalised residents is heavily over-represented in the centre (25 per cent more than average) and in the southwestern and southern sectors (21 and 14 per cent). We wish to examine the extent to which this is caused by the combined effects of housing policies at national and local levels, which have resulted in segmentation of the housing market and an unevenly composed housing market in different parts of the city. To do that, we will first consider the differences between zones and sectors concerning residents with the same tenure.

The table shows our calculations of how the group is over-represented within each tenure in the different parts of the region compared with the average representation of the group in this tenure. If housing policies are of no consequence, we should expect the same pattern of over-representation within each tenure. The table shows, however, that the pattern is somewhat different within the tenures and differs from the pattern for all dwellings. In all tenures, there is an over-representation in the centre but this is most pronounced in the owner-occupied sector and somewhat less evident in private rented accommodation. In social dwellings, the group is over-represented in ring zone 4 in strong opposition to the general trend for all dwellings.

By comparing the sectors, it becomes clear that social housing in the richer northern and northwestern sectors has nearly the same proportion of marginalised people as the average for all sectors. Surprisingly, the group is mostly under-represented in social housing in the western sector. The pattern in owner-occupied housing is closest to that of all dwellings except in the southeastern sector.

In the table, two indices of segregation are calculated:

1 the simple index of segregation that shows how the location of the chosen group differs from the location of the whole population;
2 the index of dissimulation that shows how much the group differs from the rest of the population.

We prefer to use the simple index. The latter index is calculated only to make this analysis comparable with other studies that use this index.

As shown, on the whole, segregation in Greater Copenhagen is not disturbing. The largest segregation is found between the ring zones – especially between the centre and the suburbs. There is somewhat less pronounced segregation among the different sectors in the suburbs.

An interesting fact supplied by the table is that segregation among sectors inside tenures in general is less pronounced than total segregation. The most marked segregation is found in the owner-occupied sector and the smallest in social housing. This is, however, quite reasonable, as people move into owner-occupied housing more because of market forces and solvency of households, while the composition of residents in social housing is governed by administrative measures used by local authorities and housing associations. The conclusion here is that the more market-oriented tenures – such as owner-occupied housing and to some extent private rented accommodation – are more likely to promote segregation of marginal groups than social housing. It can, however, also be seen from the figures on over-representation in the table that a segregational pattern similar to the general pattern exists in social housing in the different sectors.

Table 2.4 shows total segregation divided into two parts:

1 segregation caused by differences in the composition of the housing market in the different parts of the region;
2 residual segregation due to other factors.

Table 2.4 **Total segregation of marginalised people among ring zones and sectors, divided into segregation caused by differences in the housing market and residual segregation due to other factors, Greater Copenhagen 1996**

Marginalised	Ring zones	Sectors
	Index of segregation	
Total index of segregation	10.5	6.7
Caused by housing market*	5.9	4.6
Residual segregation	4.6	2.1
Share of segregation	Per cent	
Caused by housing market	56	68
Residual segregation	44	32
Total	100	100

* Calculated as the expected segregation among sectors, etc. in cases where the composition of residents in each tenure in the municipalities corresponds with the average for the whole region.

The calculated expected segregation caused by the location of different tenures in the region reflects the fact that we expect segmentation in the housing market and the differences between local housing markets in the municipalities to cause segregation. As seen in the table, we expect differences in local housing markets to produce a segregation index of 4.6 between sectors and 5.9 between ring zones. When compared with the index of total segregation, we conclude that housing market differences are responsible for respectively 68 per cent of the segregation among sectors and 56 per cent of the segregation among ring zones.

The residual segregation is quite small – indices of 2.1 and 4.6. One conclusion could be that given the existing structure of the housing stock, other forces that cause segregation have had only a limited effect in Copenhagen.

Segregation of Immigrants

As shown earlier (Figure 2.6), immigrants are a very segregated group in the Copenhagen Region. Table 2.5 reveals that immigrants are also very unequally distributed among tenures in the regional housing market. On average, immigrants account for 15 per cent of those renting social housing but only 3 per cent of owner-occupiers. We could therefore expect differences in the composition of the housing market to be the main cause of segregation of immigrants.

Immigrants are heavily over-represented in the centre and in the southwestern and western sectors, while ring zone 2 and especially the northern sector have much fewer immigrants. Inside the different tenures, the picture changes somewhat. In the owner-occupied sector, immigrants are more over-represented mainly in the owner-occupied flats in the centre. They are also over-represented in the southwestern sector. Social rented accommodation most closely resembles the general pattern of segregation but with a somewhat smaller over-representation in the southwestern and southern sectors. Table 2.5 shows that segregation indices within tenures are generally smaller than the indices of the total segregation among sectors and rings, except for the segregation between rings inside the owner-occupied tenure category. However, segregation is quite high in social housing, and is much higher among sectors than is the case for owner-occupied housing. This high segregation can be partly explained by differences in the kind of social housing located in the municipalities. Immigrants are concentrated mainly in social housing built after 1960 (Skifter Andersen and Ærø, 1997), which is more common in the outer rings and in the southern and southwestern sectors, and less common in ring zone 2 and the northern and western parts of the region.

Table 2.5 Proportion of residents in different tenures that are immigrants, over-representation in and segregation among zones and sectors, Greater Copenhagen 1996

Immigrants	All dwellings	Owner-occupied	Social rented	Private rented
Proportion of residents (%)	7	3	15	7
Ring zone		Over-representation, %		
Ring 1	25	70	26	10
Ring 2	-26	-13	-28	-37
Ring 3	8	-11	9	-40
Ring 4	-26	-30	7	20
Index of segregation	11.5	14	10.6	8.3
Index of dissimilarity	12.4	14.4	12.5	8.9
Proportion of residents (rings 2–4)	6	2	13	5
Sector		Over-representation, %		
North	-35	-1	-23	-19
Northwest	-16	-5	-19	-13
West	-14	-20	-27	-7
Southwest	44	28	20	-13
South	43	-1	33	98
Southeast	-47	-3	-63	-18
Index of segregation	16.7	3.8	13.5	14
Index of dissimilarity	17.7	3.8	15.5	14.7

Segregation of immigrants in the Copenhagen Region cannot therefore be attributed solely to the different proportions of tenures in municipalities' local housing markets. Table 2.6 shows that this can explain only 26 per cent of the segregation between *rings*. This is partly because differences inside the social sector – between new and old housing – are not registered. The segregation among *sectors* can be explained more effectively by the segmentation in the market (54 per cent).

Lessons from Copenhagen

This study has attempted to assess the pattern of social segregation in Greater Copenhagen and to some extent evaluate the relevance of the classic model

Table 2.6 Total segregation of immigrants between ring zones and sectors divided into segregation caused by differences in housing markets and residual segregation due to other factors, Greater Copenhagen 1996

Immigrants	Ring zones	Sectors
Segregation	*Index of segregation*	
Total index	11.5	16.7
Caused by housing market	3.1	7.6
Residual segregation	8.5	9.0
Share of segregation	*Per cent*	
Caused by housing market	26	46
Residual segregation	74	54
Total	100	100

(Burgess/Hoyt) formulated half a century ago. Another aim was to expose the effect segmentation in the housing market and differences in housing policies implemented by local governments have on segregation in general.

The social geography of Greater Copenhagen is marked firstly by a zonal structure that differentiates the population according to life-cycle stage. In general, the more distant from city, the higher the number of families and the lower the proportion of elderly residents. However, during the last 5–10 years, the inner suburbs have replaced central Copenhagen as the zone with most elderly people and fewest youngsters.

Secondly, the social pattern has a clear sectoral dimension regarding socioeconomic status: the northernmost sectors have attracted a socioeconomic elite in Copenhagen – people with high incomes, professionals, managers etc. In contrast, low incomes and marginalised people are concentrated to the south and southwest. However, the general level of segregation in Greater Copenhagen is relatively low compared with other big cities in Europe and United States.

Having said that, differences exist among municipalities inside the same sectors of the region that cannot be explained just by differences in locational attraction and general segregational forces in the city. Instead, these differences appear to be linked to differences in the composition of tenures in the housing market within municipalities.

There seems to be good reason to assume that the composition of tenures in the housing stock is of major importance for segregational patterns. As shown, more than half of the segregation of marginalised people among sectors in the region can be explained by differences in housing supply. We have also shown that there is much less segregation within tenure categories in sectors and rings than is the case for average total segregation.

Ethnicity has gained importance as a dimension during the last two decades; the most striking characteristic is the concentration in a few selected areas. This is also due partly to the high level of segmentation of the Danish housing market; as many immigrants belong to low-income groups, their opportunities in the housing market are limited to less attractive parts of the social housing sector and private rental sector. There are, however, also signs that some immigrants have either preferred to concentrate on certain estates, or that they have to some extent been excluded from social housing in other municipalities.

Two kinds of conclusion can be drawn from this evidence: First, that housing supply in the different parts of the region is not simply a response to a certain structure in demand from different groups of the population who wish to settle in various areas. It is also largely a result of local housing policies implemented by local governments in municipalities. Second, that the marked segmentation between different tenures in the Danish housing market means that differences in housing supply have a separate effect on segregation among municipalities in the Copenhagen Region. The more market-based the housing market, the higher the level of social segregation.

Chapter 3

The Appearance of Urban Decay and Deprivation in Western Cities

Cities are divided into neighbourhoods which have different qualities and are inhabited by different people. This variety and differentiation in cities is normally accepted as a positive thing. People with different needs and economic resources can choose to settle in different parts of the urban landscape in accordance with their preferences for, and willingness and ability to pay for, the qualities available. Inequality in the environmental qualities and location enjoyed by different groups is therefore not seen as a special problem, but a result of the general economic and social inequality in societies.

However, sometimes this differentiation of urban space seems to go too far and conditions in certain parts of the cities become unacceptable. These problem areas are called slums, deprived neighbourhoods or areas of urban decay. The neighbourhoods in question are characterised by widespread physical deterioration, a lack of investment in buildings and services and a high concentration of visible and invisible social problems among residents. In the worst-hit areas, a process of abandonment has begun, leaving empty apartments and half-destroyed buildings. Such unsafe environments are suitable habitats for only the most marginalised groups in society – criminals and drug users.

Slums in the USA

The worst-hit areas with the worst problems are to be found in the central parts of some US cities – just outside the central business district.

Since 1940, the development in housing quality has been measured in periodic surveys using different indicators (see Apgar, 1990). The number of 'dilapidated' dwellings, measured in accordance with certain criteria, increased by about 17 per cent in the 1960s (Stokes and Fischer, 1976). Another study showed a 1.4 per cent decline in dwellings with 'inadequate structures' for all housing in the 1970s, while showing a 3.4 per cent increase for rental housing (Apgar et al., 1987; Apgar 1991). According to this study, 20 per cent of the rental stock (comprising 30 per cent of the total stock) was in need of major rehabilitation at the beginning of the 1980s. Another source says that 2 per cent of the total stock in 1985 had severe physical problems, while another 7 per cent had moderate problems (Grigsby, 1990).

To a large degree, the problems of decay in the American housing stock are concentrated in certain urban areas. Despite years of economic growth and several urban renewal programmes (see Adams et al., 1991; Kaplan, 1991), urban decay has spread in major cities. Some neighbourhoods exhibit ongoing decay; buildings are deteriorating and many dwellings are being abandoned.

The extent of these processes can be explained partly by the special conditions prevailing in the housing market in American cities. In both Western Europe and the USA, a dramatic change has occurred in the economic conditions of cities since the 1950s. That change was caused by two trends. The first is the decrease in industrial activity, with increasing unemployment among blue-collar workers. The second is the departure of middle-class residents moving to suburbs. These two trends were stronger in the USA than in most West European cities. In Europe, moreover, a great deal of new social housing has been built in the suburbs for people with low incomes. In the USA, these groups have been left behind in the older parts of the American cities (see, for instance, Adams et al., 1991; Bartelt, 1986; Fossett, 1987). Racial discrimination against blacks and other people of colour has further contributed to urban segregation and a concentration of poor people in certain areas.

In the USA, income is distributed more unevenly than in most Western European countries, and the welfare system is less comprehensive. Under these circumstances, a larger proportion of the population cannot pay for modern, well-maintained dwellings. Housing allowances are low, and only a small proportion of the stock (4 per cent) may be construed as social housing with subsidised rents.

American experience shows that the extent of both urban decay and renewal has varied greatly over time and from city to city (see, for example, DiGiovanni, 1984). It might be expected that factors such as average household income, distribution of income, and the extent and scope of urban renewal programmes has been of decisive importance. However, American census data suggests there is a wide range of poor-quality housing and decline among cities and neighbourhoods with similar income distributions. Decay has been spreading even while real incomes rise, subsidy programmes expand and substandard housing is eliminated (Grigsby et al., 1987, p. 49).

A statistical study of the connection between abandonment and other factors in American cities (Bartelt, 1986) showed where urban decay has been most pronounced: in cities in economic decline and, especially, in old industrial cities. As might be expected, this supports the fact that a relative or absolute fall in incomes or a rise in unemployment in a city increases the risk of urban decay. The study found no connection between general population changes and abandonment.

On the other hand, the greatest incidence of abandonment and urban decay in the USA coincided with periods of high economic growth and rising incomes – especially in the 1960s. One explanation could be that increased incomes spurred the demand for owner-occupied housing in the suburbs during such periods and that this migration to the suburbs has reduced demand for dwellings in the more central parts of cities. Another explanation could be found in the theories put forward by Saskia Sassen (1991) and others: that economic development and globalisation of cities have resulted in a combination of economic growth and increasing social inequality. This could mean less ability to pay for good housing among people at the bottom of the income scale. However Sassens conclusions have later been criticised for being based on insufficient empirical material (Nørgaard, 2000) and for only being applicable to New York and especially not to European cities (Hamnet, 1994).

Despite this, it can be concluded from American experience that urban decay is most likely to occur in cities with increasing differentiation. Accordingly, cities experiencing an unstable and fluctuating economic development have a greater risk of urban decay. This is because parts of the population lose their jobs and their incomes fall, while other groups of the population have rising incomes and move away from the city centres.

European Experience of Urban Decay and Deprived Neighbourhoods

Conditions in the American housing market differ fundamentally from those in most Western European countries. European cities have a lower risk of urban decay and severe slums, welfare systems are better, and housing allowances are larger, meaning that more people can afford well-maintained dwellings.

The extensive public involvement in housing in Western Europe since World War II, supplemented by special large-scale urban renewal programmes, means that Europe has not experienced the same serious decay in, and virtual breakdown of, large urban areas. Europe has, however, seen some problems of decay in old housing and in some of the large social housing estates built in the 1960s and 1970s. And there is no doubt that the general forces of decay which can be observed in the unregulated American housing market also exist in Western Europe – they have been restrained only by extensive public involvement in the housing market.

The extent of urban problems in various European countries depends partly on the degree of social inequality, differentiation and segregation in each country (Skifter Andersen and Leather, 1999). A very segregated housing market with a high concentration of people with low incomes and social problems in certain urban areas leads to larger problems of urban decay.

The general economic and legal conditions concerning private maintenance and improvement of dwellings in these countries have also been of decisive importance. The fundamental economic conditions are not the same in different tenures and they vary from country to country. Therefore differences in the composition of the housing market in the countries and the public regulation of tenures also play important roles.

In most countries, the most problematic tenure in the older parts of the cities has been private rented housing, though the United Kingdom seems to be an exception. This is due partly to some fundamental problems with this tenure – the potential conflicts between landlords and residents, but also results from inexpedient rent control systems that deprive landlords of incentives for housing maintenance and rehabilitation.

The problems with social housing vary. In most of the countries, a combination of building problems and social problems, caused by a high concentration of residents with low incomes, has resulted in problems in high-rise estates from the 1960s and 1970s. Problems on the older estates depend on the administrative rules in the housing associations for collection of money saved for maintenance.

The conditions for housing rehabilitation in owner-occupied housing were formerly quite good. However, in areas with declining demand, e.g. fringe areas, or with a high concentration of low-income residents, some deterioration has also been observed (United Kingdom). In some countries, problems have also been observed in owner-occupied flats lacking maintenance, especially where outdoor maintenance is concerned. Sometimes, residents have insufficient incentives to keep the building in good repair or lack an effective organisation to implement the work.

Urban problems have been given different national priorities depending partly on the composition of the housing stock. For example, some countries – Denmark, France and the UK – have a much larger proportion of old dwellings built before 1945. France and the UK in particular have an old housing stock, while the dwellings in Sweden, Norway and the Netherlands are relatively new.

The extent of the problems has also changed over time depending on the general economic development and public initiatives designed to solve them e.g. the development in obsolete housing lacking bathrooms (Figure 3.1). In 1980, in most of the countries, less than 10 per cent of the dwellings had no bathroom. In the Netherlands and UK especially, very few dwellings were without bathrooms at this time. In three countries – Austria, Denmark and France – more than 15 per cent of the dwellings still lacked a bathroom in 1980. Austria and France succeeded in reducing the problem quite effectively during the 1980s while Denmark improved only a few dwellings in the period.

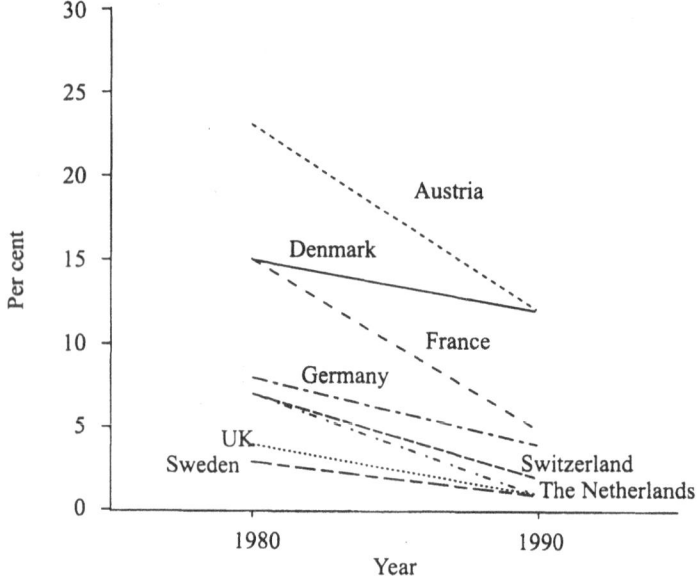

Figure 3.1 Proportion of dwellings without bathrooms

Source: Skifter Andersen and Leather, 1999.

Some of the main problems of urban decay in Western Europe[1] have been:

1   Risks of *destruction of historic buildings and neighbourhoods* largely in old inner-city areas. The problems in these districts have often been closely linked to the industrial and commercial development of the areas.

    In most of the countries, there has been an extensive effort to preserve historical buildings during the 1960s and 1970s so that remaining needs for preservation are limited.

2   A lack of improvement of *obsolete housing* from the last century and the beginning of this century. As we saw in Figure 3.1, very obsolete housing is most frequently found in Denmark and Austria and to some extent in France and Germany. These problems are often combined with:

3   Severe problems of *social and physical decay in certain older urban areas with housing from before 1920*: concentration of people with low incomes and social problems combined with unsatisfactory maintenance and deterioration of the housing stock.

These problems concern mainly high-density blocks of flats or terraced houses lacking open spaces, and dwellings with substandard sanitation. Often these properties are or have been seriously run down.

These problems have been found in all the major urban areas of Europe, but to varying degrees. In Sweden, most of the problems were solved before 1970 by extensive slum clearance activity. As in Switzerland, which also seems to have less pronounced problems, the older urban areas were smaller than those in other countries. Austria, Denmark, Great Britain, France and the Netherlands still needed extensive renewal in these areas after 1980. This was not quite as necessary in Germany, where large part of the areas were destroyed during the War, and in Norway, where cities are relatively smaller.

4   Less serious problems of *social and physical decay in housing from 1920 to 1950*. These were usually well-built properties, but they lacked either certain basic amenities or were in need of modernisation or replacement of standard amenities such as kitchens and sanitary installations. Deterioration is not usually pronounced, though it has accelerated in some areas with a preponderance of residents who expose the dwellings and estates to particularly hard wear and tear. Not all countries have experienced such problems (Switzerland, Sweden).

5   Need for *restructured economic activity and reorganised use of land inside cities*. This covers former industrial areas being transformed into housing or converted for use in service trades. Increasing environmental problems of noise, pollution, traffic etc. in cities have also been of importance.

These problems have arisen especially in highly populated and industrialised urban areas in Germany, Great Britain and the Netherlands, and to some extent also in France, Austria and Switzerland. They have not been so serious in the Nordic countries.

6   *Deterioration of single-family houses in rural fringe areas or those occupied by low-income households*. Demand for the poorest dwellings in regions in decline is typically low, unless they are attractive as holiday

homes. Deterioration has also been observed in owner-occupied housing inhabited by people with low incomes in urban areas, who cannot afford to pay for sufficient maintenance.

Deterioration of housing in fringe areas has been a special problem in mountainous parts of Switzerland, France and Norway. In Great Britain, a large part of the former private poor-quality rented housing has been sold to low-income households who have not been able to keep the buildings in good repair. In Norway and Denmark, problems of disrepair are found in some owner-occupied flats.

7 Special *social and physical problems in social housing from the 1960s and 1970s* built as large, multi-storey housing estates. These dwellings, typically with good-standard installations but poor architectural appearances, have had serious structural defects that have required relatively heavy investments in repairs. Moreover, extensive wear and tear on the buildings have occurred in connection with serious social problems among residents.

All the countries have experienced these kinds of problems, but they seem to have been most serious in France, the Netherlands and Great Britain, where high proportions of immigrants reside (Skifter Andersen and Leather, 1999). Norway had only minor problems in its mostly cooperative postwar housing estates, and Austria also had fewer problems. In Switzerland, some problems have occurred in newer private rented housing and in owner-occupied flats.

The direct observably severe problems found in the worst European areas of deprivation and decay involve:[2]

1 physical decay because of shoddy construction work, rapid attrition and dereliction, and increasing volumes of litter and rubbish in open spaces;
2 low demand, abandonment of dwellings;
3 economic problems because of overdue payments from tenants, or vacant apartments;
4 visible antisocial behaviour: crime, rioting, vandalism, drugs, alcoholics, increased noise;
5 social and racial tension and conflicts among residents;
6 high moving frequency leading to;
7 partial breakdown of normal social relations and reduced tenant activity;
8 deteriorated housing service and management;
9 deterioration of local private and sometimes also public services;

10 school problems because of a high concentration of children from poor families or ethnic groups;
11 visible signs of negative changes and unstable conditions.

The direct consequence of the emergence of these problems has been a deterioration of the environment and housing quality for people living on the estates. This has been shown by several studies (Burrows and Rhodes, 1998; Taylor, 1998; Evans, 1998; Cars, 2000). An indirect effect is that these areas gain bad reputations – places where people stay only when they have no alternative. For those who have to live in these areas, this can mean an attack on their identity and a reduction in their self-esteem. As Taylor (1998) puts it: 'For many residents on estates, community is the site of fear and blame rather than choice and pride'. Sometimes, the bad image of a neighbourhood is transferred to people living there, which leads to discrimination that reduces residents' scope for obtaining jobs and bank credit (Taylor, 1998; Dean and Hastings, 2000; Social Exclusion Unit, 1998). Other studies (Aitken, 1990) have shown that people are very concerned about the prospects of the neighbourhood where they live. Even if the actual situation is not too bad, residents are alarmed by signs that the situation is declining. Unstable conditions in a neighbourhood therefore make residents uneasy.

It is difficult to determine the extent of urban decay and deprivation in European cities. There is a gradual transition from normal well-functioning urban areas through neighbourhoods that suffer from some physical and social decay to areas with abandoned and deteriorated buildings dominated by crime and drugs. The definition of when neighbourhoods are deprived can also vary from country to country.

In England, for instance, 3,000 neighbourhoods, each with more than 100 households suffering from concentrated problems of run-down, vacant or derelict housing have been identified by the English House Condition Survey. In another study based on social data, 1,370 social housing estates in England, ranging from 50 to 5,000 households, were defined as deprived (Social Exclusion Unit, 1998).

In Denmark, 500 social housing estates with more than 230,000 residents in 250 different urban areas have been identified as suitable for publicly supported regeneration (Skifter Andersen, 1999). Moreover, seven larger mixed urban areas, each with between 1,000 and 15,000 people, have been part of special urban revitalisation programmes, and five more will be appointed. In addition, traditional urban and housing renewal programmes are continuing in the older part of the housing stock.

Notes

1 The study referred to (Skifter Andersen and Leather, 1999) compared nine countries: France, Germany, Austria, Switzerland, Holland, UK, Denmark, Sweden and Norway.
2 See, for example, Taylor, 1998, Power, 1997, Power and Tunstall, 1995, Evans, 1998, Hall, 1997, Social Exclusion Unit, 1998, Burrows and Rhodes, 1998, Kearns et. al., 2000, Costa Pinho, 2000, Cars, 2000.

Chapter 4

Explanations of Decay in the Urban Housing Market

What are the fundamental economic causes of urban decay and housing deterioration? In Western European countries, most governments have found it necessary to establish special subsidy programmes and public regulation of urban renewal and housing rehabilitation. However, the deeper reasons for this public intervention, and for supply subsidies to maintain and improve the housing stock, have not been clearly formulated. Few researchers have tried to answer the question: why has the housing market been unable to produce a well-maintained and modern housing stock?

Many economists seem to believe that housing deterioration can be explained entirely by either the existence of demand for low-quality housing or by negative effects of public intervention in the housing market that destroy the efficiency of the market (see Nesslein, 1988a and b). The argument is that if the housing market is functioning according to the assumptions of general economic theory, problems of bad and inadequate housing can occur only through lack of demand resulting from parts of the population having inadequate incomes.

Throughout Western Europe, government intervention has generally been significant, especially in the rented housing market, and has taken the form of rent control, for instance. Many economists consider this intervention to be the main reason for a badly functioning market, and an important indirect cause of failing maintenance and housing improvement.[1] The strong tradition of public intervention in the housing market may also explain why fundamental research on the economics of the housing market has been relatively sparse in Europe. It is difficult to distinguish the effects of market forces from the effects of public regulation. Accordingly, very little research has been done to identify the fundamental causes of deterioration or failing rehabilitation of the housing stock and urban areas in Europe.

The United States has a much less regulated market. Therefore, it is possible to observe processes of decay and renewal that are less affected by rent control or other kinds of public interventions used in European countries. Extensive research has been done in the housing market in the USA, and on processes of decay and renewal in cities. American research therefore allows us to discuss the possibility that general market failure exists and promotes slums and decay.

In the following sections, we will look at the traditional economic explanations of housing deterioration and urban decay first. Based on American research on actual economic conditions and mechanisms in slum areas, it will be shown that these theories are unable to explain the development in these neighbourhoods. Other explanations must be found and a new theory on processes of urban decay and renewal is formulated based on evidence from various American studies.

One conclusion from American experience is that the individual behaviour of private owners and landlords is of great importance for housing deterioration. In the last section of this chapter, evidence from a Danish study on how landlords act during rent control will be used to show that the economic situation and private motives of landlords determine maintenance levels, while market regulations are of only minor importance.

Critique of Traditional Economic Explanations of Housing Deterioration – American Experience

Dilapidation and abandonment of housing are often explained as being a consequence of a 'natural' process: as dwellings grow old, their quality decreases. After a certain time, the buildings are worn down to a quality level that is unacceptable. The dwellings are then vacated, and after some time the buildings are demolished to make way for new buildings.

However, the economic literature gives two different explanations for this deterioration. One says that for either technical or financial reasons, housing cannot be maintained indefinitely. The other explains deterioration as a consequence of market processes, with older housing in the course of time becoming obsolete and passing on to people with lower incomes who cannot afford to pay for good maintenance (the so-called 'filtering process'; see Grigsby, 1963). One could therefore divide the traditional economic explanations into a combined technical-financial explanation and a socioeconomic or market explanation.

Technical-financial Explanations for Deterioration

Some authors (Ratcliff, 1949; Muth, 1969; Quigley, 1979) have regarded decay as a consequence of dwellings undergoing natural – physically conditioned –

dilapidation. Others (Lowry, 1960; Grigsby et al., 1987; Rydell, 1970; Rothenburg et al., 1991) find no empirical evidence that dwellings cannot be maintained indefinitely.

The crucial question is whether maintenance costs increase over the course of time. If so, there may be an economically optimal life span for housing. Based on purely technical considerations about the lifetime of different parts of a building, it can be argued that maintenance costs will vary over time because of the cost of replacing these parts. But this does not necessary imply that maintenance costs will increase in the long run. Several researchers (see the survey in Margolis, 1981) believe that maintenance costs increase with building age, but no one has presented empirical proof to support this. According to Ingram and Oron (1977), it is possible to divide building capital into 'structure capital', which is infinitely durable, and 'quality capital', which is worn down with age. Margolis points out in his survey that researchers disagree on whether maintenance costs increase in the long run and that even those who agree that they do rise disagree on how much they increase.

An empirical study (Rydell, 1970) concludes that although maintenance costs escalate in the first years of a building's lifetime, they later stagnate at a level 40 per cent above the initial costs. The same conclusion can be drawn from statistics on maintenance expenses in the about 400,000 dwellings in the Danish social housing sector. Those statistics show (Figure 4.1) that maintenance costs increase with age during the first 20–25 years, but then remain stable.

Even accepting that maintenance costs increase with time, it is not necessarily unprofitable to continue maintenance indefinitely. It is a fact that the relative price of new housing has increased over time because productivity in the building sector has not increased at the same rate as in other sectors of the economy. Consequently, over the years it is becoming relatively more expensive to replace old building capital with new building capital. This could outweigh higher maintenance costs for the old capital.

It is fair to say that no convincing arguments have been presented to buttress the explanation that housing deteriorates for purely technical reasons. We can therefore conclude that the deterioration of housing cannot be explained through purely technical-financial causes.

Socioeconomic or Market Explanations

Dwellings are generally acknowledged to become obsolete in the course of time. Due to increasing incomes and acquired tastes, demand has shifted

Figure 4.1 Maintenance costs in DKK per square metre in social housing in Denmark 1990

Source: The Danish Ministry of Housing.

towards larger, better-equipped dwellings in better surroundings. For this reason, much of the old housing stock has become less desirable than new dwellings and has therefore become obsolete.

Increasing affluence after World War II resulted in growing demand for owner-occupied single-family houses in the suburbs. High- and medium-income groups moved away from city centres. Some of the vacated dwellings were abandoned and demolished. Others were occupied by people with lower incomes. This process, by which well-to-do residents in a neighbourhood are replaced by low-income households, is called downward 'succession'. Many American social scientists have seen this process of downward succession as the primary cause of urban decay (see the overview in Grigsby et al., 1987; and Rothenburg et al., 1991). The people left in these central city areas are less able to pay for good housing quality, which results in decreasing investments both in maintenance and improvement of the housing stock.

It is, however, not quite clear from this literature what the actual connection is between succession and decay, why succession has happened and why the dwellings have not been adapted to changes in demand. Small dwellings could for example be converted to satisfy demand from single residents. Moreover, the evidence of gentrification in some neighbourhoods – the process by which a worn-down urban area is renewed as people with higher incomes displace low-income groups – refutes the assumption that the ageing of neighbourhoods inevitably leads to succession as a law of nature.

Many American researchers believe that property values and rents have to be reduced when succession occurs and that this automatically leads to reduced maintenance. The argument is as follows: reduced maintenance is a rational strategy for landlords, i.e. the quality of dwellings is reduced to a lower level corresponding to the new demand from low-income groups. The first landlords to adopt this strategy in a neighbourhood make the highest profits (Rothenburg et al., 1991).

This point of view implies that a dwelling can be maintained at different levels that result in differences in quality. Maintenance activities such as painting outside walls and renewing parts of the building are not essential to its survival, and can be postponed. But other maintenance activities cannot be downgraded or postponed. Deferred upkeep threatens the survival of the building, causing damage that is far more expensive to repair.

For this reason, there are limits to how much maintenance can be reduced, unless the owners have an economic strategy for writing off building capital in a shorter time. However, American researchers who have studied specific examples of the economy of housing estates in urban areas in decay (Stegmann, 1972, Grigsby and Rosenburg, 1975) conclude that an economic strategy of fast depreciation (called 'milking') is seldom profitable. The problem is that the costs saved nowhere near compensate for the loss of building capital and rental income. Furthermore they contend that the strategy is not always feasible; local authorities can intervene when the requirements of building legislation are violated.

Moreover, several case studies of American neighbourhoods have revealed that maintenance costs do not necessarily decrease as decay in a neighbourhood increases. A study of housing in the central parts of St. Louis in the 1970s (Quinn et al., 1980) showed that maintenance costs actually increased in 70 per cent of the dwellings, while rents decreased in 62 per cent of them. A study in Baltimore at the beginning of the same decade (Grigsby and Rosenburg, 1975) also showed that maintenance costs increased in the majority of dwellings. However, a study in Newark, New York, in the 1960s (Sternlieb, 1969) showed that maintenance costs were reduced.

These apparently conflicting empirical results reflect the many and complex reasons for neighbourhood decay, including differences in the behaviour displayed by different landlords and tenants.

One important explanation for the development of maintenance expenditures, mentioned in almost all of the studies (see also Salins, 1980), is that dilapidation increases when households with low incomes and social problems move into houses. These occupants often take less care of dwellings. Sometimes there is direct evidence of vandalism, which drastically increases the need for maintenance, especially in the last stages of the process of decay. This means that slum dwellings may cost more to maintain than better-quality housing. At the same time, some of the poorer residents may cease paying rent. This means losses to the landlords until the tenants are given notice and new ones are found.

In the light of these problems, some landlords prefer to keep rents at a certain level, even if this leads to vacant apartments, instead of reducing rents. They would rather forego the income than rent the units to families with social problems and low incomes. A study of the development of rents in two American cities (Rydell, 1977) showed that landlords preferred to have empty dwellings in situations with falling demand instead of reducing rents, as that would attract low-income groups. More support is provided by several statistical studies of the connection between housing quality and rents in the USA that show low-quality dwellings with relatively high rents compared with their quality (Muth, 1969). It has also been shown that rents at the bottom of the rental market do not react properly to changes in demand (Rothenburg et al., 1991).

The American studies suggest that landlords in slum areas cannot afford to carry out the necessary maintenance for a combination of reasons: increasing maintenance needs, decreasing rental incomes and restricted access to bank credits (Leven et al., 1976). Landlords in American slum areas seem to be caught in a trap, with maintenance costs increasing while income from their property is decreasing.

There are, however, differences between the behaviour and situation of different kinds of landlords. Grigsby and Rosenburg (1975) showed that most of the major landlords in slum areas with more than 100 dwellings made a reasonable profit on their properties and could afford satisfactory maintenance. They had a rational administration and were careful about choosing new tenants. Many of these landlords had experienced a loss of capital with the drop in property values in the neighbourhood, but had paid back their loans on time.

Minor landlords were in quite a different situation. Many had some debt in their property. Their liquidity was precarious and getting worse, due to problems with bad tenants and vacant dwellings. They could not obtain any new bank loans and often could not afford to pay for sufficient maintenance. Sometimes they stopped paying property taxes (see, for example, Peterson et al., 1973; Smith et al., 1989) and – more rarely – payments on loans. In many cases, they eventually had to abandon property, either because the buildings had deteriorated too much or because local authorities were trying to collect outstanding taxes. In a following section we will show that some landlords in Europe can also be expected to behave less than rationally and make economic dispositions that will lead to deterioration of their properties.

The American studies of the 1970s demonstrated some typical problems faced by many minor landlords and owner-occupiers. Generally speaking, they had not always been able to foresee the decay of their neighbourhood and the fall in property values. Many had invested too much in their properties. Often they lost money or were unable to sell their houses. Therefore, some better-quality dwellings were also abandoned.

The American evidence referred in this section suggests that the deterioration of dwellings and urban areas cannot be regarded simply as a rational response by the housing market to changes in demand. The existence of slums cannot be explained as a simple consequence of low incomes and low housing demand.

Neighbourhood Processes of Decay and Renewal in American Cities

Neighbourhood Effects

The question is whether deterioration of old housing can be explained simply by succession or filtering. Evidence from American research on the decline of certain parts of major cities suggests that the explanations are much more complex. Sometimes, succession can be regarded as a consequence and not a cause of urban decay.

When explaining neighbourhood decay (and renewal), it is crucial to recognise that the value of a dwelling is affected by its surroundings. The outcome of investments in a dwelling therefore depends on investments in other buildings in the neighbourhood. If one landlord or owner invests and the neighbours do not, he will lose money because the general decay of the neighbourhood will reduce the value of his property and make his investments unprofitable. If the neighbours do invest, and he does not, he will make larger profits. If there are expectations of declining investments, an optimal investment strategy is to invest less than the neighbours. Empirical studies in the USA (Mayer, 1981 and 1985; Quinn et al., 1980) have clearly shown that rehabilitation of dwellings occurs much less frequently in neighbourhoods in decay. This is especially true for rental housing. In owner-occupied housing, often residents want to improve their homes instead of moving and therefore tend to make investments that are, in fact, not profitable (see, for example, Rothenburg et al., 1991; Schilling et al., 1991).

Processes of Decay

In most cases, neighbourhood decay and succession are processes that reinforce each other. The fundamental process of succession and decay is illustrated in Figure 4.2. As shown, it involves the interaction between three main factors:

1 the composition of residents in the neighbourhood;
2 the economic conditions of the properties;
3 the physical condition of buildings and the neighbourhood as a whole.

All three factors change simultaneously because they affect each other. Replacing former residents with lower-income residents means lower demand for housing from new residents who cannot afford to pay high rents. This affects the economic conditions of the properties and makes it less profitable to invest in maintenance and improvements. Therefore the physical condition of the buildings declines or the dwellings become obsolete. This means that the attractiveness of the whole neighbourhood declines and succession increases.

Finally, a new and strong factor speeds up the process, as shown in Figure 4.3. When the succession has reached the point at which a comparatively large proportion of the residents are people with social problems, the economy of the properties becomes affected by losses in rental incomes because residents sometimes cease paying rent, because the turnover of residents increases and because some of the dwellings could be vacant for longer or shorter periods. At the same time, wear and tear on properties increase because residents are less inclined to take care of the dwellings. At this point, the possibilities of reversing the process are very small and abandonment will begin to take place.

Housing is a long-term investment and expectations about the future are of decisive importance. American studies (see, for example, Sternlieb and Burchell, 1973; Stegmann, 1972) show that when expectations about decay appear in a neighbourhood, a process is initiated that is very difficult to stop and which seems to be irreversible. The starting point could be small changes

Explanations of Decay in the Urban Housing Market 63

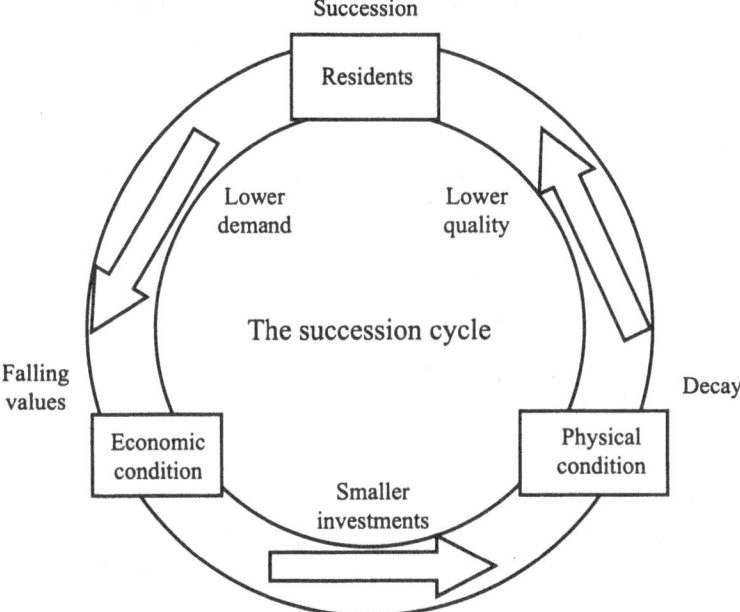

Figure 4.2 **The process of succession and decay**

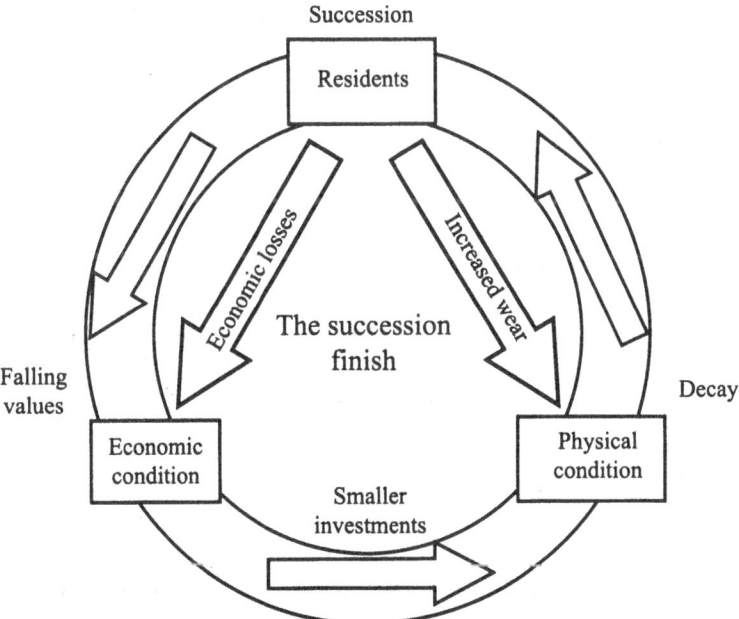

Figure 4.3 **The final succession and decay process**

in the neighbourhood, such as a few poor people – often blacks – moving in, or a small number of buildings that show signs of deterioration. Recent research (Ellen, 2000) shows that, in choosing neighbourhoods, householders care less about the present racial composition and general situation than they do about expectations concerning future neighbourhood conditions, such as school quality, property values and crime. It also shows, however, that people in the USA tend to associate a growing minority presence with structural decline.

Sometimes the process of decay could be initiated at random for various reasons, because a few property owners cannot afford to maintain their houses properly (Grigsby et al., 1987). This could give rise to expectations about a future decline in demand and land prices in the area, which leads to an actual fall in house values and investments. One reason is that banks become very reluctant to give loans in the area (so-called 'redlining'). The consequences are deterioration in the neighbourhood followed by migration of middle class residents. Instead, people with lower incomes move in and the process accelerates. Ultimately, crime and vandalism increase, and everyone who can escapes. An increasing number of dwellings are abandoned, but are not always demolished to make way for new buildings because of the character of the neighbourhood.

Inaccurate expectations among investors about the future development of a neighbourhood can promote decay and abandonment (see, for example, Stegman, 1972; Quinn et al., 1980). The problem is that investors cannot always easily foresee which part of a city is going to decline and which will not. Many factors are involved, including the expectations and actions of other investors. Therefore, some owners pay too much for their properties or invest too much in renovation and are therefore more vulnerable to economic losses caused by neighbourhood decay. These investors are the first to give up maintenance and later abandon dwellings.

Deterioration of housing has also been observed in neighbourhoods where little or no succession has occurred (see, for example, Grigsby et al., 1987). This can happen because structural changes that affect land prices – changes in transport systems, public investments, localisation pattern of industry and other trade, etc. – change expectations for some neighbourhoods and are an indirect cause of deterioration in various parts of a city. These changes in land prices can result in greater differences between the profit earned with the actual use of a site and the potential profit to be gained through its optimal use. This creates expectations of a shorter lifetime for the present buildings on the site and the economically optimal maintenance then decreases. In an empirical study (Mayer, 1981), the actual level of maintenance carried out on buildings on poorly utilised sites was shown to be lower than on other buildings. Dildine and Massey (1974) have used a theoretical model to show that optimal maintenance efforts decrease as land prices increase.

Processes of Renewal – Gentrification

While many neighbourhoods in American cities are declining, there have also been examples, since the 1970s, of neighbourhoods where decay has stopped and after few years, new investments have begun to flow into the areas. This process has been named 'gentrification', the opposite of succession, because households with higher incomes move into the neighbourhood and replace the existing residents who have lower incomes. The process is illustrated in Figure 4.4.

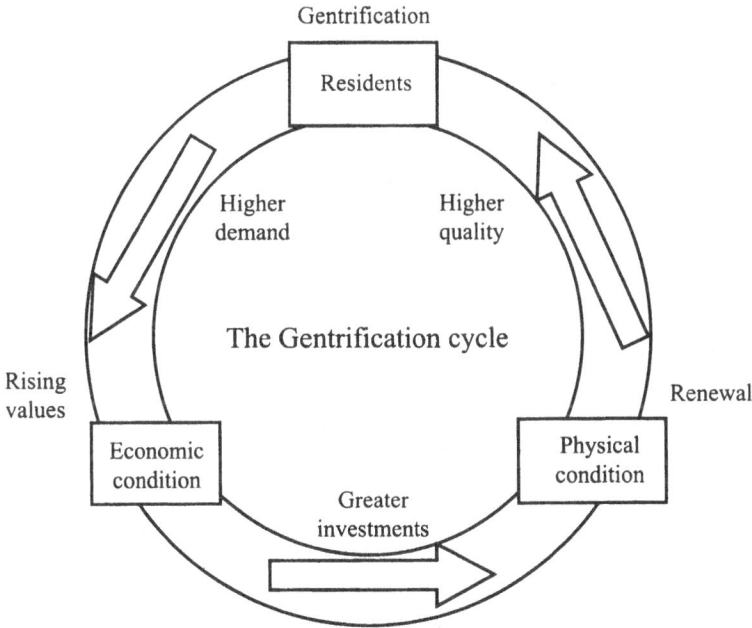

Figure 4.4 The process of gentrification and renewal

Seen in the light of the strong and self-enforcing processes of decay described above, it is difficult to understand how gentrification can take place in American cities. How can the process of decay suddenly change into a process of renewal? How can it be profitable to invest in neighbourhoods in decline?

An important reason for gentrification is the change in employment in city centres since the 1960s, with many new jobs for so-called 'yuppies' (young urban professionals). Many of these were young and single, or were couples without children who preferred living near city centres instead of moving to the suburbs.[2]

One explanation that is especially popular with geographers (see Smith and Williams, 1986; Smith, 1991) is that property prices in neighbourhoods in decay are low, which provides a basis for profitable investments if the use of a site can be changed (the so-called rent gap theory). But this does not automatically explain why gentrification takes place in certain areas and not in others, since most property prices are low in neighbourhoods in decay because investors do not expect the use of the land to be changed. If they did, the prices would be higher.

The crucial condition for gentrification is therefore a change in the future expectations of the neighbourhood (see, for example, Smith, 1989). A few young optimists who move into a neighbourhood and renovate some of the houses, or one or two investors who own several properties, can influence expectations in the area, so that more people begin to believe in renewal and rising prices. Of course, this continues only if there is a potential demand for housing in the neighbourhood from households with sufficiently high incomes.

The total amount of renewal resulting from gentrification in American cities has, however, been limited, and in most cases has not had an essential effect on the general tendencies of decline in major cities (see Nelson, 1988; DiGiovanni, 1984). Renewal is more common in neighbourhoods located near city centres, water or parks or with other special qualities. Sometimes renewal is supported by public investments in the area.

Gentrification in the USA has been more a case of some groups of people living in the city regrouping within the same city limits rather than returning to the city from the suburbs. Some researchers believe that gentrification indirectly promotes decay because poor people are displaced from the gentrified areas and concentrated in other parts of the city where succession and decay then accelerates (see Smith and Williams, 1986; Nelson, 1988). Gentrification could therefore lead to increased segregation and urban decay in cities, depending on the extent to which the gentrified areas are substitutes for the suburbs or for other neighbourhoods in the cities.

There are also indications that gentrification in the USA may be relatively temporary. Reports from New York (Marcuse, 1993) indicate that processes of decay have begun to appear in some of the gentrified neighbourhoods – called 'de-gentrification'. Gentrification in the USA could therefore to some extent be a phenomenon belonging to a certain historic epoch, disappearing with changing tastes and new economic conditions.

What Can be Learned from American Experience of Decay?

The purpose of this chapter has been to discuss what Europe can learn about the causes of decay and renewal from American research on this subject.

Segregation, poverty and the general economic development of cities that led to a concentration of poor people and social problems in certain neighbourhoods are more important causes of urban decay in the USA than in Europe. But American research indicates that explanations of urban decay are not simple, and that special conditions and mechanisms promote decay of dwellings and prevent renewal.

Housing deterioration cannot be explained simply by dwellings having a limited technical or economic lifetime or as a rational market response to demand for low-cost low-quality housing. American studies of landlords' economies in slum areas have shown that it is seldom profitable for them to pursue a strategy of reduced maintenance and faster property depreciation in response to decreasing demand.

Evidence from American research indicates instead that decay in a neighbourhood is a self-perpetuating process with simultaneous changes occurring in the composition of residents, economic conditions of the properties, and physical condition of the buildings. Immigration of people with lower incomes to a neighbourhood leads to lower demand and rent limitations, which result in less investment in maintenance. This in turn causes physical deterioration, which accelerates the migration of people with good incomes and influx of people with lower incomes.

This process is explained and influenced by several phenomena. American research has identified the following important factors:

1 The value of a dwelling depends on the quality of the neighbourhood. Renewing or refurbishing housing in a neighbourhood in decay is therefore rarely profitable. This creates strong economic mechanisms for decreasing maintenance in certain parts of the cities.
2 When the proportion of low-income households with social problems rises in a neighbourhood, wear and tear on dwellings increase, which leads to higher costs for maintaining and running the property. At the same time, losses from unpaid rents increase. Increasing crime in the area encourages middle class residents to migrate to other parts of the city.

3 Segregation in the housing market, which leads to an additional concentration of households with social problems in certain neighbourhoods, is an important cause of slums.
4 Expectations concerning the future development in a neighbourhood are of crucial importance to investors in housing and to banks financing the investments. Expectations of decay create a self-reinforcing process, with accelerating decay and more negative expectations. Decay increases when banks and authorities financing investments in housing decide to limit loans to certain neighbourhoods (redlining) – or increase the capital costs. On the other hand, new expectations of renewal can create a positive spiral of investments and positive expectations.
5 Structural changes in a city – changes in transport systems, localisation of trade etc., which affect land prices, can provoke increased risk of decay in some neighbourhoods because expectations have changed.

Can Neighbourhood Processes of Decay and Renewal be found in European Cities?

There are fundamental differences between housing market conditions in the USA and most Western European countries that have reduced the risks of urban decay and severe slums in European cities. There are better welfare systems and larger housing allowances, meaning that more people can afford well-maintained dwellings. However, it can also be shown that extensive public intervention in the housing market in many ways impedes the processes of decay described above. Figure 4.5 shows some of the interventions made in the housing market that have significantly impeded urban decay in the private housing market in European cities.

Europe has a larger social housing sector that has provided better housing opportunities for the poor and reduced their dependence on the old private rental housing stock inside the cities and therefore weakened the forces that create succession. Housing allowances have made it possible for low-income tenants to pay rents that keep up the economic basis for maintenance.

In many countries, rent control and other kinds of price control systems remove incentives for owners to maintain and improve their dwellings. On the other hand, rent control also impedes the succession and decay process because rents are often kept below market prices. In the first place, this means that segregation does not happen to the same extent because more low-income families can afford better dwellings. Some middle class people also stay in lower quality housing because it is inexpensive. Secondly, landlords' rental

Explanations of Decay in the Urban Housing Market

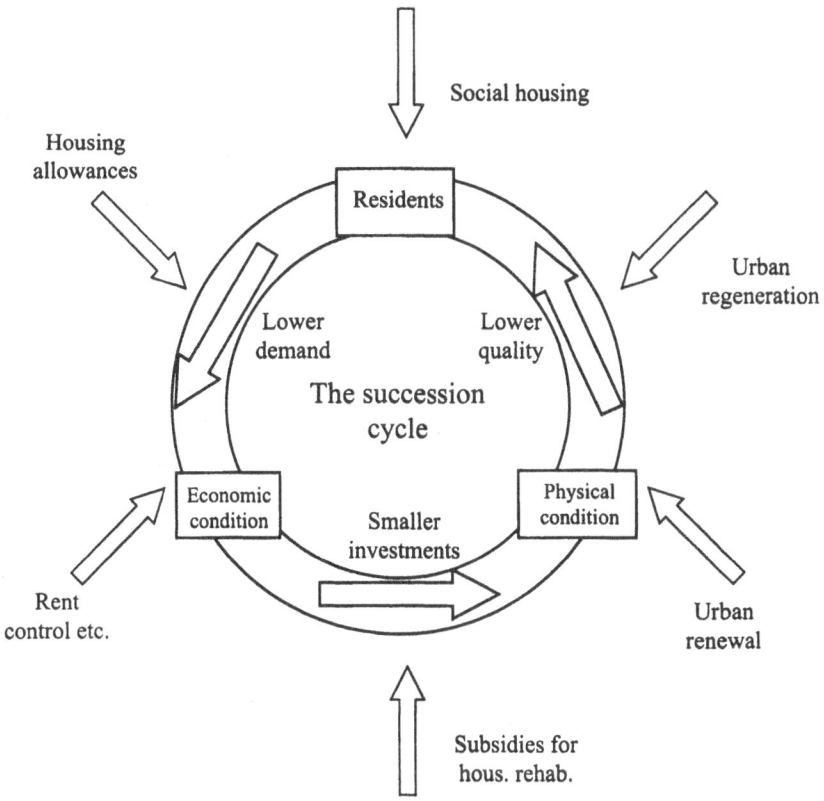

Figure 4.5 Public intervention in the housing market that impedes urban decay in Europe

income and their investment incentives are only slightly affected by succession, because newcomers with lower incomes are also able to afford the rent.

In many European countries, different policies for urban renewal and housing rehabilitation are in use (see Skifter Andersen and Leather, 1999). Some of the programmes imply public subsidies for investments in housing rehabilitation, which makes renovating properties more profitable for owners. In other cases, local authorities carry out urban renewal schemes that directly force through slum renovation or demolition. Furthermore, general public investments in neighbourhoods in decay make them more attractive and impede succession.

The extensive public involvement in housing in Western Europe since World War II, supplemented by special large-scale urban renewal programmes, means that Europe has not experienced the same serious decay in, and virtual breakdown of, large urban areas. Europe has, however, seen some problems of decay in old rental housing and also in some of the large social housing estates built in the 1960s and 1970s. And there is no doubt that the general forces of decay that can be observed in the unregulated American housing market also exist in Western Europe – they have been restricted in the last 30 years only because of the extensive public involvement in the housing market.

It is important that the development of problems of decay in the housing market in European countries is understood as interaction between market forces, which create decay, and public intervention in the market that influence these forces – directly or indirectly.

Sometimes, public intervention is the main problem. Examples include cases of local authorities creating succession in social housing estates by allocating the great majority of flats to households with very low incomes and social problems. Other examples include some of the rent control systems for private rental housing that deprive landlords of incentives to maintain and improve the dwellings.

In other cases, the negative market forces of decay are too strong. This could be the case in countries with highly segmented housing markets and with small social housing sectors. In these countries, high concentrations of low-income households in certain parts of private rental or owner-occupied housing could create greater problems of deterioration in these parts of the housing stock. However, many factors could be of importance, such as social and economic conditions in the country and elements of the general housing policy such as housing allowances and tax subsidies, rent control etc.

There is therefore no simple explanation for the causes of urban decay found in Europe. In every country, the proportion and interaction of market forces and public interventions in the market are specific.

The general forces of succession and decay in parts of the housing market also exist in Europe. These forces may become more active in Europe if a more market-oriented housing policy is adopted.

It can be concluded from some of the American studies mentioned that urban decay is partly a result of unsuitable behaviour among some of the actors on the housing market. In the next section, we will look more closely at this problem in a European context and try to expose the extent to which this is due to public regulation, i.e. rent control.

The next chapter will discuss whether special processes of social and physical decay also take place in European deprived urban neighbourhoods.

Rent Control and Unsuitable Behaviour of Private Landlords as Causes of Housing Deterioration

In economic studies of the private rental sector of the housing market, and in political debates on housing policy, it is often assumed that private landlords are basically guided by rational economic motives. This section, which is based on a Danish study of housing rehabilitation activity among private landlords under rent control shows that landlords can have many other motives for buying and maintaining rental property than those covered by an economic theory. It is concluded that despite the assumptions, private landlords do not always behave as economically rational and efficient actors, and that an understanding of structures of landlordism is essential when assessing causes of housing deterioration in the private rental sector.

In most European countries since World War II, private rental housing has followed a general trend of decline (see, for example, Harloe, 1985; van der Heijden and Boelhouwer, 1996). This development has resulted in a reduction of the private rental stock arising from the conversion of private rented dwellings into other forms of tenure and by reduced investments in the production of new dwellings. But it has also caused disinvestment in the remaining stock. In many countries, some of the most severe problems concerning deteriorated and obsolete housing are found in the private rental sector (Skifter Andersen and Leather, 1999).

However, in some countries, especially the UK, it has been a political objective for some years to revive the private rental sector as part of a new housing policy according to which the state wishes to withdraw from the housing market – so-called privatisation policies (see Crook and Kemp, 1996; Whitehead, 1996).

The fundamental idea behind this policy is that in several respects private renting can be regarded as a better means of meeting housing needs using fewer public resources than is the case with other forms of tenure. One argument in favour of increasing the amount of housing supplied by the private rental sector is that private 'landlords can be expected to be more efficient than individual owners in generating improvement, repair and management – especially where economies of scale can be achieved' (Whitehead, 1996).

Such arguments are based largely on notions of private landlords as rational economic agents who react quickly to market signals and tenants' requirements. However, such a simplified picture of private landlords does not apply to the reality revealed in recent years by studies of the actual behaviour of private landlords. These studies show many different types of landlords with varying motives for owning rental property and with differing levels of professionalism and ability to carry out efficient property administration and provide a good housing service.

This section addresses private landlords' ability to maintain and improve their properties and their motives for doing so and reveals the extent to which this is influenced by rent control. The starting point is the development of a theory on investment motives among different kinds of private landlords based on empirical evidence from a number of research projects in Denmark[3] and on available literature from other countries. The actual investment behaviour of private landlords is then illustrated using results from a survey conducted among landlords in Denmark. We will start by describing the Danish housing market and the kind of rent control in use so that this evidence can be understood in a proper Danish nationwide context.

Investment Motives among Different Kinds of Landlords

Traditional economic theory on the rational behaviour of private landlords and on the effects of rent control is based mainly on the assumption that private landlords are investors who share a long-term view of the investments made and who usually have purely economic motives.

An examination of studies from different countries, however, shows that this type of economically motivated landlord is seldom typical and that other types of landlords often dominate the private rental sector.

Finally, a theory of motives for investments in private renting and a typology of private landlords are presented based on English and Danish studies.

Economic theory on the maintenance of private rental properties and the effects of rent control The simple foundation of economic theory on the investment behaviour of landlords (see Dildine and Massey, 1974; Mayer, 1981; Moorhouse, 1982; Margolis, 1981; Kutty, 1996) assumes that landlords maximise the current value of the expected stream of profits (the share of rental income that remains after running costs and maintenance expenses are paid) arising from the ownership of a rental property. In view of the extreme durability of housing, a landlord is assumed to adopt an infinite horizon perspective. The profits expected in future periods are discounted in order to obtain their present value. Rational expectations are assumed.

Maintenance affects rental incomes and profits in two ways:

1 the quality of the dwellings is influenced by the standard of maintenance because people prefer nice clean houses and dwellings – therefore, higher rental incomes can be expected if maintenance is good;
2 the life span of the buildings, and therefore the period in which one can expect to receive rental incomes, depends on maintenance – especially the kind of maintenance that takes care of fundamental structures of buildings – roofs, walls, foundations, etc.

One basic economic problem for landlords, according to economic theory, is therefore related to the choice between different possible long-term maintenance and improvement strategies that affect the life span of the building and future rental incomes. This optimising problem can be solved if the landlord has access to knowledge on the lifetime of different parts of a building and other fundamental technical matters plus the expenses in connection with different kinds of maintenance work.

It is also important for landlords to have reasonable expectations regarding the future housing demand in the local area – will there be a future demand for the housing services that he intends to offer? Experiences in many countries with strong fluctuations in the housing market and sudden changes in public policies have certainly not made it easier for landlords to predict the long-term market conditions for private rental housing.

Finally, the economic decisions of landlords should depend very much on their expectations concerning the future price of capital. The discount factor applied when comparing future incomes with present investments depends on the potential profit of alternative investments and expectations on the future development in interest rate and inflation. Here too, rational investors face elements of uncertainty.

Rent control normally implies that the fixing of rents is not linked exclusively to the quality of the dwellings judged in market terms. It has been a common conclusion in the economic literature on the effects of rent control (Moorhouse, 1982; Niebank, 1985; Malpezzi, 1990) that landlords are expected to reduce maintenance and improvement. The argument is simple: if maintenance does not affect rental incomes, it is not profitable to maintain the quality of the dwellings. However, maintenance still influences the life span of the buildings and therefore affects the discounted value of future rental income. So even where rent control is used, there are incentives for maintenance depending on the profitability that could be obtained by alternative utilisation of the site.

It is also easy to conclude that rent control will prohibit investments in improvements if rents cannot be increased.

However, the actual effects of rent control depend very much on how the regulation is put into practice. Based on a theoretical model, e.g. Kutty has shown that certain types of regulation with built-in economic incentives in theory could have positive effects on maintenance and improvement activity compared with an unregulated situation (Kutty, 1996; see also Turner, 1990; Arnott, 1995; Albon and Stafford, 1990).

Literature on the structure of landlordism Most of the literature on private rental housing pays some attention to the existence of differences between landlords' economic backgrounds. The structuralisation of private landlordism has, however, been restricted mostly to division into the two categories: individual and company landlords, and the number of dwellings or properties owned by each landlord.

For example, this was the case in the survey of landlords in England made by Crook and Kemp (1996). In the conclusions from this research project, the authors stated that 'many landlords are generally too small to generate significant economies of scale in management and maintenance and to minimise risk through diversification' (p. 57). The survey showed that most private rented housing in England is still owned by individual and small-scale landlords for whom letting is not their main profession, business nor main source of income. Only one-quarter of the lettings were owned by companies, nearly 60 per cent by individuals and the rest by other organisations such as churches and educational institutions. Seven out of 10 lettings had owners with fewer than 25 lettings. It was also shown that only half of all lettings were originally acquired for investment reasons, that less than half of all lettings had landlords who were looking for commercial returns, and that for many landlords, private landlordism was a part-time activity.

In Australia, landlords owning a single property hold over 50 per cent of all rental properties (Yates, 1996). Another survey (New South Wales) also showed that 53 per cent of the private rented dwellings were owned by individuals. Owners of 25 per cent of rental properties were characterised as 'unintentional' landlords who did not make a conscious decision to invest in rental property. They became landlords through a variety of circumstances such as inheritance of property or a temporary change of residence.

This evidence from England and Australia is far from exceptional. Studies and figures from other countries such as Sweden (Lundström and Gustafsson, 1985) and Germany (Skifter Andersen et al., 1992) also show a domination of individual owners and small-scale landlords in the private rented sector. This is also confirmed by material from Denmark, which can be seen in the sections below.

The most extensive study on investment motives and behaviour of private landlords was conducted by Allen and McDowell.

In their book and based on earlier studies, Allen and McDowell (1989) conclude that in Britain, large-scale investor landlords left the sector in the years following World War II to be replaced by a relative increase in the importance of small-scale or resident landlordism. Moreover, they conclude that most of the large-scale investors who have continued to invest or have entered the British market, tend to be more interested in the appreciating capital values of residential property than long-term rental income.

Allen and McDowell classify landlords in six different groups based on a specification of the different characteristics that landlords display in their historical and ideological attachment to residential property and their differences as economic agents. They pay attention to the type and size of the landlords' capital, their sources of finance, their investment practices and their relationships with tenants and their property. Based on case studies, Allen and McDowell defined six different types of landlords and showed pronounced differences in their motives and behaviour. We will now compare their findings with results from the Danish studies of landlords.

Private Renting and Private Landlords in Denmark

The Danish Private Rental Market

The total share of private lettings in Denmark constitutes about 16 per cent of the total housing stock. Some of these dwellings are either single-family houses (4 per cent) or owner-occupied flats that are let out (3 per cent). Private rental dwellings in blocks of flats therefore constitute only 9 or 10 per cent of housing in Denmark.

As in most other countries in Europe, the Danish private rental sector has been in decline for many years. Before World War II it was the dominant sector, but afterwards a new trend began with more social housing being built than new private rental housing. The real blow to private rented housing came in the last years of the 1960s when increased inflation and favourable tax deductions made owner-occupied housing much more attractive. Meanwhile, interest rates were raised substantially. Unlike social housing, new private rented housing did not receive direct production subsidies, which made it difficult to build private rental housing with affordable rents, even though private tenants – like social tenants – were entitled to quite favourable housing benefits.

Moreover, the older stock decreased by about one-third from the middle of the 1960s to the end of the 1980s. Besides demolition of old and neglected buildings, the main reason was that many dwellings were converted into owner-occupied flats, which was made possible from 1966. This transformation of tenure was, however, partly stopped in the 1970s and totally prohibited after 1980. Instead, during the years that followed, a great number of private lettings were transformed into cooperatives after an act was passed by parliament. This act required landlords who intended to sell their property to first submit an offer to sitting tenants wishing to form a cooperative.

Danish rent control Since 1976, rents in Danish private rented housing have been regulated according to a principle called 'rent determined by expenditures'. Certain rules are laid down by legislation such as how to calculate rents for each different estate. The rent is determined by adding up the budgeted running costs for expenditures, such as cleaning, taxes, insurance etc. plus a certain amount per dwelling for administration. Fixed charges per square metre for maintenance are also included in the rent and there is a fixed so-called capital yield for landlords that has remained at the same level since 1976. An analysis (The Danish Government Commission on Rent Legislation, 1997) suggests that on average, rents are 30 per cent below market levels. There are, however, great differences between the provinces and the Copenhagen area, where rents can be more than 50 per cent below market levels.

Rents can be raised at any time, but the landlord has to inform the tenants in advance and provide them with written proof that the new rent is justified by higher expenses. Rents can also be raised in connection with improvements. The increase permitted is in principle – within certain limits – calculated on the basis of repayments and interest on the loans necessary to finance the improvement. In case of disagreement over the budget and rent increase, tenants can complain to a board of appeal – called the rent tribunal – which then settles the dispute.

In accordance with Danish housing legislation, the landlord is obliged to carry out necessary maintenance on his property and the rent tribunal can order him to repair building defects if the tenants complain about them. If the landlord does not follow such orders, he can be deprived of his right to administrate his property.

Tenants have basic rights, such as security against eviction and the right to complain about rent and maintenance to the rent tribunal. They also have a right to be heard in relation to proposed housing improvement. A certain procedure is prescribed whereby the tenants must be informed twice, first about the nature of the improvement and later about the rent increase. If the tenants do not wish to accept either the improvement or the rent increase, the landlord has to contact the rent tribunal for approval. If the tribunal finds the improvement unnecessary or feels the rent would become too high compared with the general rent level, permission for the improvement can be denied or the rent increase can be reduced. In practice, improvements are seldom prevented but it is quite common for rent increases to be reduced.

The expected effect of rent control on housing rehabilitation In principle, Danish rent control should encourage maintenance and improvement. Money is collected from the tenants and earmarked for maintenance, which should ensure that money is available. This should also alert tenants to how much they can demand from the landlord. When making improvements the landlord can, in principle, obtain an increased rental income that is sufficient to cover all capital expenses incurred.

In reality, the picture is not quite so rosy. A great part of the older stock has deteriorated and the process of improving obsolete dwellings is progressing very slowly. This is due partly to the rent control system.

For many years, the fixed charges for maintenance were too small, especially in the light of the major backlog of maintenance problems from before 1976 that had to be solved. In our opinion, however, the system of transferring funds to specific accounts earmarked for maintenance, controlled by the landlord but paid and checked by the tenants, has a positive effect on maintenance activity. It is difficult for a landlord to refuse a request for maintenance from the tenants if money is available in the account, and on most estates the money is used for maintenance. Furthermore, when a house is badly maintained and the tenants complain to the rent tribunal, the tribunal is often more willing to order the landlord to carry out maintenance if the account has a positive balance. Part of the money is placed in a special central fund from which payment can be made only when maintenance work has been done. This system stimulates the landlords to carry out maintenance to release their money from the fund. An analysis of the investments in improvements made by landlords (Skifter Andersen, 1995c) has shown that satisfactory returns are achieved in most cases and in some cases returns are very good.

Motives of landlords in Denmark The Danish studies show a picture of landlordism that in many ways resembles that described by Allen and McDowell. We have, however, developed a more detailed structure of motives and have identified six different types of motives that guide the way landlords run their properties:

1 *Long-term economic motives*. In the economic literature, investors in rental housing are expected to have these kinds of motives. Greatest importance is attached to property's long-term profitability and administration, and the money invested in maintenance and improvements is guided by this motive. It does not matter if there is a budget deficit for some years if the perspectives for future gains are good.
2 *Short-term economic motives*. Some landlords value an economic surplus from the property every year. This could be because they cannot raise money to finance a temporary deficit or because they depend on an income from the property to live on. This motive guides their investments and their expenditures on the property. In an economy with inflation, short-term economic motives tend to diminish investments.
3 *Speculative economic motives*. Rental housing is seen as just one of a number of possibilities for speculative investments. Expectations regarding short-term changes in real estate prices are the basis for such speculation, while the long-term profitability of the estate has little importance except for its influence on the development of current real-estate values.
4 *Incomes from building work*. For building firms, landlords linked to building firms or those who are tradesmen themselves, there is a strong incentive to buy and rehabilitate properties with the purpose of obtaining work. Small-scale landlords and tradesmen can avoid taxation of this income through do-it-yourself work.
5 *Property as a personal possession*. For some landlords, their property is not just an investment object but more a kind of personal belonging. They attach a separate importance to the appearance and quality of the house and dwellings, and it is important for them to be able to control these factors. The property is a kind of personal project, and circumstances other than simple economic factors have considerable importance.
6 *Service or social motives*. For different reasons, it is important for some landlords that the housing services provided for their tenants are of a good quality or are as cheap as possible. These motives result in housing that is cheaper or better than would be economically optimal if profitability was the only motive. This could be because the landlord has a kind of nonprofit

status or is an organisation that completely or partly aims to provide housing for certain groups. Companies wishing to provide accommodation for their employees would also fit into this category.

It was our general impression from the Danish case studies that only a minority of landlords were guided by long-term investment motives and very few landlords had these as their sole motives. This was confirmed by the survey. Based on the qualitative studies, we developed a classification of landlords in multi-storey houses in Denmark along similar lines to those used by Allen and McDowell. The following types of landlords were identified and their motives described:

1 *Informal landlords.* This group resembles the group identified by Allen and McDowell. It is a group of individuals who own a single property containing a few dwellings. The majority did not buy the property as a financial investment or as a source of income, but for other reasons, e.g. to obtain accommodation or business in the building. Sometimes they inherit the property and continue to own it either because they are unable to sell it or, like their parents, keep it for sentimental reasons.

For these landlords, the short-term economy is essential as they rarely have access to capital they can invest. The 'property motive' also has great importance because the house is seen as a personal belonging and its appearance signals the landlord's status and lifestyle. He is usually in very close contact with the tenants and it is important for him to have good relations with them, which often implies a 'service motive'.

The relationship between landlord and tenants is what we have called 'patriarchal'. Relations between the parties are quite personal and informal, but the landlord is so involved in the property that it is difficult for him to relinquish control of it and give the tenants a say. This can cause severe conflicts between the parties if tenants want more influence or if they complain to public authorities or rent tribunals.

Typically, informal landlords are personally responsible for both administration and often less extensive repairs. The houses are usually reasonably well kept but the dwellings are not always of a modern standard because it is difficult for the owners to finance improvements and because there could be a deficit in the budget for the first couple of years. In properties where relations between the landlord and tenants are not good, the landlord will not dare to suggest rehabilitation work that would involve rent increases because his lack of professionalism and insufficient knowledge of legislation makes him vulnerable to formal complaints and resistance from tenants.

2. *Small investors.* This group has much in common with what Allen and McDowell call investor landlords. These individuals have bought or inherited one or a few properties that they keep as a source of savings or continuous income. However, as this income is insufficient to live on, they also have other careers.

Long-term economic motives play a role for some of these landlords (saving) even though they rarely carefully consider what is important in terms of obtaining optimal long-term profitability. The short-term cash flow is still more important to them. Some of these landlords have left the administration in the hands of lawyers or professional administrators but most attempt to cope alone in a less than professional manner. Some have property motives. Their relationships with tenants can usually best be described by the term 'patriarchal' used above though they are less closely involved with tenants than informal landlords. The scope for conflicts with tenants is extensive because of unprofessional management.

3. *Professional landlords.* This group includes individuals and property companies that run properties as a main occupation. Living exclusively on an income from rental housing requires a certain number of properties and dwellings, so these landlords own several properties. For some odd reason, this group of landlords is not identified by Allen and McDowell in the English study.

Long-term economic motives dominate, as professional landlords have more capital or better access to finance, but cash flow can also be important in some cases. These landlords rarely have special 'property motives', as they regard their properties mainly in plain business terms.

The properties are administrated much more professionally than is the case with the previous types of landlords, and legislative rules are followed strictly. Tenants are seen as customers and are supplied only with the services they are willing to pay for.

4. *Companies with other business objectives.* In some cases, Danish firms engaged in manufacturing, trade or service also own rental dwellings. In Denmark, they are not very often 'employer landlords' as in the study by Allen and McDowell. Sometimes the dwellings are situated in buildings owned by the company for other reasons. Some of the dwellings are a relic from earlier times when placing surplus capital in housing was sometimes seen as a good investment.

The short-term economy is not of much importance, as the properties normally comprise only a small part of the company's total finances. The long-term economy is of importance only if the main motive for buying was investment.

If the company has its own premises in the property, 'property motives' encourage a cleaner, more presentable appearance. Most companies wish to avoid conflicts with tenants, either because some of their employees are living in the building or because it could result in bad press. Service motives are therefore of some importance.

5 *Speculative landlords*. These landlords have mostly speculative economic motives and no special interest in running properties or long-term profitability. The short-term cash flow, however, is of some importance because they often lack capital for their speculations. Therefore, their primary interest is to keep down expenses on the property.

They have no special interest in the appearance and quality of the property unless it improves scope for a profitable short-term increase in property values. There are no special motives for providing services for tenants as long as most of the dwellings can be let out. Conflicts often arise with tenants because rules are violated or maintenance is insufficient.

As property speculation is a risky business, these landlords often set up special companies with very limited liability that own a single building or a few properties. If the speculation results in losses, they can simply allow the company to go bankrupt.

6 *Building trade landlords*. These are landlords whose main economic activity is in the building trade. Their primary motive for buying rental property is to obtain building work. Some are short-term investors who plan to renovate the houses shortly after purchase and then sell them again. These landlords have speculative motives that resemble the speculative landlords' motives. Others have bought a portfolio of properties over the years and have a combined long-term investment and building motive.

7 *Financial landlords*. These investors have access to large capital values. Investments in real estate are only a small part of their total investments. In Denmark, the majority of this group comprises pension funds but it also includes some banks and insurance companies.

These landlords are the only ones who carefully calculate the long-term profitability of investments in rental properties and compare it with the profitability of other investments. Short-term economy is of no importance at all.

One of the motives for pension funds is to provide cheaper accommodation for their members. The service motive is therefore also of great importance to these landlords. In general, it is important for this group to avoid conflicts with tenants that may result in bad press. For these reasons a presentable appearance could also be important.

8 *Public utility landlords.* For this last group of landlords, the service motive is most important. It resembles the 'traditional landlords' identified by Allen and McDowell and contains private organisations established many years ago to provide good, cheap housing for certain groups of the population, e.g. trade unions, charitable institutions or other private foundations. In many ways, these are private counterparts to public social housing.

The only economic aspect involved is short-term cash flow. Deficits must be avoided, as there is no capital available to invest in the properties. Investments can be made only if the capital costs can be covered by an increase in rents, which demands acceptance from the tenants. In many of these properties, it has therefore been difficult to carry out necessary maintenance and improvements.

Table 4.1 gives an overview of the types of landlords and their motives. As shown in the overview in Table 4.1, the main motives normally ascribed to private landlords in economic theory – long-term considerations concerning incomes from properties – are important only to some of the types of landlords identified. For other landlords, short-term economy and speculative possibilities play a dominant role. Noneconomic motives such as property Below, we will try to show the extent of these motives among Danish landlords and their importance for housing rehabilitation based on the results of a survey among landlords.

Landlords owning old blocks of flats in Denmark and their properties The survey conducted among landlords features some more precise definitions of types of landlords needed to distinguish them from each other: These definitions are not without problems. The divisions between the first three groups are somewhat arbitrary, which means that the landlords do not distinctly belong to the ideal types defined. Some of these landlords could also have very speculative motives and some of them could cooperate with building firms, meaning they have building motives.

In Denmark, less than one third of the dwellings in the older part of the private rental stock (built before 1950) are owned by what we have called professional landlords, whom we expect to have long-term economic motives

Explanations of Decay in the Urban Housing Market 83

Table 4.1 Types of private landlords and their motives for investing and running rental properties

Motives	Short	Economic Long	Speculative	Building	Property	Service
Types of landlord						
1 Informal	+++				+++	+++
2 Small investors	+++	+		(+)	+++	+++
3 Professionals	+	++		(+)	+	+
4 Other business		++			++	++
5 Speculative			+++			
6 Building			++	+++		
7 Financial		++			+	++
8 Public utility	+++					+++

Notes

\+ Only some importance.
++ Important.
+++ Very important motive.

Table 4.2 Statistical definitions of different types of landlords

Informal landlords	Individuals owning one property with less than seven dwellings
Small investors	Individuals owning fewer than four properties but more than six dwellings
Professionals	Individual owners with more than three properties and companies with the primary purpose of profiting from rental properties
Other companies	Companies organised as normal joint-stock companies, with primary purposes other than running properties
Speculators	Companies organised with very limited liability
Builders	Building companies
Financial investors	Pension funds, banks and insurance companies
Public utility	Nonprofit companies, private funds, charitable institutions or other private foundations

(Skifter Andersen, 1994). Moreover, financial investors, who are also expected to have such motives for their investments, own 7 per cent. In both groups, each landlord has a considerable number of properties and dwellings. The properties owned by financial investors are large, with an average of about fifty dwellings. Most are new properties situated in Greater Copenhagen. Almost half of the dwellings were bought before 1980. In spite of special tax subsidies for their investments in real estate, financial investors have not therefore been very active in the market in recent years.

The professionals have relatively small properties, which are quite old and more than half are situated in Copenhagen. This group has been more active recently in the real-estate market as most of their properties were bought after 1980.

Forty per cent of the dwellings are owned by either informal landlords or by small investors who together form the largest group of landlords. As each landlord possesses only a few properties and dwellings, there are many landlords. More than 75 per cent of all landlords belong to these two groups.

The large majority of informal landlords are situated in the provinces. Some of these landlords have recently bought their properties but no more than the average for all landlords. The small investors show a similar pattern, but have relatively more often bought property in Copenhagen.

Landlords who are builders as their main occupation, are a small group with only 1 per cent of the dwellings. Each of the three remaining types of landlords possess about 7 to 8 per cent of the dwellings. Speculators and builders differ from the other groups, as expected, as in most cases they are more likely to have bought their properties recently. In fact 30 per cent of the dwellings owned by these landlords were bought within the past two years. They mostly invest in smaller properties outside Copenhagen – builders especially invest in very old housing. On average 'other companies' have the largest number of dwellings among the former groups, followed by public utility landlords. Both groups have bought their properties many years ago and seem to be a dying race. Most of the dwellings are located in Copenhagen but are younger than the average.

Average rents differ between the groups. This variation cannot be explained by differences in quality and location of the dwellings. The highest rents are found in dwellings owned by professional landlords, followed by builders and speculators – all three types of landlords have strong economic motives, as shown in Figure 4.1. The lowest rents are found in dwellings owned by other companies, public utility landlords and informal landlords to whom property motives and service motives are important. Financial investors also charge relatively low rents in spite of having many newer dwellings of good quality located in Copenhagen. This indicates that noneconomic motives are also of some importance to this group of investors.

Maintenance and improvement needs As stated above, private rented housing in Denmark is often badly maintained and lacks modern facilities. In the survey referred to (Skifter Andersen, 1994), an average of 16 per cent of the dwellings were located in buildings with large maintenance needs and only 23 per cent in buildings with no needs at all. Nineteen and 23 per cent of dwellings, respectively, had no central heating or no bathroom. Only 10 per cent needed no improvements concerning new or improved facilitates, insulation and energy consumption, open spaces etc.

The best-maintained properties in the survey seemed to be those owned by financial investors, other companies and informal landlords. Few improvements were needed in properties owned by these three categories. Dwellings lacking their own bathroom were least frequently found in the possession of financial landlords and other companies while central heating was most common in buildings owned by informal landlords and financial investors. This matches our expectations, as all three categories of landlords attach importance to the appearance of the property and to the housing service they provide. Two of these groups also have access to capital, while the informal landlords can manage some of the maintenance through do-it-yourself work or by employing moonlighters.

It is remarkable that housing owned by public utility landlords seemed to have deteriorated most. In spite of strong service motives, they have not been able to maintain their properties sufficiently due to cash-flow problems and low rents being of most importance to the tenants, who have a great influence.

Speculators and public utility landlords owned the most obsolete housing. Professional landlords also have many dwellings without bathrooms or central heating.

Investments in and Motives for Housing Rehabilitation among Danish Private Landlords, and Barriers to Rehabilitation

Two measures were used in the survey to give a picture of the landlords' rehabilitation activities. The actual activity in 1991–92 was measured by the amount spent on rehabilitation, divided into maintenance and improvement. Table 4.3 shows the average investments per square meter.

Table 4.3   Average investments per year in housing rehabilitation in 1991–92 in Danish blocks of flats built before 1950

Types of landlords	Improvements	Maintenance	All
	DKK per square metre/year		
Informal	36	42	78
Small investors	33	42	75
Professionals	61	61	122
Other companies	74	45	119
Speculators	27	35	62
Builders	186	236	422
Financial investors	57	86	143
Public utilities	17	50	67
All	47	53	101

The survey showed a large variation among the landlords regarding how much they had invested in housing rehabilitation in the two years. In nearly 40 per cent of the dwellings, no money had been spent.

A statistical analysis of variance between investments made and variables describing landlords and properties showed that the variable describing the type of landlord – as defined above – most significantly explained the variation in investment behaviour among the chosen variables. Other significant variables were the age of the buildings, the maintenance needs stated by the landlords and the year of purchase. Improvement needs, measured as lack of toilet, bathroom or central heating, had no significant covariance with investments.

When asked about their rehabilitation plans for 1993–94, 45 per cent of the landlords questioned answered that they had no intention of doing any maintenance or improvement during the two years. There did not seem to be a connection between the maintenance and improvement needs in the properties and the landlords' plans. In properties with severe maintenance backlogs, as many as 45 per cent of landlords did not intend to carry out any maintenance. In 65 per cent of dwellings in need of improvement, there were no plans to take any action.

It was not always the types of landlords with the poorest housing who did most rehabilitation work – in fact the reverse was true. The small group of builder landlords had – as one would expect – invested most in their properties in 1991–92 because it had been their main reason for buying them. But besides them, financial investors, followed by the professionals and other companies had done the most to improve their housing. Financial investors did most maintenance while other companies invested relatively more in improvements and planned to continue doing so. Looking at the plans for 1993–94, it seemed that especially the other companies were planning to do something about their remaining maintenance problems.

The speculators and public utility landlords made the smallest investments. The speculators spent little money on maintenance and would continue to do so. The public utility landlords also did little to improve their lettings in 1991–92.

The informal landlords and small investors used the same amount of money and both initiated less rehabilitation work than the average landlord. It must, however, be expected that the total level of activity – especially among informal landlords – must have been higher because of do-it-yourself work etc.

Motives for housing rehabilitation The landlords were asked why they had undertaken maintenance and improvement in the years 1991–92. Based on the earlier case studies, the possible answers in the questionnaire were split up into three main groups:

1   Economic motives:
    a) improve opportunities for letting out dwellings or selling the property;
    b) increase the sales value of the property;

c) increase profitability in general.
2 Property motives:
   a) avoid severe damage to the building/prolong life span;
   b) improve appearance of the buildings.
3 Satisfy demands from others:
   a) from tenants;
   b) from local authorities;
   c) from rent tribunals.

One conclusion from the earlier case studies was that Danish landlords often carried out maintenance because tenants had complained. Very few of the landlords had a maintenance strategy or elaborated plans for future maintenance. It was often their strategy, especially among small-scale landlords, to wait and do nothing until tenants made demands – either directly or through complaints to rent tribunals – or local authority had stepped in.

As shown in Table 4.4, economic reasons were not very important for investments in housing rehabilitation. The expected profitability of the investments was even less important. Profitability plays the greatest role for financial investors, no role for public utility landlords and other companies and a very small role for informal landlords. The fact that rehabilitation can make it easier to let out dwellings was more important. This was especially important for informal landlords, professionals and builders. On the other hand, this motive is of less importance to financial investors, public utility landlords and other companies. In general, this motive is most important in the provinces where controlled rents are not very much lower than expected market rents and private landlords are more in open competition with other kinds of housing supply. Landlords in these parts of the country have more economic incentives to embellish their properties to attract tenants. In the Copenhagen area, with a general shortage of cheaper housing, bad maintenance has little effect on reducing opportunities for letting out. These circumstances affect the answers from the different types of landlords since some are located mostly in the provinces, others – especially financial investors and other companies – in Copenhagen.

Improving sales value is especially important to informal landlords and builders, followed by speculators and small investors. It is of no importance to financial investors and public utility landlords.

It is to be expected that property motives for rehabilitation are also most frequently found among landlords with strong property motives in general (Table 4.1). This was confirmed by the survey. Table 4.4 shows that the

Table 4.4 Reasons for housing rehabilitation in 1991–92 among Danish landlords in blocks of flats built before 1950

Investors	Informal	Small inv.	Professionals	Other companies	Speculators	Builders inv.	Financial utility	Public	All
Motives				% of dwellings with motives					
1 *Economic*	50	31	42	12	45	46	31	9	34
a easier to let out	43	26	38	12	24	46	0	9	27
b higher sales val.	22	11	9	8	11	18	0	0	9
c profitability	5	12	13	0	16	18	31	0	12
2 *Property cons.*	77	76	65	81	74	52	84	96	75
a avoid damage	40	49	41	4	39	52	69	69	43
b appearance	66	57	48	81	49	34	58	49	55
3 *On demand*	39	38	50	47	60	34	89	65	46
a from tenants	33	33	35	46	54	34	84	54	38
b from loc. auth.	6	7	13	2	5	0	31	24	11
c rent tribunal	0	1	8	0	0	0	2	0	3
4 *Other motives*	12	8	14	69	4	21	14	7	16

Note: The percentages do not add up to 100, as the landlords could state up to four reasons.

Source: Skifter Andersen, 1994.

appearance of the buildings was most important to informal landlords and other companies, followed by financial and small investors. The appearance of buildings is of least importance to builders, followed by speculators, public utility landlords and professionals.

It must be assumed that landlords in badly maintained houses more often wish to avoid building damage. Moreover, this motive also involves an economic aspect, as it includes a wish to prolong the life span of buildings. This motive was most important to the public utility landlords, who often have badly maintained housing, and to financial investors who are conscious of long-term economic conditions. In total, property motives played the greatest role among public utility landlords, financial investors and other companies – the least among professionals, speculators and builders.

Tenants' demands for rehabilitation are of importance in two ways. In some properties, landlords generally attach importance to the wishes of tenants. In other cases, the main reason is that the property is badly maintained and therefore the tenants complain and perhaps threaten to make formal complaints to the local rent tribunal. Orders to carry out maintenance issued by rent tribunals are found mostly among professional landlords. Drawing on the evidence from the case studies, the smaller incidence of this among informal landlords and small investors can be explained by the more informal way they administrate their properties. These landlords rarely allow a conflict with tenants to reach a point at which a rent tribunal is called in, whereas this does not represent a problem for the professionals.

Demands from tenants have been most important for rehabilitation among financial investors, public utility landlords and other companies – all landlords for whom the service motive is important. Applications from tenants have also affected the relatively small investments made by the speculators, but it must be expected that in this case, complaints about inconvenience from bad maintenance of these building are the main reason. It is surprising that demands for maintenance from tenants are of less importance in answers given by informal landlords. The reason could be that the parties are in such close contact that the landlord is better in tune with tenants' wishes.

Demands from local authorities could also be caused by two different factors. Local authorities have the formal task of controlling whether buildings are safe and healthy and reasonably maintained. If they judge maintenance to be insufficient, they can make demands on landlords. Experience shows that local authorities in Denmark rarely do this. On the other hand, local governments in many municipalities are interested in improving dwellings suitable for elderly people, and often try to encourage private landlords to do

Explanations of Decay in the Urban Housing Market 91

this by promising special subsidies. This is probably the main reason why financial investors and public utility landlords have quite often made investments demanded by local authorities. In the case of professionals, both reasons could be important.

Barriers to housing rehabilitation In the survey, landlords were asked to identify the most important barriers to further rehabilitation of their properties. The possible answers were divided into four groups:

1. The economic profitability of investments:
    a) uncertainty about profitability;
    b) possible rent increase too small to be profitable;
    c) insufficient increase in sales value ;
    d) difficult to let out rehabilitated dwellings.
2. Cash flow and financial problems:
    a) difficult to get loans;
    b) cash-flow problems for the first few years;
    c) existing loans in the property are too big to allow new loans.
3. Rent control and other legislation:
    a) rent control;
    b) tax problems;
    c) rules for tenants' right to information and make complaints.
4. Considerations for sitting tenants:
    a) tenants cannot pay;
    b) resistance from tenants.

As shown in Table 4.5, landlords representing only about one in four of the lettings thought that rent control was an important barrier to rehabilitation. As mentioned earlier, rent control has the greatest effect in the Copenhagen area and much less in the provinces. Rent control is of least importance for the activity of informal landlords, builders and financial landlords. Rather surprisingly, it is most commonly mentioned as a barrier by the other companies – perhaps because most of their properties are concentrated in Copenhagen.

For almost 60 per cent of the lettings, landlords pointed to one or several economic barriers to further housing renewal. Only 35 per cent, however, responded that obtainable rent increases were too small. Complaints about this problem were most common among professionals, other companies, builders and speculators, while financial investors and public utility landlords rarely mentioned it.

Table 4.5 The opinions of landlords on barriers for further rehabilitation in blocks of flats built before 1950

Landlords Motives	Informal	Small inv.	Professionals	Other	Speculators companies	Builders	Financial inv.	Public utility	All
					% of dwellings mentioning barriers				
1 *Economic profit.*	**54**	**62**	**68**	**80**	**71**	**72**	**27**	**18**	**58**
a uncertainty	26	41	49	42	37	8	18	3	36
b rent incr. too small	32	33	46	40	40	47	25	17	35
c value incr. too small	21	22	13	10	30	42	26	1	17
d difficult to let out	14	8	11	8	18	21	0	0	9
2 *Finance/cash flow*	**30**	**31**	**52**	**14**	**48**	**42**	**0**	**26**	**34**
a financial problems	18	17	45	8	39	29	0	11	24
b cash-flow problems	14	15	11	8	14	33	0	6	12
c exist. loans too big	4	4	1	0	12	0	0	8	3
3 *Rent legislation etc.*	**12**	**39**	**45**	**61**	**35**	**0**	**14**	**26**	**35**
a rent control	6	26	26	55	26	0	8	24	23
b tax problems	7	16	17	27	0	0	0	2	12
c tenant particip.	4	11	12	6	9	0	5	0	9
4 *Tenant considerat.*	**21**	**19**	**20**	**10**	**23**	**29**	**6**	**37**	**19**
a tenants cannot pay	18	15	12	7	19	29	6	35	15
b tenants' resistance	3	6	11	5	9	0	3	17	7

Note: The percentages do not add up to 100, as the landlords could state up to four reasons.

Source: Skifter Andersen, 1994.

Of equal importance is the fact that landlords feel uncertain about the economic profitability of housing rehabilitation. This evidence points to the fundamental problem of private renting – the difficulty of appreciating the economic consequences of investments and foreseeing future economic conditions. This uncertainty is not found among the financial investors, who probably fully appreciate the consequences, or among public utility landlords who do not invest to generate profits. A surprisingly high proportion of the professionals and other companies feel uncertain about their investments, as do small investors, which is more to be expected. Informal landlords do not care very much about the profitability of their investments and therefore less frequently express uncertainty.

For builders and speculators, the fact that rehabilitation does not increase sales prices and that improved dwellings are more difficult to let out are greater economic barriers. These barriers are of no importance to the public utility landlords and mean little to the professionals and other companies, who have a more long-term view of their investments. A comparatively high proportion of financial landlords attach importance to the increase in sales value. This seems to show that they judge their investments not only in the light of future incomes and expenses but also look at the development of real-estate values.

It is not surprising that speculators (and builders) have financial problems and that the mortgages in their properties are too high. It is more surprising that many professional landlords complain about finance problems. It suggests that these landlords have also financed their purchase of properties and some of their cash-flow problems by taking out mortgages in their properties. Finance problems seem to be much less important among the other types of landlords – especially among financial investors and other companies, as could be expected.

As expected, cash-flow problems in connection with rehabilitation are important among informal landlords and small investors and also among builders and speculators.

For the public utility landlords, tenant considerations are by far the most important barrier to rehabilitation – especially the fact that sitting tenants cannot afford large rent increases. The economic ability of tenants is another important barrier for informal landlords, while expected resistance from tenants is of special concern to professionals.

Is Economically Irrational Behaviour among Landlords a more Important Cause of Housing Deterioration than Rent Control?

Much economic literature on private rented housing assumes that the behaviour of private landlords is guided principally by rational economic considerations and that long-term profitability is the most important motive for investments. It is often assumed that private landlords are much more efficient at maintaining and administrating their property than owner-occupiers and social landlords. However, as shown above, studies from Denmark and several other countries show that private landlords are a very inhomogeneous group with different motives and behaviour. Only a few landlords fit into the expected picture of the economically rational private landlord.

For many landlords, economic motives other than long-term profitability play a dominant role. Short-term economic conditions, such as actual cash flow, are especially important to many small-scale landlords. Other landlords have speculative motives – they buy and sell property – and the development in sales value is therefore of most importance, whereas actual and future profits are of marginal interest.

Noneconomic motives are also very important. In many cases, landlords have so-called 'property motives' that have a decisive influence on their maintenance activity. The appearance and quality of the buildings has a special, noneconomic importance for these landlords either because they are living there or have business premises or because they have a personal relationship with the property and regard is as a personal belonging.

In many cases, landlords are also guided by what could be called 'social motives' because for various reasons they feel special obligations towards sitting tenants. In these cases, the needs and interests of sitting tenants have a special influence on landlords' investment behaviour.

In many countries, the private rented sector is dominated by small-scale landlords who are not very efficient administrators and whose investments are seldom guided by rational economic motives. Some of these landlords own just one or a few dwellings ('informal landlords') or they are small investors who cannot derive a livelihood from being a landlord.

Other landlords with special motives are public-utility landlords – charitable institutions, trade unions and other private foundations – and companies with other primary business objectives than landlordism, who let to employees or have business premises in the same buildings. Other special groups are speculators – often organised as limited liability companies – who buy and sell rental property to obtain short-term gains, and builders who buy properties for work purposes.

In Denmark, a group of professional landlords with mainly purely economic motives have been estimated to own only 30–40 per cent of the lettings, based on evidence from a Danish survey comprising rental housing in old blocks of flats. However, some of these landlords also attached great importance to short-term economic conditions or to actual sales values. 'Financial investors' – banks, insurance companies, pension funds, etc. are landlords oriented mainly towards long-term profitability. Some of these – especially pension funds – are, however, also guided by social motives and property motives because they let out to employees or members of the funds or because they cannot risk bad press concerning badly maintained properties.

The Danish surveys have documented that these differences among landlords and their motives have a pronounced impact on their housing rehabilitation activity. It has been shown that a classification of landlords is one of the most important variables for explaining investment behaviour, together with variables such as building age, year of purchase and maintenance needs of the properties.

The survey showed that landlords who rate cash-flow problems or speculative motives most important (informal landlords, small investors, speculators, public utility landlords) invest less in maintenance and housing improvement than professional landlords. Small investors especially can be very passive and unwilling to invest in their properties. Often they are not very professional administrators and have difficulty estimating maintenance needs and the profitability of investments. For the majority of these landlords, uncertainty about economic consequences was a main barrier against housing rehabilitation. Often maintenance was postponed until it was necessary to avoid severe damage to buildings. For the speculators, rehabilitation is not profitable because it does not affect actual property prices in a way that makes speculation more profitable. This group of landlords had the worst-maintained properties and they carried out very little maintenance. Public utility landlords do not invest because they lack capital and wish to keep rents down.

On the other hand, some landlords with property or service motives (informal landlords, other companies, financial landlords) tend to use more money on housing rehabilitation than professional landlords because they want to own an attractive property or because they wish to provide good housing for their tenants. In the survey, property motives were most often mentioned as motives for investments.

In many cases, sitting tenants play a crucial role in keeping up maintenance activity. It became evident from both the survey and from the earlier Danish qualitative studies that many landlords did not carry out maintenance until tenants or local authorities demanded repairs. In more than 40 per cent of the cases in the survey, landlords mentioned demand from sitting tenants or local authorities as one reason for rehabilitation.

The lessons to be learned from this and other studies are that private landlordism is not always the simple answer when policy makers wish to provide efficient housing free of public subsidies. Besides general market problems that produce decay in parts of the private rental sector, as discussed in the American case, problems also arise from economically irrational and inefficient behaviour of certain types of landlords. On the other hand, some landlords also possess motives that make them take better care of their property and provide better services for their tenants than if they were guided only by strictly profit-maximising motives.

Limited effect of rent control on rehabilitation in Denmark Any conclusion derived from the reported Danish evidence on housing rehabilitation and investment motives among different kinds of landlords must include the influence of the special Danish rent control system. In principle, investments in improvements are profitable because the regulation allows rent increases sufficient to produce a reasonable profit. Moreover, special payments are collected from the tenants to pay for maintenance. The economic incentives among landlords to carry out maintenance may, however, be reduced as long as dwellings can be let out. But the survey showed that only one in four landlords mentioned rent control as one of several barriers to housing rehabilitation. The Danish rent control system does not seem to be a major obstacle to housing rehabilitation, even though it has some importance, especially in the Copenhagen area.

Notes

1 A substantial amount of literature exists on the effects of rent control. See, for instance, Downs, 1988, Malpezzi, 1990, Niebank, 1985, Moorhouse, 1982, Rydell and Neel, 1982 and Sternlieb, 1974. It can, however, be argued that rent control schemes could be designed in a way that creates good incentives for investments in rehabilitation, see Turner, 1990 and Skifter Andersen, 1992.
2 Nelson, 1988, Smith and Williams, 1986, DiGiovanni, 1984 and Schill and Nathan, 1983 are key publications on gentrification in the USA.

3 Published in Hansen et al., 1990, Skifter Andersen, 1995 and Skifter Andersen and Foerlev, 1996.

Chapter 5

Processes of Social and Physical Decay in Deprived Urban Neighbourhoods

As mentioned in the introduction, in the research literature deprived urban neighbourhoods are understood mainly as spatially concentrated pockets of poverty and their emergence is explained as a direct product of globalisation and increasing social inequality in the cities. However, evidence exists indicating that there is no simple connection between the general social and economic development of cities and the emergence of deprived neighbourhoods.

In this chapter, we will take a closer look at the nature of deprived urban neighbourhoods in Europe. In short, the chapter attempts to illustrate how the concentration of poverty generates special problems and effects that tend to reinforce each other. These self-perpetuating processes of social and physical decay are shown to take place in these areas, and have a strong and separate importance for deprivation and segregation. The character of these processes is illustrated on the basis of a Danish study of 500 deprived social housing estates.

Vicious Circles in Deprived Neighbourhoods

The starting point for a different comprehension of the causes of deprived urban areas is the concept of 'vicious circles' that are found in such areas. In Denmark, from an early stage, the understanding of deprived housing estates has been based on a perception of these estates as neighbourhoods where negative self-perpetuating social, economic and physical processes take place (Kirkegård, 1985; Vestergaard, 1998; Skifter Andersen, 1999a). Other researchers have written about 'the cycle of labelling and exclusion' (Taylor, 1998; Costa Pinho, 2000), 'independent neighbourhood effects to do with cumulative decline' (Gibb et al., 1999), 'spiral of decline in which underlying problems.. are perpetuated and compounded over a period' (Morrison, 1999), 'downward spirals and dynamics' (Lee and Murie, 1999), 'mutually reinforcing social, building and organisational problems' (Power and Tunstall, 1995) and 'self and/or mutually reinforcing tendencies ... "vicious" or "downward" cycles' (Hall, 1997).

All these statements refer to how different factors inside and outside the affected urban areas reinforce each other in a negative direction, creating increased deprivation, stigmatisation and decay. Taylor is concerned with the connection between changes in the image of estates and changes in the composition of residents, through which increasingly bad reputations lead to middle class people moving away and being replaced by poor and excluded families. Costa Pinho has studied the mechanisms leading to the creation of negative social identities and public images. Morrison sees the main problem associated with problems of drugs, antisocial behaviour, violence, crime and prostitution creating a poor reputation. Gibb et al. find that one of the main reasons for abandonment and low demand for housing in these areas is that the decaying environment prompts a high turnover of residents and failing interest in house hunters. Mumford and Lupton (1999) focus on instability and disorderly neighbourhood environments causing highly localised low demand. Power and Tunstall (1995) draw attention to high turnover and vacancies resulting in damage to buildings, loss of social cohesion and a breakdown in controls, which generate serious management problems, poorer conditions, deteriorating services and eventual chaos.

Chapter 4 described market processes of decay in North America. In Europe, these processes are influenced by the many ways in which housing policy intervenes in the housing market with measures such as housing benefits, public housing supply, rent control and urban renewal. But it was argued that the same processes exist behind the effects of regulation. A Danish PhD study (Munk, 1998) has shown that they can be found in the private parts of the Copenhagen housing market – especially in owner-occupied flats. A recent study in Helsinki, Finland (Kortteinen and Vaatovaara, 1999) showed how downward succession, like that found in American cities, has spread from areas with many low-income groups to neighbouring areas, so that over a 15-year period, these areas have experienced a change in population towards lower-status groups.

Processes of Deprivation and Decay on Housing Estates

In social housing, however, the general model of decay (Figure 4.1) is too simple, as administrative and organisational matters have a much more important role to play here than in the pure market model. Based on earlier work that evaluated efforts to improve deprived social housing areas

(Kirkegård, 1985; Christiansen et al., 1993) a new model (Figure 5.1) was constructed as a basis for studies of processes of decay in social housing estates in Denmark. The model contains one more element than the simple model: The organisational conditions of the estate. That means the efficiency of the administration of the estate, the amount of resources that residents make available and the quality of their organisation. Moreover, the economic conditions differ somewhat, as the main problems are often relatively high rents compared with the market value of the dwellings, combined with a bad economy because of rent arrears, empty dwellings and excessive maintenance and administration costs.

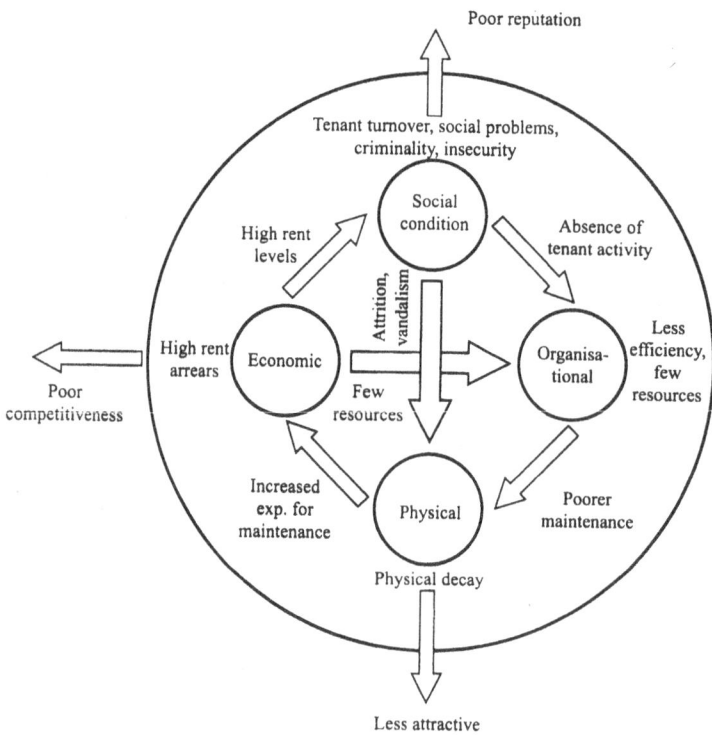

Figure 5.1 Model of processes of deprivation in Danish social housing estates

The model highlights some of the problems frequently found on Danish problem estates (Vestergaard, 1998). The social physical and financial conditions give these estates poor reputations, make them less physically attractive and less competitive on the housing market. As a result, the composition of residents changes as more unemployed and people with smaller economic and social resources move into the area. This, in turn, results in worse organisational conditions and faster deterioration of the physical appearance of the estate because of vandalism and careless use. Financial conditions are also affected directly and indirectly, which in turn affects the resources available. Together, these changes make the estates even less attractive and accelerate the process of residential succession.

As the model suggests, the interior and exterior processes of deprivation and decay can be differentiated to some extent. The exterior processes concern how the changes in the image and attraction of the estate influences the relations with the rest of the city and the composition of newcomers on the estates. The interior processes concern the changes in conditions on the estate, where negative social, physical, organisational and financial changes reinforce each other. These two kinds of processes influence each other as the interior processes change the image and attraction of the estates, while the exterior processes create changes in the composition of residents on the estates and in the living conditions for residents.

Interior Processes of Deprivation

Interior processes of deprivation in neighbourhoods can be linked mainly to the assumption that social norms, self-perception and behaviour among residents undergo changes and simultaneously influence the physical, social, organisational and economic conditions in a neighbourhood. In turn, these affect residents' norms and behaviour. Various kinds of negative interior processes are described in the research literature.

Evolution of different norms concerning family and work in deprived neighbourhoods Some of the theoretical discussions on this subject date back to the work of Massey (1994) and Wilson (1987), who formulated the hypothesis that people are influenced by the norms and behaviour that dominate in the neighbourhoods where they live. One of Wilson's central propositions was that living in a poor neighbourhood leads to social isolation of the residents and to norms that differ from those normally found in society. When the proportion of residents with deviant norms reaches a certain level, these deviant norms spread to other people in the neighbourhood. He referred to several studies of poor neighbourhoods in the USA that showed a higher incidence of: school dropouts, teenage pregnancy, births out of wedlock, resignation in the search for employment, deviance from norms of mainstream society, deviant behaviour and physically run-down buildings (see also Ellen and Turner, 1997). He argued that these conditions led to deviant norms becoming increasingly accepted in the neighbourhood, which led to resignation among residents, less inclination to search for employment and increased social isolation.

Wacquant (1993) and Friedrichs (1997) have shown that it is difficult to transfer the American findings to conditions in European cities. Friedrichs draws our attention to the fact that these effects depend a great deal on the extent to which residents are spatially restricted, for example if their action space and social network are restricted to the neighbourhood. This is the case only for certain social groups. Moreover, Friedrichs points out that the mechanisms by which people are influenced by their surroundings are far from clear. Some authors (Erbring and Young, 1979) believe social interaction is the main mechanism, while others (Skogan, 1990) argue that neighbourhood characteristics in general also have an impact on residents' attitudes and behaviour. Friederichs describes a mechanism called 'normative adjustment' that spreads certain types of behaviour, seen as antisocial or stigmatised, in a local community. He refers to a study made by Hirschl and Rank (1991) that found a positive correlation between the population density in a community and the rate of welfare participants and explained it by saying that a 'culture of poverty' existed in such areas. These researchers assume that the observation of poverty and deviant types of behaviour in a neighbourhood tend to influence the normative level of all residents and result in poverty and deviant behaviour becoming more legitimate. Friedrichs, however, stresses that more thorough research on these assumptions is needed. He also points out that different studies in poverty areas have shown that residents are a very inhomogeneous group and their social network is rarely limited to the neighbourhood. Moreover, there is often a high turnover of residents, which means that new residents with other norms could arrive continuously.

The interaction between physical decay and norms Friedrichs (1997) also refers to some American research showing that visible deterioration of a neighbourhood, including litter, attrition, graffiti and vandalism, has an impact on residents' attitudes and behaviour (Skogan, 1990). The implication is that residents can get used to a lower visible quality of their neighbourhood, accepting disorder and ugliness and after a while changing their own behaviour so that they take less care of the environment. This can create a self-perpetuating process that accelerates negative behaviour and decay and leads to increasing maintenance costs. This development resembles experience gained from areas in decay in the USA as described in Chapter 4. This process therefore also increases the economic strain on landlords, who can choose between increasing expenses or further deterioration of their properties.

A Danish study (Christensen and Benjaminsen, 2000) studied the statistical connection between variables describing different kinds of social problems and conditions, and observed physical problems in 250 deprived housing estates. The study showed that the incidence of different physical problems was correlated with the social composition of residents. Factors such as vandalism, graffiti, litter and run-down open spaces and entrances were found much more frequently on housing estates with a high proportion of people on public support. A strong correlation was also found between these physical problems and different social problems on the estates, such as crime, noisy residents, drug abuse and special problems with young people.

Spirals of social conflicts in fragmented neighbourhoods Some literature on effects of segregation claims that segregation often leads to more homogenous neighbourhoods with better possibilities for social interaction. Ethnic groups, especially, are assumed to more easily preserve their culture and identity in concentrated groups (van Kempen and Ösükren, 1998).

In Europe, however, deprived urban areas are seldom dominated by a single homogenous group (Friedrichs, 1997). On the contrary, they are inhabited mostly by a great variety of different marginalised ethnic and social groups who have very little in common. Some of these people have a culture or behaviour that deviates from general norms, i.e. they have less regard for the comfort of their neighbours, make more noise and engage in other annoying activities. Moreover, they are often less able to handle situations involving conflicts.

Modig (1985) compared the social interaction among residents in some parts of deprived housing estates with other housing areas in Sweden. He found significantly higher incidences of nuisances from neighbours and social conflicts in places with many problem households. He also found that these households in the deprived estates had less contact with other residents and a reduced sense of community spirit. For residents as a whole, he found that the social network increased with the length of residency, but paradoxically the sense of community spirit waned and the number of conflicts increased with the number of years of residency. There could be two explanations: 1) the general conditions on the estates had worsened over time; or 2) over time, residents had established an increasing number of conflicts with some of their neighbours and felt less affiliation to the neighbourhood. This is in sharp contrast to a large number of studies on peoples' relations to their homes (see, for example, Hurtig, 1995) that have shown that people normally establish more affiliation to their surroundings the longer they stay there.

In her study of five deprived housing estates in Portugal, Costa Pinho (2000) has shown that the occurrence of major conflicts depended on the specific character of the ethnic and social composition of the residents. She found three main kinds of conflicts in the areas:

1 conflicts related to drug abuse;
2 general conflicts between neighbours ;
3 conflicts between ethnic groups.

The first category represented the most serious conflicts on all estates. The second was seen as generally less serious but more damaging for the local cooperation and the local network. This type of conflict was usually expressed as arguments, insults and fights between neighbours, often also over more general matters such as the use and management of common areas and buildings. The last types of conflicts were less visible but penetrated social life in a way that weakened social relations and affiliation to the neighbourhood.

An EU project report on case studies of deprived housing estates in eight European countries (Cars, 2000) also indicated that tensions exist between different ethnic groups. However it also identifies conflicts between new and old residents. This is especially evident in areas that have undergone rapid changes, from being more ordinary housing estates to being housing for marginalised groups. Consequently, there is a clash of different norms linked to differences in age and in attitudes to the neighbourhood. Some of the most serious conflicts take place between elderly and young people.

There is therefore reason to believe that deprived neighbourhoods are relatively more subject to different kinds of conflicts between residents than other neighbourhoods and that these conflicts tend to be self-perpetuating. This seems to be connected with other processes of self-perception and stigmatisation in the areas.

Processes of conflicts, crime, insecurity and withdrawal In Costa Pinhos' (2000) study, certain types of conflicts led residents to feel insecure. In this way, conflicts have a fundamental importance for how the neighbourhood is perceived by residents. However, the study also showed that other conditions such as crime and drug abuse were more important sources of insecurity.

Various kinds of criminal behaviour are often found in deprived housing estates. Hirschfield and Bowers (1997) studied disadvantaged areas and showed a significant relationship between different variables representing social cohesion and levels of certain types of crime. This study indicated that crime rates are much higher in areas with fragmented populations.

Insecurity has several important consequences for neighbourhoods. Safety is of fundamental importance if people are to identify with their neighbourhood and participate in local affairs. Insecurity can often lead to isolation. Costa Pinhos' study showed that people who felt insecure often preferred to stay at home, especially at night when they felt most insecure. In this way, conflicts, crime and insecurity can encourage residents to be more reluctant to participate in social life and organisational matters both within their communities and outside. Moreover, a study by Dean and Hastings (2000) showed that friends and family living outside the neighbourhood were more reluctant to visit residents when crime had been reported there.

Internal and external stigmatisation It is a well-known fact that most people who stay in the same place for a longer time more or less identify themselves with their neighbourhoods (Knox, 1995). That is one reason why few people express dissatisfaction with their home and neighbourhood when asked. This is also often the case when residents in deprived areas are interviewed (see, for example, Kearns et al., 2000, Gottschalk et al., 2000). Often there is no direct link between the problems found in an area and the dissatisfaction expressed. In areas with major problems concerning crime and insecurity, however, satisfaction expressed is considerably lower.

The consequence of this identification with the neighbourhood is that the self-understanding of residents is often influenced by the image and problems of the neighbourhood. In her study in Portugal, Pinho (2000) identified how important the image of the neighbourhood was for the self-identity and self-understanding of the residents. She found that problems in the areas, such as conflicts, crime and bad external image, were internalised in the residents' perception of their own identity so that a process of self-stigmatisation took place. People tended to blame themselves for the problems in their neighbourhood and the resulting negative self-images affected their ability to be socially active. Pinho concludes that this process of self-stigmatisation seems to favour a defensive life strategy through which people are less active in their search for jobs and less inclined to participate in social life in the neighbourhood. Another study of three deprived housing estates in England made by Dean and Hastings (2000) showed that residents testified to the fact that their lives were impoverished economically, socially and emotionally by the tenacity of the estate's problem reputation.

There is some evidence that neighbourhood stigma transferred to residents also has severe consequences for their contact with the outside world. Some of the residents interviewed by Dean and Hastings said they felt they had experienced discrimination. It was more difficult for them to get insurance and bank credit and they also claimed that employers lost interest in their job applications when they heard where they lived. They also felt that family, friends and colleagues were critical of the estate and that they always had to defend the place where they lived. They tried to avoid telling people their address.

Reduced possibilities of social cohesion and participation in management Studies (referred to in Hirschfield and Bowers, 1997) have shown that deprived housing areas are more likely to have a weaker organisational base and are therefore at greater risk of social disorganisation.

General experience from deprived social housing estates shows that levels of social cohesion and participation in the affairs of the neighbourhood are lower than in many other places (Cars, 2000). Musterd and Ostendorf (1998) have also conducted a study of deprived areas in the Netherlands that showed a clear connection between the degree of concentration of poverty and reduced social participation. The main explanation for this is, of course, that poor people are generally less socially active, but Pinhos' study also indicated that self-stigmatisation and insecurity have a separate importance in reducing social activity. Moreover, as described above, social fragmentation in the areas – the fact that many areas are inhabited by many different social and cultural groups – and the conflicts involved, also reduce incentives for social cooperation within the neighbourhood.

The possibilities for mobilising residents to contribute to improvements and management are therefore relatively worse in deprived neighbourhoods. This is not simply a consequence of segregation, but might also be attributed to special social and mental processes taking place among residents in the areas.

School problems American studies of deprived neighbourhoods, in particular, but also some European studies, have revealed the special problems that emerge in local schools (Massey, 1994; Saltman, 1991; Friedrichs, 1997). Children coming from poor and stressed families often display problematic behaviour and possess deviating norms. Schools that are dominated by such children therefore tend to be less attractive places with less effective teaching. It is more difficult to attract good teachers to such schools (Hjärne, 1991), which further reduces the quality of teaching and some of the more active parents try to move their children to other schools, private or public. Schools with many children coming from immigrant families also experience language problems.

These school problems are self-perpetuating and influence the attractiveness of the whole neighbourhood. When families with children are looking for a new home, they pay great attention to the quality of schools in the neighbourhood.

Reduced private services Private services follow market forces and are available where demand is sufficient. When residents in a neighbourhood are replaced by people with lower incomes, the demand for many services decreases and perhaps changes. As a result, the supply of service facilities such as shops, banks, cafés and cinemas disappear (Cars, 2000). In some cases, public facilities are lacking because the residents in the area are unable to stand up for themselves and let their needs be known (van Kempen and Özükren, 1998). Deans and Hastings also showed that residents in some depressed housing estates were very unsatisfied with both public and private services and felt that they paid higher prices than elsewhere.

In this way, reduced incomes not only affect individual families but also whole neighbourhoods. Deteriorating services reduce the attractiveness of the neighbourhood and contribute to further deprivation of the area.

A Danish Study of Processes of Deprivation and Decay in Social Housing

In this chapter, we will throw some further light on processes of deprivation using a Danish study of 500 social housing estates. The main purpose of the study, conducted at Danish Building and Urban Research, was to evaluate the effects of the efforts made in connection with a Danish government programme to stop processes of deprivation and decay (described in Chapter 7).

The Tested Model of Processes of Deprivation

A model of processes of decay in the areas was formulated and tested. The tested model is shown in Figure 5.2. The model describes the expected relations between some of the internal and external problems and conditions on the estates studied. The purpose was to identify some of the central mechanisms leading to spirals of decline.

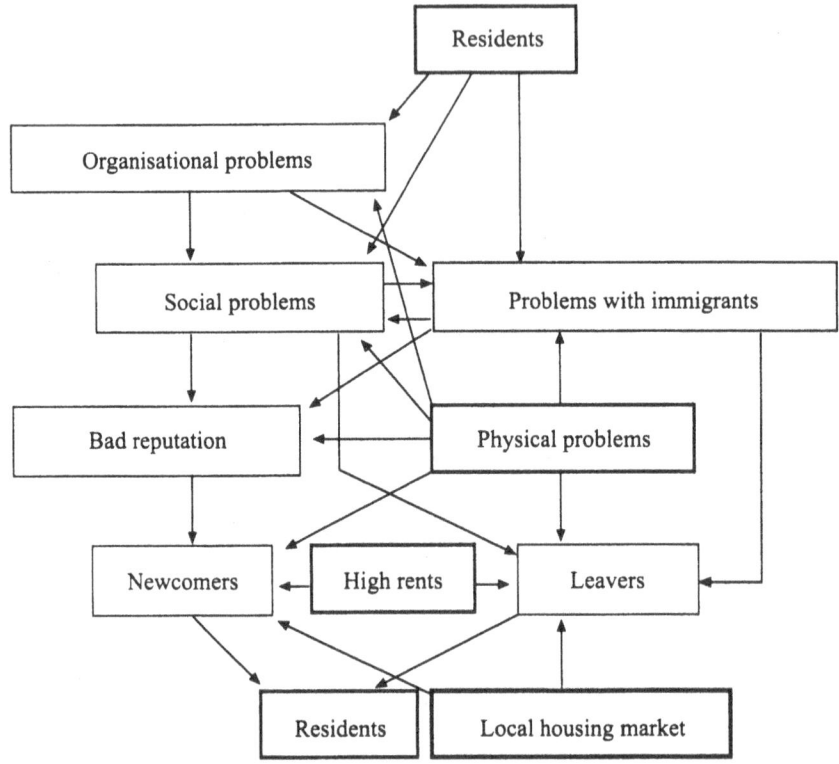

Figure 5.2 The tested model of processes of deprivation

The elements in the model can be divided into: a) *given circumstances*; b) *observed problems*; and c) *residential changes*. *Given circumstances* are:

1 the local housing market conditions;
2 the rent level on the estates;
3 their physical appearance and amenities.

Observed problems are:

1 passivity and low engagement in the affairs of the estate among residents;
2 social and behavioural problems of different kinds (including crime, vandalism, drugs and conflicts);
3 special problems in connection with immigrants;
4 bad reputation of the estate.

Finally *residential changes* involve the initial composition of residents, the mobility rate of different groups, and the composition of new residents moving to the estates.

If you compare this figure with Figure 5.1, you will see that some of the connections in this figure are missing. It has therefore not been possible to investigate the effect of social and organisational conditions on the physical environment because these processes are more long-term.

The core hypotheses in the model are as follows:

1 The *activity level and engagement of tenants* are supposed to be determined by the composition of residents and by the physical conditions on the estates – especially by the extent to which there are common facilities on the estates where activities can take place. In Danish social housing, tenant involvement is crucial because tenant democracy is highly developed. Every estate is a closed economic system administrated by a board of people elected by and from among the residents. If these boards do not function well, the estate's problems become worse.
2 *Social problems* are seen as a product of the composition of residents, the physical conditions on the estates and organisational problems caused by a low activity level among residents. Moreover, special problems in connection with immigrants are assumed to have a possible effect on social problems in general.
3 It is expected that *problems in connection with immigrants* are explained by the composition of residents. It is, however, also assumed that the physical conditions on the estates and their organisational problems have an effect. Social problems in general could also tend to increase special problems in connection with immigrants.
4 *Bad reputations* should be caused by the physical appearance and perhaps peripheral location of the estates. Bad reputations could also be influenced by social problems and by many immigrants.
5 *High moving frequency* – especially among residents not belonging to the marginal groups of society – is assumed to be explained by problems experienced on the estates connected with physical conditions and location, with social problems and with the consequences of many immigrants being present. The rent level of the estates, compared with the local rent level, also has an effect on people moving, which is also influenced by conditions on the local housing market, i.e. what are the alternative housing choices?
6 Finally, the *composition of people moving to the estates* should be explained

by the estate's reputation, physical appearance, location and amenities, by the rent level and by local housing market conditions.

The change in residents, and therefore the new composition of residents, is a function of who moves in and out of the estates, and the vicious circle of deprivation is then complete.

Data and Methods used in the Study

The data used in the Danish study comes from two main sources:

1 Public data registers provided data on residents in 1994 and on people moving in and out of the estates in the period 1994–96. Denmark has a special housing and building register from which it has been possible to obtain data on the estates and their rents. From this register, it has also been possible to obtain data on local housing markets defined as municipalities.
2 Two surveys with almost identical questions were carried out among tenants in the elected boards on the estates and among their housing associations. The answers from each estate were combined to describe the problems and conditions in each area. The respondents were asked to rate different problems in their estate on a scale from no problems to very serious problems.

In relation to the elements in the model described, the following data were available.

Data on residents, newcomers and leavers The data contained information on age, family status, education, employment, job description, duration of unemployment, source of income from the public, nationality and place of birth and also duration of stay on the estates. This data was combined to divide the residents into life-cycle groups and into different social groups: early pensioners, welfare recipients, old-age pensioners, students, part-time employed with low and medium-high incomes, respectively, and residents in full-time employment with low and medium-high incomes.

Some special problem and resource groups were also defined. The problem groups were young and middle-aged single men without work and single parents without work. The resource groups were identified as people in employment aged between 25–65, living as couples and with a further and higher education, or those classed as superior employees or self-employed residents.

Data on the estates and their physical problems The public registers provided data on the size of the estates (number of dwellings), year of construction, dwelling size, rents, building types and municipalities' locations. The municipalities were divided into four groups according to the degree of urbanisation:

1 Copenhagen and its suburbs;
2 the five biggest cities outside Copenhagen and their suburbs;
3 other towns with more than 15,000 inhabitants; and
4 other municipalities.

From the two surveys, evaluations were extracted of the spatial location (in relation to transport and services), the visual appearance of the estate, the balance of small and large apartments, the technical conditions of the buildings, the open spaces and the quality of common facilities.

Data on social problems and problems connected with immigrants In the surveys, the respondents were asked to evaluate the following problems: alcoholics, drug-users, mentally ill, special problems with young people, noisy residents, conflicts between residents, vandalism, crime and other social problems. In some of the analyses, these evaluations were combined to form a common indicator of social problems.

Regarding immigrants, respondees were asked to evaluate:

1 difficulties in connection with their integration;
2 other problems as a result of having a large proportion of immigrants among the residents.

Data on residents' activities and organisation The respondents in the surveys were asked to give their opinion on three matters:

1 the extent to which residents were engaged in activities on the estate;
2 the range of social activities;
3 the quality of the tenants' democracy on the estate.

Data on the reputation of the estate The respondents were simply asked the extent to which their estate had a bad image among locals.

Data on the local housing market Based on data from the public registers, the following information on the municipalities was produced: proportion of different tenures (owner-occupied, private renting and social renting), average rent level for renting and price level for owner-occupied dwellings, mobility and social composition of people moving to and from dwellings in the municipality.

Methods The procedure followed in the study was to construct statistical models explaining the variation among the estates of each of the four types of problems in the above theoretical model and identify moving frequencies and composition of newcomers. The independent variables were chosen in accordance with the hypotheses described above. Moreover, where high correlation existed between independent variables, the weakest variables were omitted.

The data has been weighed in accordance with the number of dwellings on each estate.

Two different statistical methods were used. Multiple linear regressions were used for the models explaining mobility, composition of newcomers, and for the index for social problems. The results shown are standardised beta coefficients.

In the other cases, the statistical properties of the independent variables made it difficult to use this method, so instead logistic regression was used to reveal whether the problems were serious or not. R-statistics (see Norusis, 1993), which can be used when coefficients are not too small (no logic variables), represent the results from the models. The R-statistics represent the survey results and show the correlation between the variables in question. The tables below show the results of the best regressions found. Only significant variables are shown (at a 0.05 per cent level).

What Factors are Important when Explaining Vicious Circles?

Data from 500 housing estates has enabled us to test the model described above to shed light on the actual connections between the different factors in the model.

In the following section, we will describe the results of the analyses that show what factors statistically explain the observed problems and the residential changes. The explained variables are respectively:

1 social activity among tenants;
2 extent of social problems;

3 problems with integration of immigrants;
4 bad reputation of the estates;
5 mobility rate among different groups;
6 composition of newcomers.

Factors contributing to residential social activity and commitment As shown in Figure 5.2, we expect the degree to which residents are active in social life in and management of the estates to depend mainly on who lives in the area, but also on the physical properties of the estates.

Many Danish housing estates have common facilities and premises where meetings and activities can take place, but they are of very different quality and are lacking on some estates. Rather surprisingly, one result of the analyses (Table 5.1) showed the very strong importance of these facilities for social life on the estates. These findings are in contrast with much literature in recent years that points to weak connections between physical design and social life in housing areas.

Table 5.1   Results from two statistical models (logistic regression) explaining the extent of social activities and active residents on the estates (R-statistic * 100)

Significant variables	Dependent variables	
	Social activities	Active residents
	*R-statistic * 100*	
Proportion of singles <30 years	–	7
Proportion of couples 30-60	10	14
Proportion of subord. funct. or skilled workers	1	6
Part-time employed, low income	5	5
Part-time employed, medium-high income	5	4
Duration of stay > 5 years	2	5
Unsatisfactory common facilities	-41	-38
Size of the estate	9	12
Year of construction	-9	-4
Proportion of dwellings not in blocks	3	1

Source: Skifter Andersen, 1999b.

The size of the estate and the year of construction are also of importance. Social activity is strongest on the older and larger estates. The first variable could be interpreted to mean that social activity on the estates grows over time. The other variable suggests that activity grows with size but does not indicate the extent. Compared with the number of residents, the activities on the larger estates could therefore be relatively smaller and social networks weaker.

The analysis also shows – as expected – that the social composition of residents is of importance, but perhaps not quite in the way expected. The groups usually regarded as the most resourceful residents – educated people with higher positions on the labour market, or high incomes – had no significant importance for the level of social activity on the estates. Instead, it was the presence of 'middle groups' – subordinate functionaries and skilled workers and part-time employees – that appeared to be important. The group of residents aged 30 to 60 living in couples was of special importance. Moreover, social stability is of importance measured as the number of residents who had stayed on the estate for longer than five years.

Factors explaining the extent of social problems Social problems are a complex issue and many variables were used in the study to describe them. The study showed (Skifter Andersen, 1999b) that there was some correlation between the problems but also between different combinations of problems. A common index of social problems was constructed as a simple average of the scores for every single indicator (crime, abuse, vandalism, etc.). This index proved to be highly correlated with nearly all the indicators. Table 5.2 describes the results from a statistical model explaining the variation in this index. As very much expected, variables describing the composition of residents are shown to be of great importance. The proportion of residents on early pension or welfare benefits is especially important, but single unemployed parents are another vulnerable group.

Immigrants seem to contribute to social problems, but the effect is small and newcomers contribute most – refugees etc. These results therefore indicate that the massive social problems observed in many Danish housing estates with a large number of immigrants are not caused mainly by the immigrants but more likely by the remaining Danes living there. This conclusion is supported by the analysis of newcomers below.

A more surprising result is the strong effect of the physical properties of the estate. The quality of common facilities and outdoor areas seems to have an important influence on the extent of social problems. The explanation could be that these facilities, as shown above, support social activities and social networks, which again restrain social problems on the estates. But as shown in the table, the extent of social activities also has a separate influence.

Table 5.2 Results from a multivariable regression explaining social problems, measured by a combined index

	Beta coefficients * 100
Physical variables	
Unsatisfactory common facilities	19
Unsatisfactory outdoor areas	21
Size of the estate	19
Year of construction	-16
Proportion of dwellings not in blocks	-11
Proportion of dwellings >100 m^2	1
Degree of urbanisation	8
Social activities	
Few social activities	10
Few active residents	13
Residents, proportion of	
Immigrants from poor countries	3
Immigrants arrived after 1990	5
Children of immigrants	2
26–40 year olds	6
Early pensioners	20
Welfare recipients	12
Full-time unemployed	7
Single unemployed men, 18–25 years	4
Single unemployed men, 41–65 years	7
Single unemployed parents	16

Note: $R^2 = 0.4$.

Source: Skifter Andersen, 1999b.

Less surprisingly, social problems are more frequently found in larger estates and in blocks of flats from the 1960s located in the more urbanised parts of the country.

Factors explaining insufficient integration of ethnic minorities Problems with integrating ethnic minorities seem to be increasing in Denmark even if they are small compared with the situation in countries such as France and the United Kingdom. In this survey, the analysis of problems with integration is based on the evaluation of the problems expressed by both the housing associations and by the elected boards of tenants.

The proportion of residents belonging to an ethnic minority varies very much from estate to estate up to 70 per cent of residents on one estate were immigrants from developing countries or from former communist countries. The statistical analysis (Table 5.3) shows, as expected, that integration problems increase with the number of immigrants – but only if they come from developing countries. The proportion of immigrants who have recently arrived in the country – often refugees – is also of importance. Moreover, it seems as if many children of immigrants – especially in the age group 12–17 years – increase the problems. More unexpected is the fact that it is of little importance whether the immigrants are employed or outside the labour market.

Table 5.3   Results from a statistical model (logistic regression) explaining problems with integration of immigrants (R-statistic * 100)

	R-statistic * 100
Physical variables	
Unsatisfactory common facilities	3
Unsatisfactory outdoor areas	3
Size of the estate	19
Year of construction	-11
Proportion of dwellings not in blocks	-8
Proportion of dwellings <50 m^2	1
Proportion of dwellings >100 m^2	-5
Degree of urbanisation	8
Few social activities	3
Residents, proportion of	
Immigrants from Eastern Europe	-2
Immigrants from developing countries	18
Immigrants arrived after 1990	8
Immigrants arrived before 90	-4
Children of immigrants	9
Immigrants 12–17 years old	9
Immigrants on early pension	-1
Immigrants on welfare benefits	3
Immigrants full-time unemployed	3

Source: Skifter Andersen, 1999b.

Integration problems are – like social problems – more common in blocks of flats on larger estates from the 1960s located in more urbanised areas. The quality of common facilities and outdoor areas has some importance but is not as pronounced as for social problems.

Conditions leading to bad reputations Estates that are seen as unattractive have bad reputations. However, opinions of the reputation of an estate depend largely on the angle from which the estate is seen. A Dutch study (Rijpers and Smeets, 1998) has identified three different kinds of reputation:

1. the reputation among residents (internal image);
2. the reputation among people living outside the estate (external image);
3. the reputation that residents believe is found among people not living on the estate (self-reflecting image).

The Dutch study showed marked differences between these three types of images. While the external image was mostly influenced by the visual quality of the estate and by the frequency of social problems, the self-reflecting image depended more on the composition of residents and less on visual quality. As the Danish study is based on the judgements of key persons on the estates – housing associations and the elected boards of tenants – we can suppose that our variable for bad reputation most closely resembles the self-reflecting image.

Table 5.4 shows that the physical appearance of the estate – as in the Dutch study – is of considerable importance. Both the visual quality and size of the area and type of buildings matter. More unexpectedly, an isolated location and high rents contribute to a bad reputation. The composition of dwellings is also important. If there are too many small dwellings, the estates are seen as less attractive. The most important social variable reflects problems caused by having many immigrants on the estates. Unlike the Dutch study, this indicates that the composition of residents – especially the proportion of ethnic minorities – influences the image of an estate.

In terms of social problems, it seems that the self-reflected image is most influenced by conflicts among residents and by problems concerning vandalism and noisy residents. Alcoholics and drug addicts seem, a little surprising, to be of minor importance only.

Another interesting result is that bad reputations vary very much according to the degree of urbanisation. It appears that estates with given social or physical problems have a much worse reputation in less urbanised parts of the country, i.e. in small and middle-sized towns. One explanation could be that in smaller towns these areas constitute a much more marginal part of the housing market

Table 5.4 Results from a logistic regression explaining when estates had bad reputations (R-statistic * 100)

	R-statistic * 100
Estate variables	
High rents	8
Isolated location	18
Bad visual appearance	10
Unsatisfactory common facilities	1
Unsatisfactory outdoor areas	1
Size of the estate	21
Year of construction	1
Proportion of dwellings not in blocks	-5
Proportion of larger dwellings >100 m^2	2
Proportion of smaller dwellings <50 m^2	16
Degree of urbanisation	-21
Social problems	
Many alcoholics and drug addicts	3
Too many immigrants	15
Problems of vandalism	7
Problems of crime	4
Problems of noise	8
Many conflicts among residents	12

Source: Skifter Andersen, 1999b.

because most of the population there is living in owner-occupied housing. Moreover, residents may be more aware of people who have social problems and where they are living. Therefore, the external image of the areas could be worse and have a negative effect on the self-reflected image.

Factors explaining mobility rates for different groups on the estates In Denmark, a high rate of mobility among residents has been seen as an important indicator of problem estates, especially if it is high among the groups of residents that are important to social life and tenants' democracy. If social stability decreases, social relations among residents are weakened and it is much more difficult to keep tenant organisations running, which is very important in Danish social housing. Moreover, high mobility increases administrative expenses and sometimes makes it difficult to find new residents, which leads to empty dwellings.

The mobility rate in the 500 deprived housing estates studied was 35 per cent higher than the average for all dwellings. High mobility rates were found particularly among people in employment and with more extensive social and economic resources.

A number of multivariate linear regressions were constructed to explain the variance in mobility rates among all residents and some subgroups of residents, shown in Table 5.5. The analyses show that the mobility rate is determined partially by factors outside the estates. The composition of the housing market (proportion of owner-occupied housing in the municipality) is of significant importance, as is the degree of urbanisation, with mobility being much higher on the estates in less urbanised municipalities. Both variables express similar conclusions, i.e. that in smaller towns dominated by owner-occupied housing, these estates are a marginal part of the housing market often used as a temporary residence. Earlier Danish studies (Skifter Andersen and Ærø, 1997) also show high mobility in social housing in small and middle-sized towns.

A bad reputation has a significant importance for mobility rates in the model, though surprisingly enough, not so much for employed people and residents with many resources. One reason is that the variable is weakened by the fact that some of the factors explaining bad reputation are also present in the model, i.e. the physical and social conditions. High frequency of moving is therefore found mainly in blocks of flats in larger estates with bad visual appearances and isolated locations. The more affluent groups – residents in employment or with high resources – especially, react to the visual quality of the buildings, and less to the location and size of the housing area. A little surprisingly, mobility is highest in the newer estates than in the older estates from the 1960s.

Mobility rates for employed and high-resource groups in particular – those with better incomes – are influenced by the difference between the rent level on the estates and the average rent level in the municipality. These groups, who do not get housing benefits and have more housing choices, more often react to high rents by moving away.

Among the social variables, a high proportion of immigrants increases mobility rates. This is especially the case for employed and high-resource groups. Social problems, as measured by our index, do not seem to have a marked influence on these groups' leaving patterns. This could be due to the correlation with bad reputation.

Factors influencing the composition of newcomers The last element in our

Table 5.5 Results from four multivariable regressions explaining moving frequencies for different groups (standardised beta coefficients * 100)

	All	Age 41–65	Employed	High-resource groups
Isolated location	7	1	3	2
Bad visual appearance	9	7	13	10
Size of the estate	16	11	8	9
Year of construction	10	18	7	10
Proportion of dwellings not in blocks	-15	-3	-14	-14
Proportion of larger dwellings >100 m^2	-4	6	-8	-9
Proportion of smaller dwellings <50 m^2	6	6	10	3
Degree of urbanisation	-21	-6	-28	-10
Rent level compared to local level	7	6	12	13
Index of social problems	2	8	–	-9
Proportion of immigrants Eastern Europe	3	3	–	0
Proportion of immigrants developing countries	6	19	12	14
Bad reputation	15	12	5	9
% owner-occupied in municipality	18	10	16	11
% social housing in municipality	1		4	-2
R^2	0.29	0.23	0.30	0.18

Note: High-resource groups = people living in couples with employment and middle to higher education.

Source: Skifter Andersen, 1999b.

model to be analysed is what factors explain the composition of people moving into the estates. One of the major problems in deprived estates is that for several years, newcomers have been dominated by people on early retirement or welfare – often with social problems and few social resources.

The composition of newcomers is influenced by the rules for allocating social dwellings in the Danish social housing sector. These rules are quite relaxed concerning the social and family status of newcomers. It is difficult for small households to get larger apartments, but in practice there are no limits on incomes. More importantly, dwellings should always be allocated in accordance with a waiting list. The lists in these estates are usually relatively long (only a few of the estates had empty dwellings). It is therefore often difficult for people with acute housing needs to gain access to social housing. This means that some of the potential groups of new tenants – people getting a divorce or migrating to the city – cannot be attracted.

Table 5.6   Results from two multivariable regressions explaining how large a proportion of newcomers were employed or high-resource groups (beta coefficients * 100)

	Employed	High-resource groups
Bad reputation	-4	-3
Index for social problems	-11	-4
% of immigrants from developing countries	-35	-39
% of immigrants arrived after 1990	-12	-8
Size of estate	–	-2
Proportion of dwellings not in blocks	5	19
Proportion of large dwellings >100 m^2	7	10
Year of construction	-15	-3
% in municipality that moves to owner-occupied	-8	-12
% in municipality that moves to social housing	23	19
The group's proportion of in-movers in municipality	41	18
R^2	0.42	0.33

Source: Skifter Andersen, 1999b.

The analyses show (Table 5.6) that the number of employed people and high-resource groups among newcomers to the estates is largely determined by the conditions in the local housing market. If these groups constitute a relatively large proportion of all newcomers to dwellings in the local municipality, there will also be a relative larger proportion moving into the deprived housing estates. The composition of the housing market also has a major influence. In municipalities with a great deal of (cheaper) owner-occupied housing and less social housing, fewer employed and high-resource groups move onto deprived housing estates. Estates lacking larger dwellings or those dominated by blocks of flats have special difficulty in attracting these groups.

Surprisingly, the variables describing the physical quality and location of the estates had no significant effect on the composition of newcomers. The size of the estates also had little or no effect.

A bad reputation does have an effect – especially if the variable describing the proportion of immigrants among residents is omitted. It appeared, however, that the best model was found by introducing the proportion of immigrants among residents in the statistical analysis, which is not quite in accordance with the model of deprivation we are examining. The results shown in the table indicate that when there are many residents in an estate belonging to ethnic minorities, this has a strong effect on who will move in, especially if many of these immigrants have recently arrived in Denmark. This evidence supports the uncomfortable conclusion that some Danes do not want to live together with other ethnic groups. It also reveals a difference between the self-reflecting image, in which immigrants played a minor role, and the external image that could be found among newcomers. Housing associations and elected tenants living among immigrants therefore underestimate the prejudices among Danes against ethnic groups from developing countries.

Finally it can be seen that, as expected, social problems also have some effect on newcomers.

Concluding Evidence on Self-perpetuating Processes of Deprivation in the Danish Study

The purpose of the study was to throw light on the nature of self-perpetuating processes of deprivation and decay that take place in vulnerable housing estates in Europe, by means of empirical evidence from 500 Danish social housing estates.

Based on earlier Danish research, a model for processes of deprivation was formulated. It presumes how social problems, problems associated with immigrants, social activity of residents, mobility rates and social composition of in-movers are connected to the social composition of residents, the physical conditions of the estates and the conditions in the local housing market.

The statistical analyses in the study have shown that relationships between these factors exist in such a way that conditions on the estates tend to worsen over time. A socially distorted composition of residents increases social problems and – if there are many immigrants – encourages special problems connected with integration. Together, these problems result in a worse reputation for the estates and increase mobility rates among residents in employment. Moreover, the poorer reputation has an effect on the composition of newcomers, so that fewer people in employment and with social resources move in and are replaced by more newcomers who are outside the labour market. Together these changes in mobility rates and the composition of newcomers result in a change towards an even more distorted composition of residents that in turn affects social problems and reputations and a vicious circle is established.

Some of the more interesting results of the analyses are:

1 As could be expected, problems tend to be the worst in larger estates with blocks of flats built in the 1960s – this relates to social problems, integration of minorities, the reputation of the estate and mobility rates. Only social activities among residents tend to be more extensive in larger estates.
2 The groups of residents most important to social activity levels on the estates are not those with the greatest resources in traditional terms – employed with better education – but the middle groups of skilled workers and subordinate functionaries – especially people with occasional occupations.
3 Good common facilities are important not only for social activities. They also help to reduce social problems and to integrate minorities. Good outdoor areas also have an effect.
4 A high proportion of minorities among residents has only a small effect on social problems on the estates. The problem is that more Danes with social problems are found on estates with many immigrants because this influences the composition of newcomers.
5 Problems concerning integrating minorities are especially likely on estates with many refugees and other immigrants who have recently arrived. Many young people belonging to minorities also increase problems.
6 Bad reputations are caused largely by isolated locations and the bad physical appearance of the estates: size, house type and visual qualities. But the proportion of residents belonging to ethnic minorities is of decisive importance. The analyses indicated that this factor is an even more important factor concerning how the estate is judged by potential

newcomers. The extent of social problems is important for the 'self-reflecting image' – the image that residents have of what they think is the reputation among outsiders.

7 The mobility rate among residents – especially among the more resourceful groups – is influenced by the reputation of the estate, by its location and physical appearance and by rent levels. Social problems and proportion of minorities play only a minor role, but are of some importance to resourceful groups.

8 For newcomers belonging to the more resourceful groups, location and physical conditions play only a minor role, except for the proportion of larger apartments not situated in blocks of flats. Bad reputation (the self-reflected image) also has a minor effect. The dominant factor is the proportion of ethnic minorities, which to a large extent decreases the number of employed people and special resource groups among newcomers. The extent of social problems also has a negative effect.

There are some marked differences between the processes in the more and less urbanised parts of the country, partly because of a difference in the character of the housing market. In small and middle-sized towns, the owner-occupied sector dominates and the amount of social housing is limited. The estates found here have a much more marginal position on the market and the mobility rate is higher. This can be explained partly by the fact that the reputations of the estates are worse, other things being equal. Problem estates seem to be more conspicuous in smaller communities. Also, the number of high-resource groups among newcomers is smaller in municipalities with large owner-occupied sectors. On the other hand, social problems and problems concerning integration of minorities tend to be smaller on estates in less urbanised municipalities.

Chapter 6

Understanding Deprived Neighbourhoods – the Connection between Segregation and Neighbourhood Decay

Many studies have understood deprived – or depressed – neighbourhoods as 'pockets of poverty' – a spatial concentration of poor and socially excluded groups (see introduction). One of the main points of this book is that such a perception of these kinds of neighbourhoods is too narrow to give a complete understanding of this phenomenon and its implications for cities as a whole.

In the preceding chapters, we have described how self-perpetuating processes in vulnerable neighbourhoods result in negative changes in the qualities of the neighbourhoods, which make them increasingly diverge from conditions in the rest of the city. The most important of these changes are:

1 *physical changes*: attrition and dereliction of buildings, facilities and open spaces;
2 *social changes*: crime, conflicts and visible social problems leading to low status and bad reputation;
3 *financial changes*: disproportion between rents and housing quality, reduction in the quality of management and private services because of lack of economic resources;
4 *organisational changes*: lack of social resources resulting in a break down of community.

Simultaneously, changes occur in the reputation and status of the areas. These changes could be called 'exclusion of places', which refers to Berghman's (1995) notion of spatial exclusion as 'not so much to spaces where there are poor persons as to 'poor spaces' themselves'.

Deprived Urban Areas Understood as Excluded Places

The studies of deprived neighbourhoods cited – and experience from slums in the United States – suggest that a revision of the understanding of the nature of deprived housing estates as simply pockets of poverty is needed. We should be more concerned about the dynamic processes of deprivation and decay at work than the actual status of the areas. Most importantly, we must establish the direction in which the processes move and their speed.

The perception of places is based on a subjective point of view, i.e. different people give places different meanings. The understanding of a place differs especially between people living there and outsiders (Knox 1995). Outsiders have a different knowledge of and affiliation to a neighbourhood to residents. In the words of Bourdieu (1993), the image of a place among outsiders – especially deprived neighbourhoods – is 'more based on ghostly figments of the imagination nourished by emotional experiences than on knowledge of realities'. Research on people's preferences for living in different parts of a city (reviewed in Knox, 1995) shows that these are not a simple function of physical qualities and location but also depend very much on how the social and cultural content of places are perceived.

When visible signs of social and physical decay appear in neighbourhoods, and especially if they receive bad press, a rapid change will occur in how the places are perceived by outsiders. It is therefore reasonable to talk about these places being *excluded* from the mental maps of possible living environments for the majority of the urban population. We could talk about exclusion of these places.

Exclusion of Places Creates Segregation

To realise the importance of this exclusion of places, we need to look at the fundamental causes of segregation described in Chapter 2. We argued that *segregation is not a simple consequence of social inequality, but a product of both social and spatial differentiation.*

Segregation is initially created as a consequence of decisions taken by individual households. In their search for a location, people choose between places that have different perceived qualities regarding housing, physical and social environments, access to transport, jobs, services and natural beauty, and status and cultural identity. When these qualities are more unevenly distributed in space, which means that differences between 'bad' and 'good' or 'ordinary' areas are more obvious, segregation will tend to become stronger because the incentives for house hunters to choose or drop certain urban areas will be increased.

Segregation is therefore influenced very much by the development of spatial differentiation in cities, and perhaps this is more important than the development in social inequality and social exclusion. Segregation and increasing spatial inequality are mutually self-perpetuating processes because the status and cultural identity of urban areas are determined by the composition of the people living there. Spatial differentiation leads to segregation, but at the same time, segregation creates spatial differences. The above-mentioned self-perpetuating processes of physical and social decay in urban areas at the bottom of the urban hierarchy therefore make a special contribution towards increasing the qualitative differences between these areas and the rest of the city and thereby add to segregation.

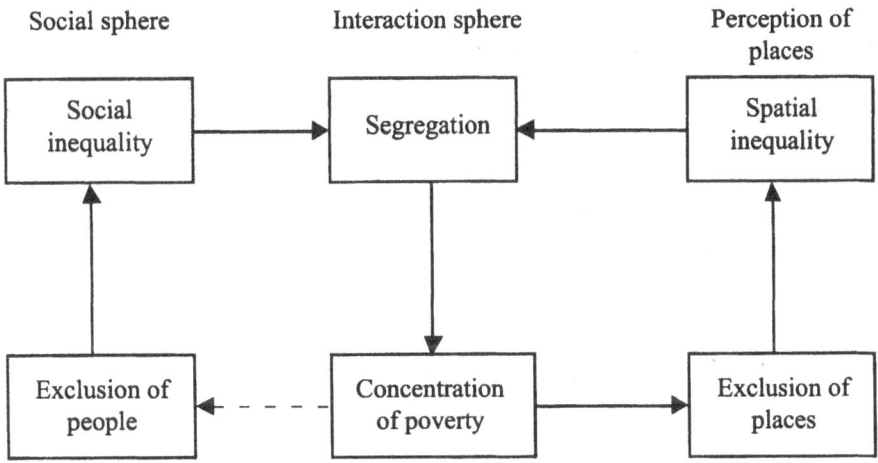

Figure 6.1 Model of the connection between segregation and deprived neighbourhoods

Figure 6.1 is an attempt to illustrate these considerations. The model does not include the basic causes for social and spatial inequality but only looks at the connection between segregation and deprivation of neighbourhoods.

Segregation takes place as interaction between social and spatial differentiation and leads to concentrations of poor and excluded people – or special ethnic groups – in certain parts of cities. As concluded above, such concentrations lead to changes in the qualities of the neighbourhoods and to exclusion of the places as possible living areas. This exclusion of places then further adds to spatial differentiation in the cities and increases segregation.

Another self-perpetuating process is suggested in the left side of the figure and suggests that living in deprived housing estates could lead to further social exclusion of people staying there, which again tends to increase social inequality. As described in the introduction, this has actually been the main point of discussion among researchers considering deprived housing areas as synonymous with spatial pockets of poverty.

The Need for a New Understanding of Neighbourhood Decay

The conclusion from this discussion is that problems of deprived areas should not be considered simply as spatially concentrated pockets of poverty that have arisen as a simple product of social inequality and segregation. For several reasons, this view is a dead end. First, it is static and does not involve the dynamic processes taking place in these areas – the so-called vicious circles – that tend to aggravate the situation over time. Second, it does not take into account the relationship between the areas and the city that surrounds them. And third, it leads to a view of the problems on the estates that underestimates the consequences for residents. Finally, the potential purposes of area-based efforts cannot be identified correctly and their effects can be misinterpreted. One of the main reasons for disagreement on the effects of area-based initiatives is therefore inadequate understanding of the nature of these urban areas.

This book proposes an alternative understanding. Segregation is seen as a product of both social and spatial inequality, and deprived urban areas are understood as 'excluded places' that contribute to increasing spatial inequality and segregation. This exclusion of places is due to social, cultural, economic and physical changes in the areas that cause them to diverge increasingly from the rest of the city. The development in these areas tends to make 'ordinary' people flee to other parts of the city making room for an increasing concentration of low-income and socially excluded groups and therefore increasing the spatial division of social groups. This effect is even more serious when looking at the segregation of ethnic minorities where the forces at work are much stronger.

The exclusion of a place is a dynamic process that can be fast, slow, stopped or even sometimes reversed. But in most cases, there are strong forces that, when the process has reached a certain point, tend to speed up the process regardless of the general development concerning economic growth and social inequality in the city. That is why increased deprivation of urban areas also takes place in many cities where incomes in general are rising or inequality among citizens has been reduced.

Measures to save these housing estates should therefore also concentrate on fighting against exclusion of places more than exclusion of people. Social exclusion should be combated mainly by general policies and only for special reasons by area-based measures. With this understanding as a starting point, in a subsequent chapter, I will discuss European literature on area-based initiatives and experience gained from some Danish initiatives.

Chapter 7

Efforts to Combat Urban Decay

As shown in this book, problems of urban decay and deprived neighbourhoods are a result of segregation. A way to combat these problems could then be to take action against the causes of segregation, especially against social inequality. For some researchers (see introduction) such action is the only efficient type of measure against deprived neighbourhoods. However, a main point in the preceding chapters has also been that urban decay in itself is an important cause of segregation and that segregation and decay are processes that are intertwined. It can therefore be claimed that efforts to combat urban decay and deprivation also reduce segregation. It is therefore a main point of view in this chapter that so-called area-based initiatives – social, economic and physical efforts in deprived neighbourhoods – have an important purpose in combating segregation and decay, and that they can work.

The first part of the chapter gives an overview of general policies for traditional physical measures in the older parts of cities – urban renewal and housing rehabilitation – based on a recent study of nine European countries (Skifter Andersen and Leather, 1999). Next, an important question in connection with these policies is discussed: To what extent should they concentrate on generating a process of economic growth and gentrification in the neighbourhoods concerned? Must it be accepted that residents are displaced from their homes and replaced by wealthier people, or should the efforts instead benefit people living in these areas? This subject is illustrated by evidence from a Danish study of the social consequences of urban renewal.

The last part of the chapter concerns policies against deprived social housing estates. European experiences based on recent research are discussed that tend to conclude that the purposes of these policies are not very well defined and that the effects are questionable. Danish policies in recent years are described and their effects illustrated using results from a Danish research evaluation that seems to have reached a different conclusions to most other studies.

Urban Renewal Policies in Europe

Cities, housing areas and dwellings can be regarded as living organism that deteriorate over time while also growing, developing and changing. Our physical surroundings currently have to be kept up and adapted to changes in needs and economic conditions. Sometimes, however, market processes of maintenance and renewal do not take place at a satisfactory speed and extent, as shown in preceding chapters. Then cities decline and housing becomes obsolete and deteriorates. Often, governments have felt inclined to take action. Most governments in Europe have found it necessary to subsidise and regulate the processes of urban renewal and housing rehabilitation and many countries have implemented special renewal programmes for deprived urban neighbourhoods.

The Diversity of Urban Renewal Policies

In a publication on Urban Renewal in a European Perspective (Priemus and Metselaar, 1992) based on questionnaires answered by government agencies in nine countries, it was concluded that there was little agreement among the countries on the meaning of the concept of urban renewal and on the kinds of problems and activities it concerned. It was also concluded that: 'Goals and motives of urban renewal policy differ to no small extent per country' (p. 18) and 'urban renewal legislation in the countries cannot be described by means of a generally applicable model' (p. 24). Another recent book (Skifter Andersen and Leather, 1999) concluded that public policies for housing rehabilitation and urban renewal in European countries appeared to be from totally different worlds. Every country has its own way of understanding this policy area and the kinds of problems it concerns.

Why does such large deviation exist between Western European countries concerning policies and practice in this field? One of the main causes is that urban renewal and housing rehabilitation actually affects a lot of different but connected problems and activities. The angle from which the field has been looked at, and therefore the starting point from which programmes and legislation have been worked out in the countries, have differed considerably.

However, it appears quite clear (Skifter Andersen and Leather, 1999) that problems of urban decay differ significantly from country to country, as do the conditions for solving them. In every country, urban problems appear in a specific geographical, economic and political context, and the possible instruments for solving the problems are often linked to the present national structure of public administration and policies. General housing policies and the character of housing markets are of special importance.

Finally, it is obvious that even if urban problems are alike in character, divergent political priorities and objectives for urban renewal could lead to quite different policies in practice.

However, a probable hypothesis is that an important cause of differences between countries is that general uncertainty exists among policy makers (and researchers) in Europe on the fundamental causes of problems of urban decay and the role the public should play in solving them. Clear answers have not been formulated for the fundamental questions of why market forces are not always able to create the necessary renewal of housing and urban areas, and how governments can most efficiently regulate the market so that renewal takes place. As a consequence, urban renewal has sometimes been organised as an isolated public task, planned and implemented by public agencies almost as if market forces did not exist. Even though all countries have found it necessary to establish special subsidy programmes and public regulation of urban renewal and housing rehabilitation, it seems as though many countries lack a clear understanding of the purpose of these policies and the extent of their application.

This was also mirrored in the above-mentioned study (Priemus and Metselaar) that showed it was difficult for governments to give precise information on the needs for urban renewal activities in their countries. They were seldom able to give a clear picture of what policies they would implement in the future. Urban renewal and housing rehabilitation policies seem to some extent to be ad hoc measures aimed at urban problems that are observed but hardly understood.

The Historic Development of Policies

Some general trends have, however, been clear in most of the countries since World War II. In the first period, until the start of the 1970s, slum clearance involving demolition of old buildings and construction of new ones dominated in many countries. This was followed by urban renewal programmes more oriented towards preserving existing buildings and urban areas and making it possible for residents to stay after renewal. More general programmes of urban revitalisation and restructuring were also initiated. At the same time, programmes supporting housing rehabilitation in single properties located inside or outside selected areas were started in many countries.

A new and unexpected field of urban renewal appeared in the 1980s in large post-war social housing estates. Increasing problems in these areas caused by technical defects and social unrest made it necessary for public authorities to intervene.

This experience in some countries caused the understanding of urban renewal to change from being a finite task, i.e. to remove or renew old and obsolete housing, to a continuous effort to solve problems of combined social and physical decay in vulnerable neighbourhoods. Moreover, in most countries it has produced a stronger consciousness of social processes as the root of urban decay. The interaction between physical and social agendas in relation to renewal has, increasingly, come into focus and new policies that strive to develop an integrated approach have been put into use.

General trends for housing policies in Europe – with withdrawal of the state from housing – have also penetrated this policy area in recent years. Even if the countries have had different starting points, some of the same general trends are evident. In the older stock, renewal of housing in whole districts is becoming less important as most of the heaviest slums from before the beginning of the century are being removed. Instead, programmes directed towards single properties are dominating. On the other hand, renewal of whole districts of post-war social housing has become more and more common. This mirrors the general change in the focus of housing rehabilitation policies from being directed against physical problems in older housing to social problems in post-war housing. In most countries, this is followed by decentralisation, which gives local authorities more influence. There is also a trend towards more importance being attached to preventive policies. Regulation of tenures is being changed to make it more attractive for private actors to invest in renewal. Programmes are becoming increasingly selective and means tests more common. The level of subsidies has become lower and it has become more difficult for residents to stay in their dwellings after renewal.

Explaining Differences in Policies

Skifter Andersen and Leather (1999) revealed five special factors that characterise and explain different national policies. These are:

1. basic view of the physical level on which to solve problems: city/district/property level;
2. function of policies: preventing or curing decay;
3. kind of public intervention: direct or indirect intervention, or regulation of conditions for tenures;
4. role of local authorities: centralised/decentralised control;
5. general/selective programmes: priority of certain geographical areas, buildings, tenures, building works or residents (means tests).

The weight they attached to broader urban problems compared with housing deterioration and obsolescence in general were important to the design of policies and the instruments chosen in the countries. The extent to which these housing problems are seen as part of general social and economic processes in geographically defined urban areas is also important. One of the main questions is if it is reasonable to renew single buildings alone, or if there are combined physical, social and economic problems in urban areas that must be solved simultaneously. In the latter case, urban renewal projects must comprise whole urban areas, and housing rehabilitation must combine physical, social and economic measures covering a whole neighbourhood.

In principle, the function of chosen policies can be either preventive or curative. Preventive policies aim to support market conditions for running maintenance, improvement and renewal of dwellings and urban structures, created by private actors. Curative policies, on the other hand, are put into effect when preventive policies have failed, and when problematic deterioration and obsolescence have occurred in certain dwellings and urban areas. It is striking that preventive policies are rarely seen as an integrated part of policies against housing deterioration and that they are often missing altogether. The actual regulations and programmes put into use in the countries have mainly aimed to cure specific problems of housing deterioration and obsolescence, while few policies exist with the direct purpose of facilitating maintenance and improvement activities on market conditions in different tenures.

The first two factors mentioned largely determine the third factor, the kind of intervention chosen to promote renewal in the market. That is if the intervention implies direct strong public involvement, if it indirectly puts more weight on supporting private initiatives or if it simply tries to regulate the conditions of tenures to facilitate market processes. Direct intervention is used mainly in connection with plans for renewal of whole urban areas where acute problems have to be cured and where it is important to simultaneously improve the whole area. There are, however, also examples of direct intervention used for single properties. Indirect regulation is used mainly to promote renewal of single properties. It can have a preventive purpose, but is used mainly to cure problems that have become or are going to become urgent, even if they are not always the most heavy and complex problems of decay. Regulating conditions for tenures has a primarily preventive purpose.

Knowledge of motives and barriers for investments among different kinds of landlords is an important basis for the design of housing policies and especially for rehabilitation programmes. This knowledge could form the basis for two different kinds of policies:

1   general regulation of landlordship;
2   differentiated policies directed towards different kinds of landlords.

The first kind of policies concern promoting the spreading of the types of landlords that are best suited to providing good, cheap and well-maintained housing and limiting the number of landlords who have undesirable motives and behaviour. Financial landlords and companies with other primary economic activities than private letting represent especially attractive types of landlords (see Chapter 4). One example of such a policy in Denmark concerns special tax deprecations for investments in housing made by pension funds. The least welcome landlords must be those dominated by speculative motives and to some extent small investors. Here capital gains taxes or demands concerning a licence or certification of the ability of new landlords to run rental property in a professional way could be relevant.

The second kind of policies comprise programmes that give different incentives and regulate different types of landlords in a way that addresses the different motives and behaviour among those landlords. Programmes must be implemented in a way that pays attention to the cash-flow and financial problems found especially among small-scale landlords and public-utility landlords. Among the latter group, a higher level of subsidies could be relevant. It is also necessary to actively seek out and give advice to small-scale and other landlords who are passive and unprofessional.

Finally, another strategy could be to support demands from tenants for better maintenance by giving them better opportunities to get organised and exert some influence.

The fourth point refers to the role of local authorities. In some countries, both the influence on and responsibilities for urban renewal have been decentralised at a local level. This implies that local governments have greater freedom to decide which dwellings should be renewed and how this should be done, but it also often implies that they have to pay a greater share of expenses by themselves. In other countries, there is stronger control from central governments. In these cases, detailed rules on how to carry out rehabilitation have been elaborated by the state, and local authorities are much more dependent on money from the state.

Alternatively, programmes could be general, i.e. they could cover a large number of dwellings in the stock, or they could be more selective. In the latter case, programmes could be restricted to certain geographical areas, or to certain parts of the housing stock, for example buildings of a certain type or age. There could also be separate programmes for different tenures taking into account that the economic conditions differ in these categories. Furthermore, programmes could specify the kind of building work that should be supported, or could give different kinds of support for different work. Finally, programmes could be selective concerning the people supported. In many countries, means tests are required for subsidised housing rehabilitation so that only people with low incomes or those in grave need receive support.

National Main Strategies for Urban Renewal

Based on the above-described criteria, three different main strategies followed by European countries[1] can be identified (Skifter Andersen and Leather, 1999).

Strategies of general housing renewal The first is called a strategy for general housing renewal. Countries such as Austria, Denmark and Sweden have followed this strategy. Typically, housing rehabilitation programmes in these countries are very general. Nearly all dwellings are covered by a few general programmes and very few means tests are required. Few centrally fixed rules exist about which housing should be renewed and how it should be accomplished. In Denmark and Austria, this is mainly left in the hands of local governments – in Sweden, in the hands of property owners. In Austria and Denmark, area renewal has played an important role and these programmes have taken the form of direct intervention. In Sweden, programmes are indirect and include only single properties. Such programmes are also found in Denmark and Austria. In all three countries, tenants' rights and security are important, which implies that rules for tenant participation and high subsidies may guarantee that residents stay in dwellings after renewal.

Significantly, the strategies chosen by these three countries agree well with their general housing policies. In all three countries, housing is largely seen as a public good and the state is extensively involved in housing. Denmark and Austria still have severe problems in housing from before 1920 in certain parts of some cities. This is why the two countries still need area renewal and direct intervention. Sweden had solved most of these problems by the early seventies. This was partly because the problems were smaller, but also because of extensive slum clearance activity after the war. The countries all have strong local governments and a tradition for decentralisation of influence.

In all three countries, the subsidy levels have been quite high. In spite of this, Denmark and Austria still have some of the greatest housing rehabilitation problems among the countries with which they are compared. One reason is that market conditions for private investments – especially in private rented housing – have not been very favourable. For Denmark, this is due partly to unfavourable general economic conditions for investments in private rental housing, though importantly, the regulation of tenures has been governed by objectives other than those encouraging housing rehabilitation. It could be said that the preventive policies have been inadequate. Another reason is that direct regulation and high economic security for residents result in high expenses per dwelling. Therefore only a limited number of dwellings can be renewed within a limited public budget.

Strategies of strong central priorities We have called the second main strategy a strategy of strong central priorities. Especially the UK and France have followed this strategy, but we have also placed Norway and the Netherlands in this group, even though these countries share some similarities with the first group.

All these countries have developed complex systems with many different programmes directed towards selected parts of the housing stock. The UK, France and Norway have made widespread use of means tests. Local governments are involved in programmes for urban restructuring or area renewal in all the countries, but their influence is – except in Norway – restricted by detailed rules fixed by the state. The dominant form is indirect intervention – even in area renewal schemes. In Norway, some direct intervention has also been found. Tenant influence has been less important than in the first group of countries, but has attracted some attention in the UK and Norway. The Netherlands has previously emphasised residents' rights to stay in their dwellings, but this has been less important in recent years.

An important explanation for the chosen strategy in some of these countries is that there is a tradition for weak local governments and strong central control. This concerns especially France, the UK and to some extent the Netherlands. However, in recent years there has been a trend in some of these countries towards more decentralisation. Especially in Norway and the UK, housing is considered as more of a public good. Consequently, these countries have tried to limit public involvement in housing rehabilitation to the most urgent problems and reserve subsidies for people with low incomes.

Some of the countries – especially the UK and France – still have major physical problems in the older housing stock. In Norway and the UK, this is because only comparably small resources have been used – the level of subsidies has been relatively low. In the Netherlands and parts of the French rental market, strict rent control has hampered private investments in rehabilitation. The use of indirect intervention, selective programmes and means tests have in some ways made subsidies more efficient in these countries. More private investments have been generated by the subsidies. Moreover, the amount of money spent per dwelling is lower. The disadvantages of centralised systems, especially in France and the UK, have been that local authorities have had more difficulty in coherently renewing urban areas. It has also been difficult to prioritise the most needy dwellings and areas at a local level, which tends to make programmes less effective. Another problem in these countries has been that low-income groups have often been expelled from renewed housing as a consequence of a low level of subsidies.

Strategies of limited public involvement We have called the last of the three main strategies a strategy of limited public involvement. Especially in Switzerland, but also in Germany (West), the programmes devised have been quite limited. Indirect intervention is the rule, except for the German urban renewal programme, which is aimed more at urban restructuring than at housing rehabilitation. Local authorities have a great deal of influence. Germany is the only country to give special tax subsidies (deprecations) supporting all investments in housing and reducing the need for indirect regulation. Tenants have no special rights and the amount of direct subsidies is small.

In both countries, traditionally the state has a more reduced role than in the other comparison countries, and a more liberal housing policy is implemented than in most countries. It is, however, important to notice that the general conditions for housing investments in both countries have been very favourable because interest rates have been low. This has made it easier for market forces to work and has reduced the need for public housing support. As a result, housing rehabilitation problems have also been reduced and most of the older stock has been renewed without subsidies. This has been supported by liberal rent control systems. The disadvantage is that poor people have often been expelled from renewed housing, and housing in general – especially in Switzerland – has become quite expensive.

Explanations for the chosen strategies From this comparison of countries in the field of urban renewal and housing rehabilitation policies, it can be seen that in spite of different starting points concerning urbanisation and housing stock, there is a connection between the applied policies and the general housing and welfare policies. Countries such as Denmark and Sweden, where housing is seen partly as a public good, also tend to consider housing rehabilitation as such and great importance is attached to security and the influence of sitting residents. In other countries such as the UK, Norway and France, where housing policies are regarded mainly as a means of solving housing problems for the poorer sections of the population, housing rehabilitation policies are much more oriented towards selected people and dwellings in which renewal on market terms is not expected to take place without public support. The tendency of complex and selective programmes and strong government control in these countries is also a result of a tradition for local governments to have weaker influence.

It is also apparent that problems of urban decay and housing deterioration and therefore the need for public support for renewal are influenced a great deal by general housing market conditions in the countries. In countries such as Germany and Switzerland, general economic policies have ensured low interest rates, which have favoured housing investments. Especially in Germany, general tax incentives have been given to support investments in rental housing while regulations for the private rented sector have been liberal. Together, these conditions have made extensive housing renewal possible without or with small government subsidies. In other countries, high interest rates and inexpedient regulation of tenures have impeded renewal of market conditions to a different degree and have therefore increased the need for public involvement.

The different strategies applied by the countries all have advantages and drawbacks. The strategy of general housing renewal is very cautious when residents are financially secure and have considerable influence. Moreover, the strategy facilitates a coherent renewal in selected urban areas to solve connected social, economic and physical problems. The negative consequences of the strategy are that high subsidies are needed with a smaller number of private investments. With limited public budgets, this means that it takes a long time to implement renewal of the neediest part of the housing stock and some of these countries are therefore still in considerable need of renewal. The strategy of central priorities results in more efficient use of subsidies where only the neediest are supported and more private capital is involved. The price is that it is much more difficult to coherently renew selected urban areas and therefore stop self-reinforcing slum processes in vulnerable neighbourhoods. Moreover, tenants are often financially insecure. This problem is even more pronounced in the strategy for limited public involvement, which has generally resulted in high rents in Germany and Switzerland.

Social Renewal or Gentrification?

Urban renewal and housing rehabilitation programmes intervene in processes of decay in neighbourhoods and change the quality and price of housing. This can lead to poorer residents being expelled because of increasing rents and more well-to-do households being attracted, depending on the kind of intervention used.

For this reason, in all the countries, two main views comprise the core elements of the discussion of the objectives of public intervention in, and economic support for, urban renewal and housing rehabilitation. One view emphasises that urban renewal should consider existing residents in the areas and in this way concentrate on redistributing resource opportunities to low-income or 'deprived' groups directly. In this view, gentrification in these areas is seen as a negative outcome.

The alternative view is that public investments in urban renewal should encourage economic growth and stimulate immigration of higher-income groups who will improve the tax base of the municipalities and contribute further investments in housing rehabilitation. It is believed that the benefits of this growth and improvement will 'trickle down' to those on low incomes. Gentrification is therefore seen as a desirable and positive outcome (see the discussion in Bailey and Robertson, 1997).

Some researchers are of the opposite opinion and argue that gentrification indirectly promotes decay because poor people are displaced from the gentrified areas and concentrated in other parts of the cities where succession and decay accelerate (see Smith and Williams, 1986; Nelson, 1988). Gentrification could therefore lead to increased segregation and urban decay in the cities, depending on the extent to which the gentrified areas are substitutes for the suburbs or for other neighbourhoods inside the cities.

However, it can also be argued that conserving the existing population structure after renewal will lead to future decay in the areas. This argument is supported by experience gained from many new social-housing estates where the quality of dwellings – and sometimes also of the environment – is high, but where problems of both social and physical decay occur. These problems can be described partly by physical conditions such as peripheral location, impersonal and alienating environment and lack of variety. But the main problem is the bad reputations these estates have acquired because of the social composition of residents that often leads to higher frequencies of social problems, crime and vandalism (see Chapter 5). If an important objective of urban renewal is to stop future decay, it is therefore important that a certain change should occur in the composition of residents – from a biased dominance of groups with low social status and a high incidence of unemployment and social problems to a more mixed population with residents belonging to different status groups.

The Social Effects of Urban Renewal – Experience from Denmark

The following section illustrates the possible social consequences of urban renewal using experience gained from urban renewal in Denmark. After a short description of urban renewal policies in Denmark, results from a study on the social effects of these policies will be described.

Problems of Housing Decay in Denmark and Public Policies against it

In some parts of the Danish housing stock, maintenance and improvement activity has been inadequate and dwellings have deteriorated. Except for those on some newer social housing estates, these dwellings are found mostly in private rented tenements or cooperatives built before 1950 and with a concentration in tenements built before 1920.

At a *national* level, the main objectives for public involvement in housing rehabilitation and urban renewal have been to preserve and upgrade older very low standard housing to up-to-date housing. This implies extensive renovation of each property with often very high building costs for dwellings renovated under the Urban Renewal Act. Capital costs for these investments would be very high and would lead to high rents if they were to be covered solely by an increase in rents after renewal.

However, the Urban Renewal Act contains strong social objectives to improve housing conditions for poor people, as the worst dwellings usually have a large proportion of low-income residents. One important objective has been to enable sitting residents with low incomes to stay in the area or alternatively to choose a similar up-to-date dwelling in another area. Therefore, very high subsidies have been allocated to urban renewal in Denmark. Rents are increased corresponding to only 5 per cent of investments in housing improvements, while state and local authorities pay the remaining capital costs for investments in improvements and repairs. Moreover, all residents have the right to obtain special individual housing benefits. Previously, the benefit covered the total increase in rent during the first year, and was then reduced gradually over five years. This means that there was no increase in net rents for the first year. These social objectives for urban renewal in Denmark have been very costly, as the subsidisation has varied between 50 and 80 per cent of building costs – the highest level in Europe (see Skifter Andersen and Leather, 1999). The disadvantage of this policy has been that only a relatively small number of dwellings have been renovated per year because public funds have been limited and Denmark therefore still has quite a large number of dwellings lacking basic facilities such as bathrooms.

The national objectives have been reflected clearly at a *local* level (in municipalities). Up-to-date housing has been the main goal for the majority of local governments (Hansen and Ærø, 1996). Most have given high priority to bad housing areas with low-income groups. However, some municipalities – especially The City of Copenhagen – have also seen urban renewal as part of a general urban policy to create economic growth and attract better taxpayers. In these municipalities, the gentrification aspect of urban renewal has been more in focus.

A Danish Study of the Effects of Urban Renewal

The main purpose of the study conducted at the Danish Building Research Institute (Skifter Andersen and Ærø, 1998) was to investigate if the social goals have been fulfilled for housing rehabilitation under the Urban Renewal Act. The following questions had to be answered:

1 to what extent does renewal benefit residents living in the dwellings before rehabilitation took place, i.e. how many original residents are left after renewal?
2 are some residents expelled from their dwellings because of the renewal and who are they?
3 what are the consequences of the renewal for residents who move away?
4 does renewal change the composition of newcomers – to what extent is succession stopped and replaced by gentrification?
5 what are the economic consequences for municipalities of the change in composition of residents?

One major methodical problem in the study was how to sort out the effects of urban renewal from all the other factors that affect population changes in older and poor housing. To make this possible, we compared the social development in the renewed dwellings with a population of dwellings with the same standard and composition of residents as those in the renewed dwellings before renewal. However, the comparison dwellings had not undergone renewal or rehabilitation.

In principle, the study includes all dwellings in rental housing and cooperatives in blocks of flats renewed under the Urban Renewal Act in the period of 1990–96. Some properties renewed in the City of Copenhagen in the period of 1986–90 under the older Slum Clearance Act were included.

Data on dwellings and residents was extracted from data registers established by the Statistical Office of Denmark. Denmark has a special register of all properties, buildings and dwellings that includes data such as amenities, dwelling size and rents. This data can be combined with data on the residents and their incomes, employment and social benefits obtained from other registers.

Data has been extracted for three different points of time – 1 January 1986, 1990 and 1996, respectively. This method enabled us to record which households had moved away in the periods of 1986–90 and 1990 to 1996, which of them stayed, and which new households moved in. It was also possible to collect data on the dwellings that households have moved away to and the housing situation of newcomers before they moved in.

A logistic regression was used to assess the impacts of different practices in urban renewal and to explain the differences in social changes in renewed and unrenewed dwellings depending on investments and rent increases, and establish whether rehousing was used.

Did Urban Renewal Benefit or Expel Existing Residents?

The Urban Renewal Act affords residents a strong influence based on the notion that most of them will remain after renewal. For example, they can veto some improvements if they do not wish to pay more. Another consequence of their strong influence is that it is very difficult to merge small flats into larger ones.

It is well known from the research literature that mobility is closely connected to the life cycle of the family (see, for example, Kending, 1984; Pickwance, 1973). In the study, we therefore split up the households into the following life-cycle groups:

1 young singles without children, aged under 30 years;
2 middle-aged singles, aged 30–60 years;
3 elderly singles, aged over 60 years;
4 young couples without children, aged under 30 years;
5 middle-aged couples, aged 30–60 years;

6   elderly couples, aged over 60;
7   young families with children, the eldest person under 40 years;
8   other families with children, the eldest person over 40 years;
9   other mixed households with more than one family.

Based on the employment situation of the person in each household with the highest income, we have also defined seven socioeconomic groups – three with members in employment split up according to household income and four with no person in employment split up according to the source of their main income. These groups are:

1   early retirement or welfare benefits;
2   old-age pensioners;
3   students;
4   unemployed residents;
5   employed, low household income (below DKK 120,000 for singles and DKK 200,000 for couples);
6   residents in employment with medium incomes (DKK 120–250,000 for singles and DKK 200–400,000 for couples);
7   residents in employment with high incomes (more than DKK 250,000 for singles and DKK 400,000 for couples).

In general, there has been quite high mobility during the period of renewal. Another Danish study of mobility (Ministry of Housing, 1997) has shown that an average 36 per cent of Danish households leave their homes within a period of six years. However, more than half (56 per cent) of the households living in these properties in 1990, before renewal began, had left in 1996 after renovation. This result questions the appropriateness of giving very high priority to the wishes of existing residents – especially their opposition against the merging of small flats. However, the mobility of different groups differs greatly, as shown in Figure 7.1.

Among the younger households without children, mobility was very high – more than three out of four households moved away. Also less that one-third of the young families with children were left. On the other hand, two thirds of the elderly households stayed in their dwellings.

This pattern is mirrored among the socioeconomic groups, with the highest mobility found among students and the lowest among old-age pensioners. Also, households in employment with low to medium incomes often move away, while the higher income groups more often tended to stay.

Efforts to Combat Urban Decay 145

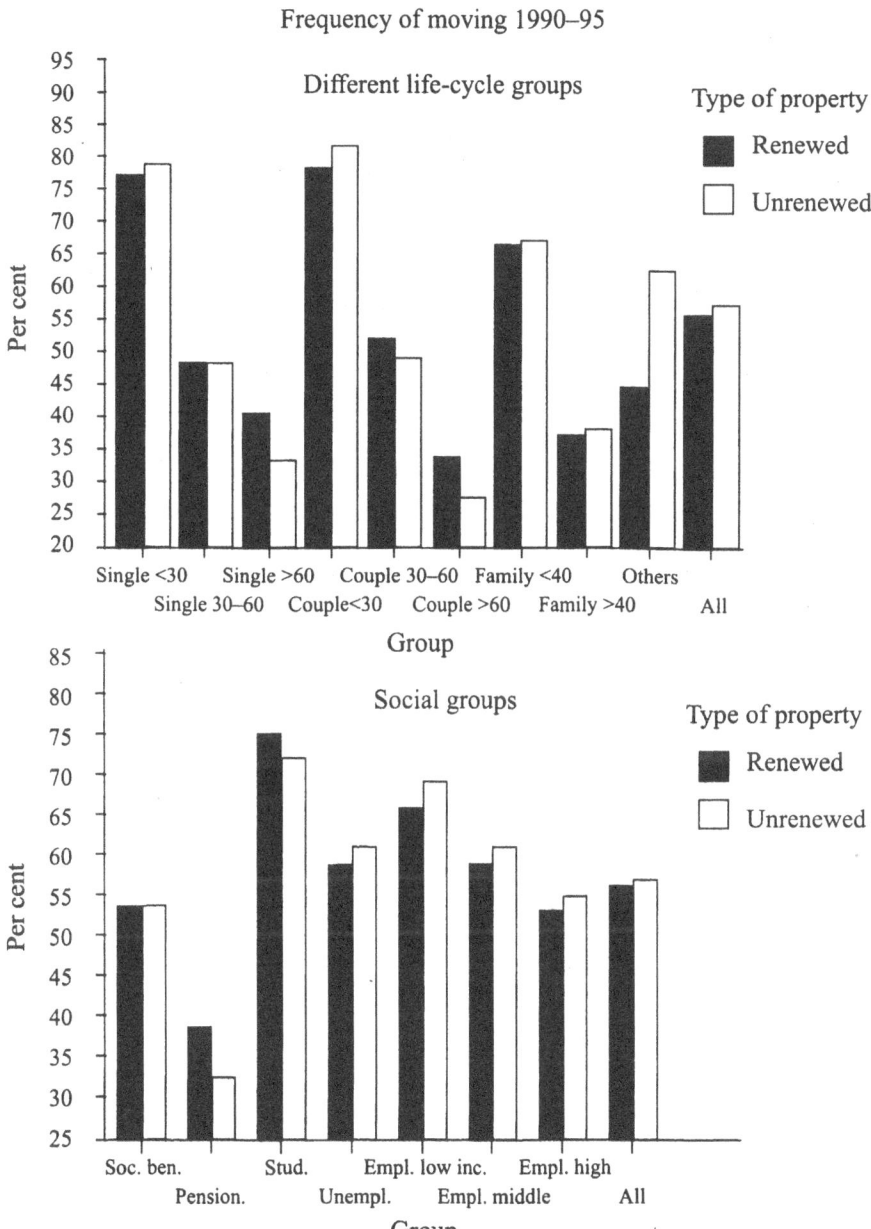

Figure 7.1 Percentage of residents in 1990, before renovation started, who had moved out before 1996

Source: Skifter Andersen and Ærø, 1998.

Are residents expelled? The study suggests that Danish urban renewal in the first period did not expel residents. The rate of mobility in the period of urban renewal was nearly the same in the renewed dwellings as in the unrenewed property. As can be seen from Figure 7.1, the main difference was that a greater part of the elderly moved away whereas younger people were more likely to stay.

A more thorough test of the hypothesis that mobility was the same in renewed and unrenewed dwellings was carried out using a logistic regression on 22,000 dwellings/households – of which 4,600 dwellings were renewed. This model also explains mobility in poor housing in older blocks of flats in general. The variables put into the model are shown in Table 7.1. Some of these variables had no significant influence on mobility. The analysis showed that the renewal variable was not significant at all, as the significance level for the Wald statistic was as high as 0.56 and the R-statistic less than 0.0000. The test therefore confirmed that there was no difference between the mobility in renewed and unrenewed dwellings.

The variables, significant at a level of 0.05 per cent, in the best model found in the logistic regression are shown in Table 7.2. The model classifies 96 per cent of the households that moved in the right group and 70 per cent of those that did not move. It has a model chi-square of 15,202 with significance of below 0.0000. The R-statistics show that the most important variables explaining variation in mobility in poor older housing are – in order of importance: size of the dwelling; income; couples; age; location of dwelling; employed; and household stability. The least important variables are: duration of stay, tenure and housing standard before renewal. These results are influenced by correlations linking some variables. Some correlation exists, especially between income, age and employment and between duration of stay and age.

The practical importance of these results is illustrated by the calculation in the last column of the expected change in mobility caused by a factor of change in the variables shown in column three.

As seen, mobility falls with age, marriage, stability of households and duration of stay, all of which agrees with other studies of mobility. It is also likely that mobility increases with increasing incomes because these dwellings are small and poor quality which is why people want to move on to better accommodation when they can afford it. The model seems to show that people in full-time employment are less likely to move, but this could be a result of the correlation with income.

The results also indicate that mobility is highest in small dwellings, in municipal dwellings and private rental housing, and outside the larger cities.

Table 7.1   Variables in general logistic regression explaining mobility in poor housing in older blocks of flats

Dependent variable:
- *Moving* or not in the period 1990–96?

Independent variables:

Household characteristics:
- *Age*: age of the oldest person in the household?
- *Children*: with or without children?
- *Couples*: couples or singles?
- *Stability*: were the same people living together before and after?
- *Income*: total income of the household?
- *Employed*: at least one person employed?
- *Duration* of stay: number of years the household has lived in the flat?

Dwelling characteristics:
- *Dwelling size*: number of square metres?
- *Age of building*: number of years since erection?
- *Bath*: is there a bathroom?
- *Central heating*: is there central heating?
- *Private renting*?
- *Cooperative housing*?
- *Nonprofit housing*?
- *Municipal housing*?
- *Copenhagen*: location in municipality of Copenhagen?
- *Large cities*: location in one of the three largest municipalities outside Greater Copenhagen?
- *Provincial towns*: location in municipalities in the provinces with more than 20,000 inhabitants?
- *Other municipalities*: location in municipalities not mentioned above?

Urban renewal characteristics:
- *Renewed*: indication of renewal or not in the period?

The effects of different kinds of renewal To test if different kinds of renewal had any importance on people moving away, we constructed another model to analyse the 4,600 dwellings renewed in 1990–96.

Table 7.2 Main results of the best logistic regression explaining mobility in poor housing in older blocks of flats 1990–96

Significant variables	R-statistic	B-coeff.	Factor of change	Calculated change in mobility %
Age	-0.052	-0.019	10	-5
Couples?	-0.099	-0.8079	1	-19
Stability?	-0.031	-11.2	1	-50
Income (DKK 1000)	0.100	0.0032	100	8
Employed?	-0.037	-0.3816	1	-9
Duration of stay	-0.006	-0.0024	10	-1
Dwelling size (m^2)	-0.121	-0.019	10	-5
Central heating?	-0.017	-0.1517	1	-4
Municipal?	0.023	0.688	1	17
Private rented?	0.025	0.398	1	10
Cooperative?	0.010	0.342	1	8
Copenhagen?	-0.048	-0.499	1	-12
Larger city?	-0.050	-0.544	1	-13

Source: Skifter Andersen and Ærø, 1998.

Besides the variables characterising households and dwellings named in Table 7.1, the following variables were used to characterise the renewal effort:

Table 7.3 Variables characterising renewal work

- Investments in *improvements* in DKK 1000 per m^2
- Investments in *repairs* in DKK 1000 m^2
- *Maximum rent* after renewal without benefits, DKK per m^2 per year
- Maximum *rent increase* in per cent
- *Rehousing:* were the households rehoused during renewal or not?

Investments in improvements increase the quality of dwellings but also increase rents in the long run. Repairs can also to some extent improve the utility value of the building and are not paid for by increased rents in Danish urban renewal. Repairs could therefore have an effect on reducing mobility. Finally, it was to be expected that rehousing would increase mobility because some of the households do not want to return if they have been moved away to another dwelling where they can stay.

The resulting regression is very similar to the one shown in Table 7.2. The same household and dwelling variables are significant, with nearly the same coefficients. Of the variables characterising the renewal activity, only two were significant, as shown in Table 7.4.

Table 7.4 Significant renewal variables explaining mobility in renewed dwellings 1990–96

Significant variables	R-statistic	B-coeff.	Factor of change	Calculated change in mobility %
Rent increase DKK/m^2	0.070	0.003	100	6
Rehousing?	-0.120	-1.0417	1	-24

Source: Skifter Andersen and Ærø, 1998.

The size of investments in repairs and improvement, respectively, had no influence on households' decisions to move away from their dwellings. The final level of rent after renewal and after removal of the special housing benefits had no effect either. The expected relative increase in rents had a small effect, which brought a greater increase in mobility. On average, the maximum rent increase was DKK 130/m^2 per year, corresponding to an increased mobility of about 8 per cent.

Provisional rehousing did not increase mobility. On the contrary, a greater part of the residents not rehoused moved away – probably because of the inconvenience of building activities.

Mobility in the years after renovation A major explanation of why renewal had no importance for mobility in the renovation period is that the special housing benefits mean there is only a small net rent increase in the first couple of years after the renewal is finished. In the following years, this support is gradually reduced and rent payments increase to the final level within five years. We examined the effect of this reduction by analysing data obtained from 1990–96 on the mobility of households living in some properties in Copenhagen renewed in the period 1986–90 and comparing it to a similar sample of properties from Copenhagen that were not renewed. Figure 7.2 shows the mobility, in the six years after renovation of the dwellings, of the original residents living there before renovation started and who stayed after the renovation period.

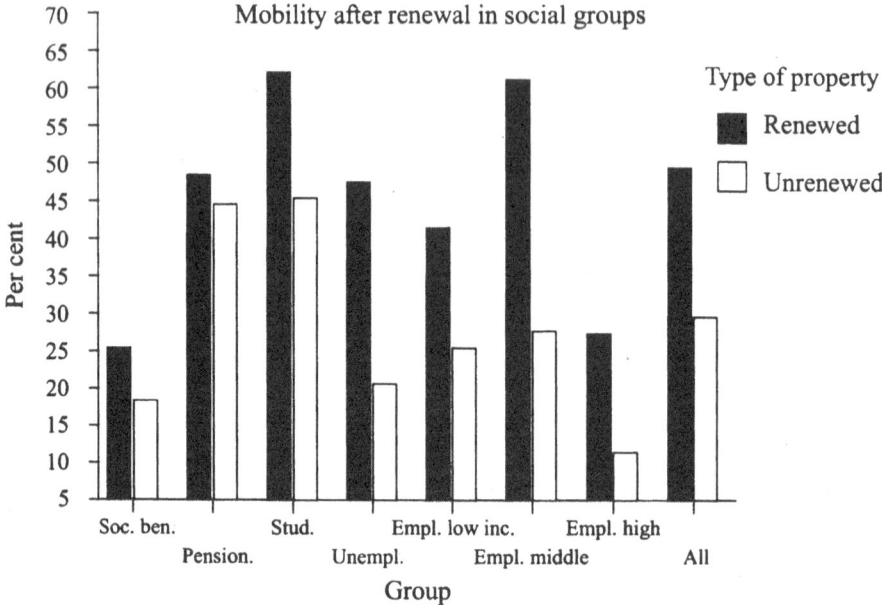

Figure 7.2 **Percentage of original residents living in the properties in 1986, before renewal, and still resident in 1990 after renewal, who moved away in the period 1990–96**

Source: Skifter Andersen and Ærø, 1998.

The figure shows that mobility among the original residents increased significantly in the renewed dwellings in the years after renovation compared to the unrenewed dwellings. If we assume that the mobility of the two groups would have been the same without renewal, it can be concluded that 20 per cent of the original residents were either expelled from their dwelling in this period or have chosen to move because they find the dwellings too expensive compared with their quality. The latter explanation is the most important as mobility has been higher, especially among households engaged in active employment. Among households living on pensions or welfare benefits, much smaller differences exist between the mobility in renewed and unrenewed dwellings. One explanation is that these groups can obtain other kinds of housing benefits when the special benefits are removed.

It can therefore be seen that also in the longer term, quite a few residents have been expelled from the renewed properties – mainly people living on unemployment benefits or people in employment with low incomes – while pensioners and receivers of social benefits have rarely been expelled.

Changes in the Socioeconomic Composition of Residents

As a result of some households moving out and others moving in during the period 1990–96, some changes occurred in both the renewed and the unrenewed properties. Figure 7.3 shows the changes over the period in the proportion of households of different socioeconomic groups – the difference between the percentage before renewal and the percentage after.

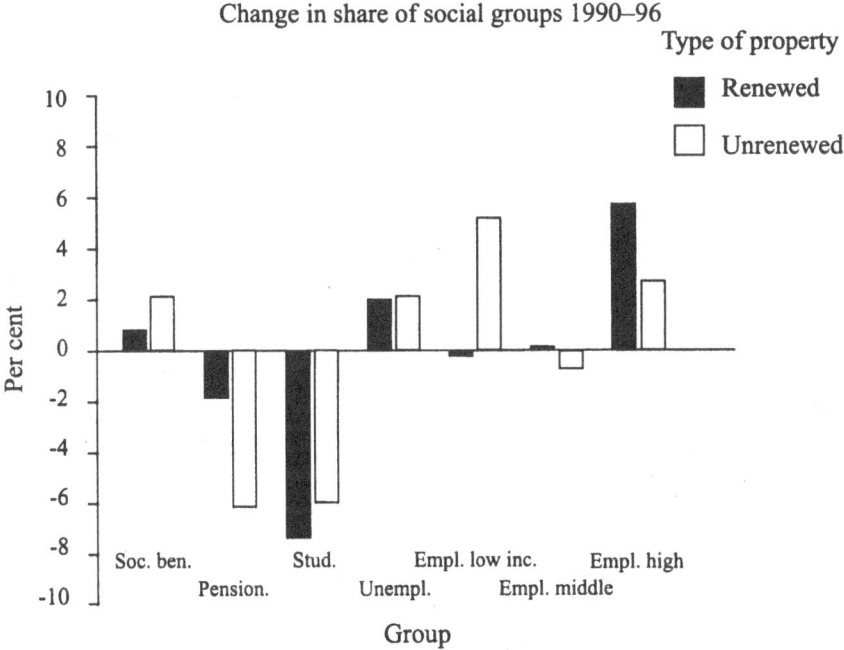

Figure 7.3 Changes in the proportion of different social groups among residents in 1990–96

Source: Skifter Andersen and Ærø, 1998.

The unrenewed properties showed signs of continuous social decay with an increase in the proportion of people on early retirement and welfare or on unemployment benefits. Residents in employment with low incomes increased in particular. Old-age pensioners and students in particular have disappeared.

Some changes have also occurred in the socioeconomic composition of residents in the renewed properties, but the changes are not comprehensive. The proportion of families with children and households in employment with higher incomes has to some extent increased at the expense of students. There has been no decrease in the number of people on early retirement, social benefits, or the unemployed. This is due to the effective Danish housing benefit schemes, which mean that the latter groups can get relatively high housing benefits to pay for the increasing rents, while people in employment and students cannot.

Compared with the unrenewed properties, the changes in the renewed properties can be summarised as:

1 an increase in the proportion of families with higher incomes among the newcomers, combined with a decrease in the number of these families leaving the properties;
2 a decrease in the number of old-age pensioners leaving;
3 a cessation of the growth in the proportion of people in employment with lower incomes found in the unrenewed properties;
4 an increasing number of students leaving;
5 fewer households with early retirement or welfare among newcomers;
6 no change in the proportion of unemployed and people in employment with medium incomes.

The renewal has therefore stopped, and to a minor extent reversed, social decay in the urban areas affected by urban renewal. On the other hand, social changes have been only small. Compared with the total population, the composition of residents in the renewed dwellings is still very atypical, with a strong domination of single households and people with low incomes or without employment.

Factors that Influence Gentrification in Renewed Dwellings

Even if the renewed dwellings on average attract only relatively few households with better incomes, there are great differences depending on the kind of dwellings, their location and tenure and the renovation carried out. A statistical analysis was therefore made to find the main factors leading to gentrification. Once again, a logistic regression was used to explain when newcomers were households in employment with medium to high incomes. The following independent variables were used:

1 *dwelling size* in m^2;
2 *age of building*;

3   indication of tenure: *private rented, cooperative, municipal, nonprofit*;
4   indication of location: *Copenhagen, large cities, provincial towns, others*;
5   investments in *repairs* in DKK 1000 per m^2;
6   investments in *improvements* in DKK 1000 per m^2.

Significant variables in the resulting model are shown in Table 7.5.

Table 7.5   **Significant variables explaining gentrification in renewed dwellings 1990–96 (independent variable is 'newcomers employed with medium-high income or not')**

Significant variables	R-statistic	B-coeff.	Factor of change	Calculated change, %
Dwelling size	0.156	0.019	10	5
Private rented	0.050	0.296	1	7
Cooperatives	0.096	0.722	1	17
Large cities	0.058	0.359	1	9
Repairs	0.023	0.027	5	3

Source: Skifter Andersen and Ærø, 1998.

The analysis showed that the age of buildings and size of investments in improvements had no significant influence at a 0.05 per cent level. This is a little surprising, as one would have expected dwellings in the oldest, historic part of the cities to be more attractive to households with good incomes. The missing effects of improvement investments can be explained by that fact that nearly all dwellings are of the same standard after renewal and investments therefore only mirror the condition of the buildings before renewal. Meanwhile, rents could be higher when investments are high.

Dwelling size is the most important variable explaining variation in high and medium households among newcomers (high R-statistic) and the difference between the composition of newcomers between small and large flats is considerable. Household income from newcomers to flats over 100 m^2 was DKK 275,000 on average and the proportion of employed residents with medium-high incomes totalled 68 per cent. Among newcomers to the smaller dwellings (less than 60 m^2), the average income was DKK 133,000 and only 38 per cent had medium-high incomes. The dominant groups among newcomers to smaller dwellings were people on social benefits or early retirement and employed people with low incomes. The same tendencies can be found among newcomers to the unrenewed dwellings but are not as strong as for the renewed dwellings.

Tenure also seems to have an effect, as gentrification more often takes place especially in cooperatives and also in private rented housing, while it is less common in nonprofit and municipally-owned housing. The proportion of 'gentrifiers' is 62 per cent in cooperatives, but only 42 per cent in municipal dwellings.

In terms of location, gentrification is more pronounced in Copenhagen and larger cities than in provincial towns and smaller municipalities.

Finally, it seems as if investments in repairs have an influence, but it is very small.

What can be Learned from the Danish Study of the Effects of Urban Renewal?

The Danish study had two objectives:

1 to investigate if further succession occurs in poor housing in the inner areas of Danish cities;
2 to clarify the consequences of public-supported housing rehabilitation for changes of the residents in such dwellings: has succession stopped and to some extent been replaced by gentrification?

The study showed a high turnover of residents in poor housing in older blocks of flats in Denmark and signs of further decay in unrenewed properties because of tendencies for more residents with low incomes or those marginalised from the labour market being present. These results indicate that some kind of public intervention and support for renewal is still needed in the older parts of the cities to prevent further decline.

The Danish Urban Renewal Act has been seen as an instrument for eliminating slums in the cities and for stopping further urban decay in some older neighbourhoods. At the same time, it has been governed by strong social objectives that benefit the poor and secure residents against being expelled from their dwellings. This has been implemented by giving very high subsidies to reduce increases in rents. The Danish system has also been characterised by a view of urban renewal as a once-and-for-all task that involves renovating very run-down properties to quite a high new standard comparable with new housing.

Together, these conditions have resulted in expensive renovation work at great expense to the public and only relative few dwellings have been renewed under the Urban Renewal Act. Because the process has been so slow, older parts of the cities – especially in Copenhagen – have undergone further deterioration while waiting for urban renewal and Denmark still has a relative high proportion of dwellings lacking basic amenities such as bathrooms (about 10 per cent).

Local governments also contribute towards shouldering the costs and at a local level, there has been some interest in using urban renewal as part of a general urban policy to attract private investments and more well-to-do residents. These objectives imply gentrification in the renewed dwellings.

This study has shown that urban renewal in Denmark has stopped further decline in the socioeconomic status of residents in the renewed properties. It also shows that the social objectives have largely been fulfilled – only a few residents have been expelled and not until after some years when the special benefits have been reduced.

Some gentrification has happened, but the total changes in the composition of residents have been relative small, even though there has been a high turnover, as in other dwellings in older blocks of flats. A relative high proportion of newcomers are people with low incomes and households without employment, living on benefits and pensions. As a result, the composition of residents after renewal is still very different from the national average and dominated by singles and low-status groups.

These results indicate that the expensive Danish urban renewal system has failed to some extent. The social composition of the renewed dwellings can result in a negative image of the areas, which can give rise to future processes of decay, as has been seen in newer social housing estates. Another bad sign is that the turnover of residents in the years after renovation is very high and that the better-off households are especially quick to move out again. Among the employed households living in the properties just after renovation implemented from 1986–90, very few were left six years later (about 15 per cent). The situation in the renewed properties is similar to problem estates in newer social housing in this respect.

It can therefore be argued that gentrification has been too limited in Danish urban renewal and that the renewal effort has failed to prevent renewed decline in the future to some degree.

One of the great mistakes in Danish urban renewal is the limited amount of merging of small dwellings into larger flats. Most of the renewed dwellings are too small for households with children or with higher incomes and they are – even if subsidies are high – still expensive for singles who cannot obtain housing benefits compared with other dwellings on the market. If larger dwellings were produced, they could be expected to attract more households with children and employment to the areas. Merging of up to 60 per cent of the small flats would not be in conflict with the objective of securing sitting households as the high turnover of residents nevertheless means that only few remain after renewal.

The most significant change needed, however, is a shift in the Danish renewal strategy. The current system leads to investments that are too heavy and cannot be covered by increasing rental incomes and property values. This places the renewed dwellings – in spite of high subsidies – in a position on the housing market from which they cannot compete on equal terms with most of the rental sector, except by appealing to people who receive high housing benefits. The system must be changed from expensive total renovations of properties to a cheaper model, in which only the most necessary repairs and improvements are made. Moreover, the initiative and decision-making should be moved from local authorities to property owners and residents who are in a better position to rank priorities so that the renewed dwellings are better positioned to compete on the housing market.

Policies against Deprived Housing Estates in Europe

Many European governments have initiated programmes with area-based initiatives to fight against problems in deprived urban areas. But in the research literature, there has been much disagreement on the effects of these programmes, with some researchers believing that the purposes of such initiatives are questionable and the effects doubtful. One of the main reasons for this disagreement is that there have been different conceptions of the purposes of the programmes and of the urban problems they aim to solve.

Earlier in this book, I argued that a clear understanding of the fundamental causes for deprived urban areas appearing has been missing in both the research literature and in the strategies formulated for area-based initiatives. I have shown that deprived urban neighbourhoods have generally been understood as spatially concentrated pockets of poverty that emerge as a direct result of increasing social inequality in cities. I also referred to evidence that there is no simple and direct connection between the general and economic development of cities and the emergence of deprived neighbourhoods and argued that other explanations had also to be found.

Such an explanation was found in the fact that self-perpetuating processes of deprivation, decay and stigmatisation can be observed in these areas. On the basis of a Danish study of 500 deprived social housing estates, the character of these processes was illustrated. It was argued that acknowledgement of such processes leads to a new understanding of deprived neighbourhoods as being '*excluded places*' that become isolated from surrounding cities in the sense that they are seen as 'no-go' areas. The dynamic negative development in deprived urban neighbourhoods makes them increasingly diverge in character and status from other urban areas. It was also argued that these increasing differences between the qualities of different parts of a city result in increased segregation and even stronger concentrations of poverty and deprivation.

This section first briefly outlines some of the literature on area-based initiatives in Western Europe and evaluations of their effects. The Danish urban policy and area-based initiatives in 500 social housing estates in the last part of the 1990s are then described and the effects of these efforts are analysed based on a recent Danish research evaluation. Finally, the purpose and effects of area-based initiatives are discussed seen in the light of an understanding of deprived urban areas as excluded places.

The Character of Initiatives and Strategies Used

It is difficult to gain an overview of policies in this field in different countries because much of the literature is not written in English. The description in this section is therefore based mainly on experiences from countries such as Great Britain, Sweden, Denmark and the Netherlands, which might be insufficient.

A review of some of the recent literature available[2] in the field – mainly based on British experience – shows that the following kinds of initiatives have been implemented:

1 physical renovation and embellishment;
2 improved management and housing service for residents;
3 active marketing and attempts to counteract bad press and bad reputations;
4 change of tenure or extended disposal of dwellings;
5 support for private service facilities;
6 special measures against crime – cooperation with police and other local institutions;
7 mobilisation and empowerment of residents and communities;
8 direct social support for socially weak groups – integration measures for immigrants;

9   attempts to attract new private firms and workplaces to the neighbourhood;
10 education, job training and other attempts to attract employment for residents.

These area-based initiatives rarely seem to have been chosen in connection with any clear strategy. Attempts to classify the efforts and their purposes are also rare in the literature. Hall (1997) distinguishes between 'inward-looking' and 'outward-looking' approaches. This division is based on an understanding of the problems of the estates as either 'internal' or 'external'. Internal problems are seen as related to the nature of the estate, while external problems are related to 'structural factors' and to the relationship between the estate and the city. Hall argues that regeneration policies have tended to focus on solving internal problems and have therefore been inward looking. He calls for outward-looking approaches that aim to overcome physical and social isolation directly, improve access to employment, and place more emphasis on strategic, city-wide or linked partnerships.

Cameron (1998) also argues for a division of initiatives into 'looking in' (community development and empowerment) and 'looking out' approaches (jobs and training, etc.) and finds that the policies of the 1990s – in opposition to those of the 1980s – contain both approaches.

Parkinson (1998), who has looked at programmes in five countries, concludes that all countries are increasingly using area-based approaches. He describes the general development in the initiatives as shifts from physical approaches in the 1980s to what he calls 'welfare approaches' in recent years, with more emphasis on economic dimensions and employment. He also stresses the great differences between the countries.

Bearing in mind the discussion in the preceding chapters on how to understand deprived urban areas, I will argue that dividing initiatives into inward-looking and outward-looking approaches is inadequate. This concept reflects a static view of the estates, in which the dynamics of segregation and population changes are not taken into consideration.

Instead, I will propose three other types of strategies:

1   *Efforts against exclusion of neighbourhoods*: initiatives that focus on how to stop and reverse the self-perpetuating processes in the areas that make them increasingly stigmatised and unattractive compared with the rest of the city.
2   *Area-based efforts against social exclusion:* as a supplement to general welfare policies, it can sometimes be relevant to concentrate efforts in

deprived urban areas for two reasons: i) to combat special effects produced by area deprivation that tend to increase social exclusion; and ii) because local private resources could perhaps be mobilised to support public efforts.
3   *General efforts against segregation:* initiatives that attack conditions that tend to increase segregation. These could include, for example, differences between tenures or rules for allocating dwellings in social housing.

This way of structuring initiatives runs transversely to the divisions that comprise inward-looking and outward-looking initiatives. Some of the outward-looking initiatives, such as job training, belong to the second type of strategy, while others, e.g. changing the physical relationship between the estate and the city, could belong to the first type. Some initiatives could belong to both types of strategies. For instance, community development and empowerment could aim both to support residents individually and the neighbourhood in general. At the same time, the strategies support each other. Improvement of neighbourhoods also benefits people living there and can therefore reduce social exclusion. Efforts against social exclusion can lead to an improved neighbourhood image.

Experience Gained from Area-based Initiatives

Just as the programmes and initiatives applied have been very diverse, the experience gained and evaluations of initiatives have also varied considerably. Parkinson's (1998) study of experiences from five European countries concludes that 'considerable disagreement about the merits of area-based approaches' exists. In his opinion, one of the causes is faulty knowledge about the effects of area-based initiatives.

Parkinson reaches a positive evaluation of some of the English initiatives, especially the City Challenge Programme, and finds that the UK has had more success with its initiatives than any other country. But he also states that it has been 'difficult to find conclusive evidence yet in any country of identifiable improvements in the economic and social circumstances of these areas'. Some other judgements have been quite negative. The British government's Social Exclusion Unit (1998) has therefore concluded that none of the English initiatives have 'really succeeded in setting in motion a virtuous circle of regeneration' and 'only for a few areas have improvements lasted. Most areas have either not improved or worsened'. Taylor (1998) is also quite negative in her appraisal of initiatives in difficult-to-let estates. She states that 'successive regeneration initiatives appear to have made little impact on the most difficult to let estates'.

Power (1997) has been more positive in her evaluation of the initiatives in twenty estates in five countries. One reason could be that she had other objectives and expectations concerning the effects. The studied estates had very serious problems. They underwent a rapid decline and several were to some extent given up by local authorities. The positive conclusion from Power was based on the fact that:

> ... the 'patchwork approach' that addresses physical, organisational, financial and social problems together has prevented ... precarious communities from continuing on their downward trajectory, arresting decay and re-stabilising conditions.

But she found that there are still unsolved questions on the estates and it is a question of whether the achieved stability will last. Evans (1998) in his evaluation of the English 'Housing Plus' programme, which combines physical, financial and social measures, finds that the combined effect of the HP initiatives was 'impressive'. There was 'a dramatic turnaround' in the resident's confidence on the estates and a sharp decrease in the number of residents who wanted to move. There was also a good connection between the extent of the efforts and growth in community confidence. However, his critique of the programme was that there had been a quite modest scale of initiatives in relation to the severity of problems, which made 'the overall response quite patchy'.

Some of the more negative evaluations have concerned initiatives that have been too narrow in scope. It is a general conclusion (Social Exclusion Unit, 1998; Hall, 1997; Musterd et al., 1999; Parkinson, 1998; Christiansen et al., 1993) that physical improvements alone are unsustainable.

There is also evidence that isolated efforts to combat social exclusion by trying to get residents back into employment have only a limited effect on the general problems of an area. Special job-creation initiatives for people living on deprived estates are costly and difficult to operate. If they are carried out without other measures to improve the quality of the estates, they simply prompt people to move away if they get jobs (Taylor, 1998; Hall, 1997). The estate is then left with empty apartments, or new households without employment move in. Isolated efforts to create work places in the neighbourhood through construction work or by encouraging new firms to locate there have therefore proved to have little effect on the estates as a whole (Cameron, 1998; Hall, 1997).

Another general conclusion is that effects of initiatives are time dependent. It takes a long time to create the partnerships and community involvement that are essential for success (Taylor, 1998). Residents need time and are often brought into the process far too late. Short-term initiatives are therefore doomed to fail. There is a danger that these kinds of initiatives will lead to a public focus on the failures of the estates, which increases stigmatisation and causes a worse reputation (Marsh and Mullins, 1998; Taylor, 1998) without producing noticeable positive effects.

Policies against Deprived Housing Estates in Denmark

Like other European countries, from the beginning of the 1980s, Denmark has experienced increasing problems in a number of large social housing estates built after the war. However, for different reasons, the problems have not been as widespread as in countries such as Great Britain and France. Denmark is a country with quite limited economic inequality (the Gini coefficient for income distribution is below 0.40) and welfare payments have been extensive. Social exclusion increased in the 1980s, but falling unemployment rates in the 1990s have to some extent rectified this. Another important factor is the organisation of the social housing sector. Extensive decentralisation of power to tenants and housing estates has in many ways helped the troubled areas to manage the emerging problems.

As in many other countries, public initiatives in deprived areas in Denmark in the 1980s concentrated on physical initiatives. Evaluations of this work showed that they had a positive effect but that increasing social problems made them insufficient to make permanent changes in the situation on the estates (Vestergaard, 1998).

A new generation of policies was introduced in 1993 because of a change in government and the fact that emerging problems with immigrants in certain neighbourhoods appeared on the public agenda. The new government set up a so-called 'Urban Committee' consisting of ministers from five different ministries. Before long, the committee had drawn up an action plan consisting of 30 proposals for initiatives. These initiatives can be grouped as:

1 physical renovation;
2 *rent reductions* and economic rehabilitation;
3 *social empowerment*: employment of special social workers and support for social activities, especially among immigrants and socially excluded residents;

4   special *education initiatives* for immigrants and refugees, including efforts to solve problems following a concentration of foreign speaking children in certain schools;
5   measures against *crime*;
6   new rules and an institutional framework *regulating immigration* and housing for immigrants;
7   new rules *regulating the assignment* of dwellings;
8   increasing state *funds for local authorities* with problem estates.

The initiatives were scheduled to take place from 1994 to 1998. Various sources provided funding for the initiatives. The main contributions were to come from the Ministry of Social Affairs (DKK 175m), the Ministry of Housing and Urban affairs (DKK 20m), the Ministry of Education (DKK 100m), local governments (DKK 305m) and the National Building Fund (DKK 205m), which is a fund financed by contributions from all social housing in Denmark. Moreover, remortgaging of a number of loans on the estates provided DKK 6.3 billion for investments in renovation and rent reductions.

The main initiatives were investments in physical upgrading (DKK 6bn), rent reductions, etc. (DKK 441m), social workers and activities (DKK 420m) and education initiatives (DKK 100m). In reality, it is doubtful whether local authorities have provided DKK 305m for social initiatives as anticipated. It has not been possible to control their real contributions, but the evaluation indicates that it has been rather lower than planned. The resources actually used for the social initiatives could therefore be much lower.

In total, about 500 housing estates (administrative sections) with 115,000 dwellings were identified for support. Some of these estates were located in the same urban area. There were, however, major differences between the severity of problems and the extent of the efforts on the various estates. For political reasons, some of the money was spread to local authorities and estates where problems were limited. On these estates, a few social initiatives were implemented while on other estates an extensive combination of physical, economic and social initiatives were implemented.

The Strategies used by the Urban Committee

Like many other political initiatives, the Urban Committee was provoked by current problems brought to the light by the press, local authorities and housing associations. There was no formulated coherent strategy or understanding of the problems behind the initiatives.

When looking at the proposed initiatives and the expressed grounds for them, it could be argued that there were at least four different strategies embedded in the initiatives. These strategies have subsequently been called:

1 *local network strategy:* strengthening local networks to combat social exclusion;
2 *improved competition strategy:* improving competitiveness for the estates on the housing market;
3 *reduced segregation strategy:* changing the assignment of dwellings to combat segregation;
4 *reduced consequences strategy:* reducing undesirable consequences for the municipalities.

The *local network strategy* aimed to establish permanent cooperation between the housing estates, local authorities and other local actors to solve problems on the estates. The intention was to strengthen the activity of and social relations between residents in the areas to improve living conditions for deprived tenants and immigrants living on the estates. The initiatives should reduce social problems through locally-based efforts and by mobilising local resources. The main aim of this strategy was to support both social workers on the estates and social activities, and also to answer the demands for local cooperation between local authorities, housing associations, tenants' local organisations (estate boards, etc.) and other local parties.

The *improved competition strategy* aimed to help the estates to compete in the housing market to attract groups other than the poor and jobless and also to reduce the high moving frequency on the estates. The most important initiatives were physical renovation and rent decreases. However, support for social activities was also seen as an instrument to increase the quality of life on the estates and to improve their reputations.

The *reduced segregation strategy* consisted primarily of changes in rules and administrative practices to limit a concentration of marginalised people and immigrants on these estates. It subsequently proved difficult to implement these initiatives because they could be seen as discrimination against the groups that one wanted to keep away from the estates.

Finally, efforts to *reduce the consequences* were concentrated on support for schools with many foreign-speaking pupils, on education and training of immigrants and on increased funds for municipalities with problems.

These strategies fit well into the theoretical frame outlined in the section above. The 'local network strategy' matches what I have called area-based initiatives against social exclusion. The 'improved competition strategy' fits into initiatives against exclusion of places. And the 'reduced segregation strategy' is similar to the initiatives against segregation. The Danish initiatives on deprived housing estates can therefore be properly understood within the outlined theoretical framework.

Effects of the Danish Initiatives against Deprived Housing Estates

Research Evaluation of the Work of the Urban Committee

An extensive research evaluation of most of the initiatives taken by the Urban Committee (UC) was conducted from 1997 to 1999. Several research institutes and private consultants have been involved, but the Danish Building Research Institute has, in cooperation with the Danish Institute of Social Research, put in most effort and completed the overall evaluation.[3]

Parkinson (1998) has proposed three reasons why knowledge on urban regeneration projects is insufficient. They are:

1 faulty evaluation projects;
2 the effects are entangled and difficult to unravel;
3 evaluations have often been conducted too early for any effects to be seen.

The Danish evaluation suffers somewhat from the last problem – partly because the ministries wanted an early evaluation and partly because the initiatives were delayed. The first two problems are limited by the scope of data and the methodology used. The amount of data collected has been extensive and advanced statistical methods have been used to isolate the effects of different kinds of initiatives. Moreover, the development on the estates has been compared to the development on the local housing market and especially to that on other social housing estates.

The main sources of the evaluation have been:

1 applications for support and action plans;
2 case studies from 20 estates and municipalities;
3 interviews with 2,000 residents on 40 estates;
4 surveys among housing associations, estate boards, social workers and local authorities in all estates (about 500);
5 data from central registers on residents on the estates before and after the

initiatives, and also on movements in and out of the estates;
6 data from central registers on the development in the housing market in the municipalities and at a national level.

The evaluation included an analysis of the problems encountered on the supported estates before the initiatives were started up, and how they interacted. A model was constructed about the relationships between these factors and tested through statistical analyses (see Chapter 5). The analyses clearly showed that negative developments of these factors have mutually reinforced each other. On the basis of this model of spirals of deprivation, a new model was constructed (Figure 7.4) to show how we expected the different UC efforts to directly and indirectly influence conditions on the estate.

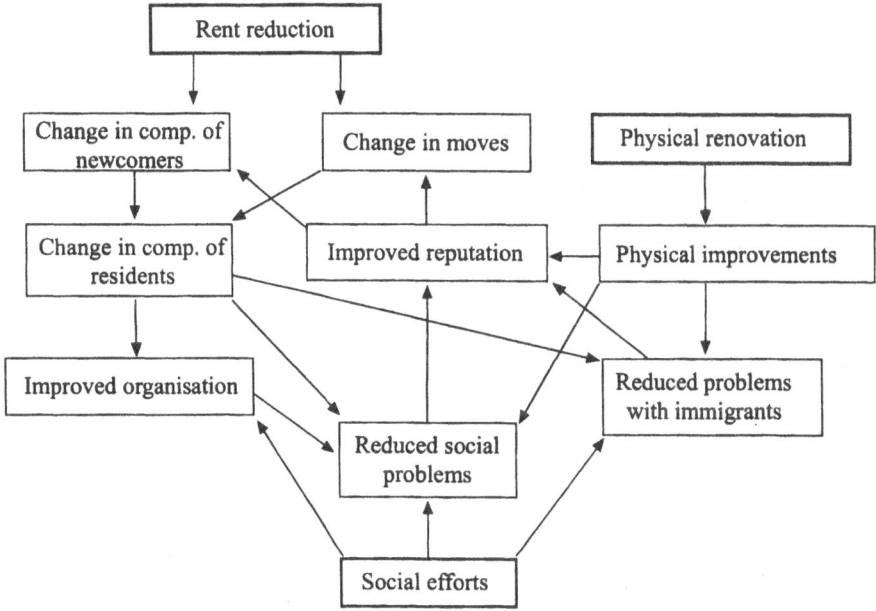

Figure 7.4 Model of the expected relations between Urban Committee efforts and changes in conditions on the estates

The model assumes that *rent reductions* should reduce moving frequencies and empty flats, and also influence the composition of both new tenants and leavers, leading to a change in the composition of residents towards more people in work and fewer immigrants and socially excluded residents. This change in residents should directly result in fewer social problems and fewer special problems in connection with ethnic groups, and also indirectly through an increase in tenants' activity and improved organisation because of increased social resources among tenants.

The physical initiatives consisted of repairing building damage, beautification of buildings and improvements of open spaces and common facilities. These improvements were expected to improve the appearance and reputations of the estates, which should, in turn, influence the number of people moving in and out of the estates. Improvement of common facilities and open spaces was also expected to contribute to better tenant organisation and fewer social problems.

The social initiatives were expected to increase social activity, make more residents active and improve tenants' organisation. This should improve the reputations of the estates. Moreover, parts of the social initiatives should be directed against socially excluded residents and immigrants, which was expected to reduce social problems.

Were the Initiatives Effective?

Overall changes in the supported estates The data for the evaluation was collected in 1996–97 at a point when the initiatives had been functioning for only a short while. This was also because it took much longer than expected to implement the initiatives.

The main conclusion of the evaluation is that a negative social, physical and economic development on the estates has been stopped, and that the efforts of the Urban Committee have prevented problems from escalating. But the problems have yet to be removed entirely. Figure 7.5 illustrates how housing associations and section boards have judged the extent of different problems on the estates, and the development after the initiatives have been started.

It may be expected that the positive effects have been overestimated by the housing associations because they are somewhat responsible for the work.

The figure shows that the physical initiatives have directly improved visual appearance, facilities and open spaces on a number of estates. Nearly 60 per cent of estates with serious problems and bad appearances, corresponding to one third of all estates, have therefore been somewhat or much better in this matter. The activity level of tenants has increased considerably, reducing problems caused by tenant passivity.

In about one-fourth of the estates, serious problems concerning crime and vandalism have been reduced. A similar number of serious problems have remained unchanged or become worse. The improvements are probably linked

Efforts to Combat Urban Decay

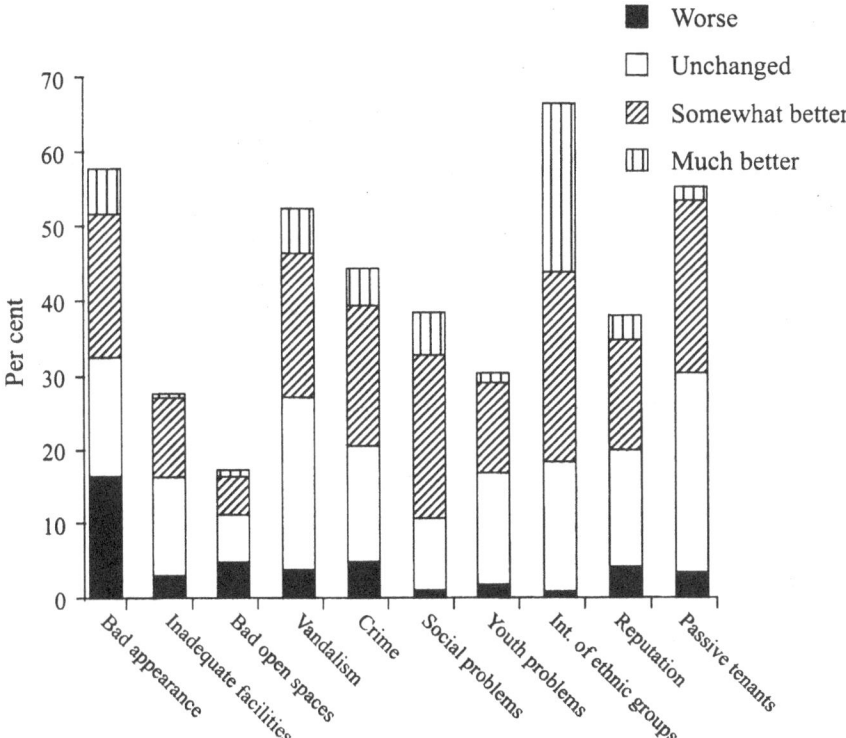

Figure 7.5 Proportion of estates (dwellings) that had serious problems in 1994 before the initiatives started, and the proportion of these where the situation became better or worse 1995–97

Source: Skifter Andersen, 1999b.

remained unchanged or become worse. The improvements are probably linked to special efforts targeting young people. These problems have been reduced on more than 50 per cent of the estates with serious problems involving young people. Fewer assessments conclude that social problems in general have been reduced. On 30 per cent of the estates with serious problems, the problems have been reduced, while on 10 per cent, they have increased.

Integration of immigrants is the only case in which more estates have experienced increasing problems than decreasing problems. This appears to be linked to an increasing number of immigrants from developing countries on the estates.

A major indicator of the degree of 'exclusion of the place' is the reputation of the estates. It can be argued (Rijpers and Smeets, 1998), that there are at least three different kinds of reputation:

1 reputation among residents;
2 reputation among outsiders;
3 the reputation that residents believe is found among outsiders.

I have previously argued (Skifter Andersen, 1999c) that the evaluation of the reputation in this study is comparable to the third category. The figure shows that nearly 40 per cent of the estates found that a bad reputation was a serious problem before the efforts started and that 55 per cent of these found that this problem was reduced, corresponding to 20 per cent of all the estates. Only a few estates have deteriorated.

Vacant dwellings were only a serious problem in very few of the estates, which points to problems in the Danish estates being more limited than is the case in e.g. England, where vacant dwellings and 'low demand' are a major problem (Mumford and Lupton, 1999; Morrison, 1999; Gibb et al., 1999). Moreover, the number of vacant dwellings was further reduced after the efforts of the Urban Committee began. Waiting lists for the estates have also grown. This development can only partly be ascribed to the initiatives, as there has been a similar trend in the social housing sector as a whole.

High mobility among tenants and a development of the composition of residents towards more excluded and marginalised people were common in many of the estates before the initiatives of the Urban Committee began. We collected data on the development of this trend in the beginning of 1998, where the social initiatives had already been operating for two years and the reduction of rents had been in effect for an average of a little more than one year. The physical improvements had been finished for an average of eight months. Many had not been finished at all at this time.

Despite the fact that the initiatives had not had long to work, it has been possible to identify positive changes on the estates, as shown in Figure 7.7. On average, moving frequencies have been reduced by 6 per cent (relatively), with the most noticeable reduction among residents in employment. This can be compared with the fact that nationally, mobility has remained unchanged among dwellings, even in other newer social housing estates. Actually, the mobility rate is now lower on the supported estates than on newer social housing estates on average.

The composition of newcomers has also changed towards more employed people. This is remarkable, as the inertia is strong in the systems that distribute dwellings to house hunters. Newcomers are chosen mainly from waiting lists. On most estates, people have been registered for several years.

Development in moving frequencies and composition of residents

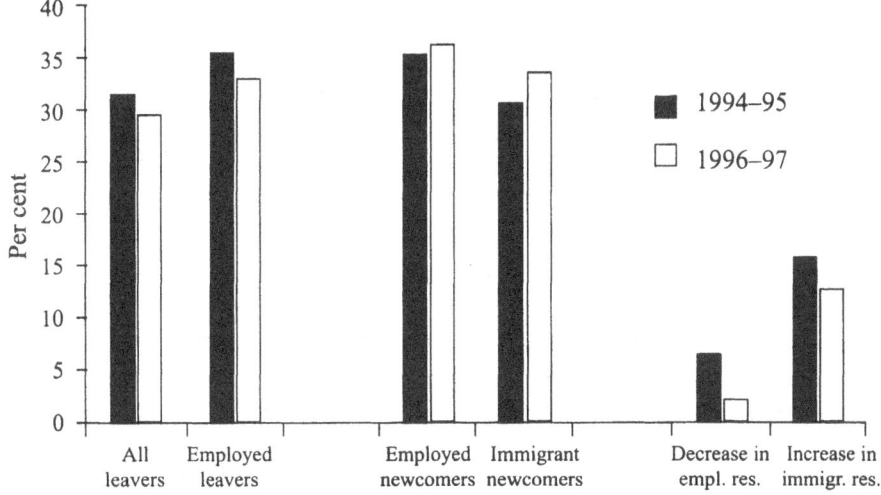

Figure 7.6 Moving frequencies for all residents and for residents in employment in the two periods 1994–95 and 1996–97, proportion of newcomers who were employed or immigrants, the relative decrease in the proportion of residents who were employed and the increase in the proportion of immigrants in the two periods

Note: The changes shown are due only to population changes, as they are adjusted for changes in sitting residents' employment.

Source: Skifter Andersen, 1999b.

The effect of these changes in movements in and out of the estates has been a pronounced reduction in the earlier sharp decrease in the proportion of employed people (and increase in the proportion of excluded residents). It can be foreseen that the composition of residents will quickly become stabilised and perhaps a positive change in the proportion of employed will occur. The figures shown are averages for a large number of estates on which some have had small and limited efforts and others have had large and multifaceted initiatives. A more specified study of the data has shown that the greatest changes have been found among the estates that previously had the most negative development in mobility and residential changes. This is linked to the fact that these estates have also benefited from the most extensive efforts.

On the other hand, the number of immigrants among newcomers has increased. This is the main reason why housing associations feel that problems concerning integration have increased. One explanation is that the number of immigrants among house hunters in general has increased even more and that this development has been even more extensive on other social housing estates. However, the rate of increase in the number of immigrants among residents has been successfully reduced by initiatives, as shown in the right-hand columns.

The Effects of Different Kinds of Strategies and Initiatives

The local network strategy A condition for support from the Urban Committee was that applications were prepared in cooperation by social housing associations and local governments. Applications were required to contain a thorough description of the situation on the estate and a detailed action plan prepared by both parties together. Another demand was that in each case, a steering committee should be established with members from both the housing estates and from the local authorities.

One of the important results of the *local network strategy* is that in many municipalities, permanent cooperation has been established between local authorities and the tenants' elected boards of the estates, in which other local actors are often involved. In some municipalities, the programme has also succeeded in orienting local authorities' social work strategies more towards neighbourhood-based efforts. In many other municipalities, however, there has not been much change in local authorities' strategies, and cooperation with the estates has been weak.

It subsequently emerged that the demands relating to applications had both positive and negative consequences (Skifter Andersen, 1999a). The positive effects were that cooperation was established between the parties that in many cases functioned in practice. The negative aspects were that the action plans were of limited use and produced conflicts with tenants later on because they were prepared in a hurry and tenants were rarely involved. On many estates, the action plans were either completely changed or discarded altogether when tenants and their local organisations came into play.

On some of the estates, efforts have succeeded in involving and directly benefiting vulnerable and deprived tenants. However, many of the social activities have targeted all tenants and these general activities have rarely involved either the weak groups or immigrants. Only activities aimed especially at these groups have been to their direct benefit. Some of the most successful activities targeted young people and have reduced problems involving crime and vandalism.

Three criteria were used in the statistical tests of the effects of the local network strategy:

1 changes in the activity level of tenants;
2 changes in the extent of social problems;
3 changes in problems involving integration of ethnic groups.

Table 7.6 Results from two logistic regressions explaining causes for increasing activity levels among tenants and an increasing number of social activities (R-statistic * 100)

	Activity level	Number of social activities
Problems of low activity before initiatives	27	18
Increase in the proportion of residents with occ. occupations	1.4	
Increase in the proportion of residents 26–40 years old	6	
Improvements in common facilities	8	25
Improvements in open spaces	28	24
Size of estate (no. of dwellings)	8	-11
Year of construction	7	
Proportion of dwellings in semidetached buildings	3	-10
Degree of urbanisation	-7	
Expenses for social workers DKK/m^2	7	2
Expenses for social activities DKK/m^2		8

Note: Logistic regressions explaining when some estates have experienced a positive change in situation. The database contains 400 cases. As there are no logic variables, the models therefore use R-statistics as results for the purpose of simplification. All the results shown are significant at a 0.05 level.

Source: Skifter Andersen, 1999b.

The statistical analysis shows that expenses used for social activities or social workers – as could be expected – have a significant effect on the development in the activity level of tenants (see Table 7.6). The extent of social activities has been increased and the tenants have become more active as a result of the

Table 7.7 Results of a linear regression explaining the causes of reduced social problems (Beta coefficient * 100)

	Stand. Beta coeff.
Social problems before initiatives	15
Increase in the proportion of residents on welfare	-3
Increase in the proportion of full-time unemployed residents	-2
Increase in the proportion of refugees	-6
Increase in the proportion of other immigrants	-2
Improvements in common facilities	3
Improvements in open spaces	8
Size of estate (no. of dwellings)	7
Year of construction	-3
Proportion of dwellings in semidetached buildings	8
Degree of urbanisation	-5
Expenses for social activities DKK/m^2	1
Expenses for social workers DKK/m^2	8

Note: This linear multivariable regression explaining changes in and index of social problems constructed on the basis of the evaluation of several kinds of problems on the estates. Four hundred cases were used as data, corresponding to the number of estates where all data was available. The standardised beta coefficient is shown. All the results shown are significant at a 0.05 level.

Source: Skifter Andersen, 1999b.

efforts. A statistically significant connection can also be found between these social initiatives and the positive development in social problems (Table 7.7), and in the development in problems with integration of immigrants (Table 7.8). A positive development has been seen, especially on estates experiencing major problems before the initiatives started. The conclusion here is therefore that even if many of the social activities have not targeted the most needy groups, they have contributed to solving social problems and integrating immigrants.

Similarly, a significant positive social effect was caused by physical efforts made to improve common facilities and open spaces (Tables 7.6–7.8). This indicates that physical area-based efforts do have an effect on social exclusion to the extent that they encourage social life in the area.

The strategy of improved competitiveness The criteria used to test the effects of the strategy were:

Table 7.8 Results of a logistic regression explaining causes for decreasing problems with integration of immigrants

	R-statistic * 100
Problems involving integration before initiatives	14
Increase in the proportion of immigrants in total	2
Increase in the proportion of refugees	-5
Increase in the proportion of children of immigrants	-4
Increase in the proportion of residents living on early pensions	-6
Increase in the proportion of full-time unemployed residents	-6
Improvements in common facilities	12
Size of estate (no. of dwellings)	10
Year of construction	11
Proportion of dwellings in semidetached buildings	-8
Degree of urbanisation	8
Expenses for social activities DKK/m^2	1
Expenses for social workers DKK/m^2	12

Note: This logistic regression explains when some estates have experienced a positive change in situation. The database contains 400 cases. As there are no logic variables, the models therefore use R-statistics as results for the purpose of simplification. All results shown are significant at a 0.05 level.

Source: Skifter Andersen, 1999b.

1 improved reputation;
2 reduced mobility rates;
3 an increasing proportion of employed people among newcomers;
4 an increasing proportion of employed among residents.

The following section describes the evaluated effects of the rent decreases, renovation efforts and social initiatives, respectively. We study both the direct effects and the indirect effects in agreement with Figure 7.4.

A direct sign that *rent reductions* have had an effect on mobility rates is that the number of persons moving fell 13 per cent on average on the estates where rents were reduced, yet remained unchanged on estates without rent decreases. The results of the statistical analysis are shown in Table 7.9 (a logistic regression of factors explaining when residents moved away or stayed). This shows that rent reductions have had a very significant effect on mobility on the estates. It also shows that the effect depends on how long ago the reductions were implemented. Another statistical analysis (not shown) has

Table 7.9 Results of a logistic regression explaining why people move out of the estates

	R-statistic * 100	B-coeff.	Significance	Factor of change	Change in mobility rate
Age (no. of years)	-6.5	-0.018	0.0000	10	-4
Male?	-1.8	-0.147	0.0001	1	-3
Children in household?	1	0.1131	0.0112	1	2
Unstable household?*	3	12.1000	0.0000	1	69
No. of years in dwelling	-3.6	-0.0165	0.0000	5	-2
Income (1000 DKK)	4.2	0.0022	0.0000	100	5
Immigrant?	-5	-0.5443	0.0000	1	-10
Size of dwelling (m^2)	-3	-0.059	0.000	10	-1
Semidetached?	-1.5	-0.1836	0.0011	1	-4
% immigrants in estate	2.1	0.0058	0.0000	10	1
Mobility rate municipality	10	0.0449	0.0000	5	5
Variables representing efforts					
Investments in renovation (1000 DKK/m^2)	1.13	0.13	4E-04	1	3
No. of months since renovation	-1.8	-0.0077	0.003	8	-1
Rent decrease (DKK/m^2)	-1.8	-0.008	0.0000	54	-8
No. of months since decrease	0	0.0028	0.411	14	1
Exp. for social initiatives (DKK/m^2)	-0.6	-0.0019	0.027	36	-1
Rent decrease* time since	0.92	0.0002	0.003	756	3
Rent decrease* social initiatives	1.1	0.000061	4E-04	1944	3

Table 7.9 cont'd

Notes

1 * = households dispersed by divorce, etc.
2 This logistic regression is based on data on all grown up residents aged over 17 corresponding to 160,000 cases. The results are explained by the B-coefficient and by the change in mobility rate (or proportion of employed newcomers) created by a change in the independent variables corresponding to two times their standard deviation.

Source: Skifter Andersen, 1999b.

also indicated that the rent reductions have had an especially powerful effect on the mobility of residents in employment.

In general, few of the estates had problems involving low demand and empty dwellings. The analysis of the effects of rent decreases on the demand for dwellings on the estates therefore focused on the extent to which the estates attracted more residents in employment. As seen in Table 7.9, the size of the rent reduction had a very significant effect on whether newcomers were employed or not. The analysis showed, however, that the effects of the rent reductions depended a great deal on two other variables:

1. the price level of owner-occupied housing in the local market;
2. the proportion of immigrants among residents on the estate (interaction in regression).

This indicated that rent reductions affected only the composition of newcomers in larger urban areas where real-estate prices are relatively high and owner-occupied housing is more expensive. In the smaller towns, where social housing has trouble competing with cheap owner-occupied housing, rent reductions did not affect the composition of newcomers. Moreover, the effects were small or missing altogether on estates with a high proportion of immigrants. On these estates, it seems that economic incentives alone cannot improve their inability to compete, which is mainly a result of their social and cultural image. It has not been possible to construct a statistical test of the effects of rent reductions for the changes in the composition of residents. But it is obvious that when there are positive effects on both lower mobility rates of residents in employment and on the proportion of employed newcomers, there will also be an effect on the proportion of residents in employment. A simple cross tabulation (Table 7.10) shows that estates with reduced rents have experienced much greater differences in population changes before and after the rent reduction than on estates without.

Before the reductions (in 1994–95) the number of residents in employment on the estates where rents were reduced decreased sharply – a greater decrease than in the other estates. After the reduction in 1996–97, this decrease was strongly reduced to a level below the level of the other estates. As seen, the increase in the number of immigrants has also increased in the other estates while it has been reduced on estates with no rent reductions. Furthermore, the growth in people marginalised from the labour market has been reduced much more on the estates where rents were reduced. These changes cannot all be ascribed to rent reductions because they largely coincide with physical

Efforts to Combat Urban Decay

Table 7.10 Results of logistic regression explaining when newcomers were in employment

	Unit of measurement	Coefficient	Significance	R-statistic * 100	Factor of change	Change in proportion of employed
Size of dwelling	m²	0.0056	0.0000	5	50	7
Rent/m²	DKK/m²	0.0002	0.0018	1.2	100	0
Semidetached?	0/1	0.1885	0.0000		1	5
Year of construction	Year	-0.0076	0.0000	-3.3	10	-2
Social problems (Index)	0/100	-0.0032	0.0000	-2.2	50	-4
Proportion of immigrants	%	-0.0141	0.0000	-6	30	-10
Proportion of newcomers in municipality	%	0.0275	0.0000	6	25	16
Comp. of local housing market*	%	0.0094	0.0000	4.3	20	5
Local price level for owner-occupied dwellings	DKK/m²	0.0002	0.0000		-1863	-9
Rent decrease	DKK/m²	0.0078	0.0000	1.7	35	7
Investments in renovation	1000 DKK/m²	-0.0001	0.0000	-1.2	2	0
Expenses for social initiatives	DKK/m²	-0.0009	0.4664		36	-0.8
Rent decrease* price level		0.000008	0.0000		65205	12.6
Social initiatives* proportion of immigrants		0.0001	0.0070		1080	2.7

Notes

1 * = proportion of dwellings in municipality that are social housing.
2 This logistic regression is based on data on all grown up newcomers. The results are explained by the B-coefficient and by the change in mobility rate (or proportion of employed newcomers) created by a change in the independent variables corresponding to two times their standard deviation.

Source: Skifter Andersen, 1999b.

renovations. The same kind of cross tabulation can be performed for these efforts, so the changes must be seen as combined effects of these two kinds of initiatives.

Table 7.11 Relative changes on estates with and without rent reductions in the number of residents in employment, immigrants and marginalised from the labour market, respectively

	Employed	Immigrants	Marginalised*
		Percent	
Estates with no rent reductions			
Relative change 1994–95	-3.4	13.0	8.2
Relative change 1996–97	-2.6	19.0	5.7
Difference	0.8	6.0	-2.4
Estates with rent reductions			
Relative change 1994–95	-10.2	13.2	15.6
Relative change 1996–97	-2.3	11.5	3.9
Difference	7.9	-1.7	-11.7

Note: * = residents aged over 17 in full-time unemployment or whose main income comes from early pension or welfare benefits.

Source: Skifter Andersen, 1999b.

The rent reductions have also had an indirect effect through the changes in residents that have occurred. Table 7.11 shows that the development in the reputations of the estates depends on the changes in the proportion of immigrants. It also depends on the development in social problems, which in turn depends on changes in the proportion of marginalised people, refugees and other immigrants (Table 7.6).

Physical renovation of some estates included embellishment of buildings and open spaces and improved common facilities. However, statistical analyses showed that the correlation between our measurement of the efforts – investment per square metre of housing space – is not very well correlated with the qualitative evaluations of the physical improvements that were obtained from the surveys. This can be explained partly by the large amount of money used to repair building defects, though this does not contribute much to the utility value of the estates.

Table 7.12 Results of logistic regression explaining causes for improved reputation

	R-statistic * 100
Problems involving bad reputation before initiatives	18
Bad location	9
Bad visual appearance before initiatives	2
Improvements in social problems	16
Improvements in problems with integration of immigrants	8
Increase in proportion of immigrants	-6
Size of estate (no. of dwellings)	-4
Year of construction	10
Proportion of dwellings in semidetached buildings	2
Degree of urbanisation	-2
Improvement of visual appearance	10
Number of months since renovation finished	10
Expenses for social initiatives	9

Note: This logistic regression explains when the situation on some estates has changed. The database contains 400 cases. As there are no logic variables, the models therefore use R-statistics as results for the purpose of simplification. All results shown are significant at a 0.05 level.

Source: Skifter Andersen, 1999b.

As seen in Tables 7.8 and 7.9, it has been difficult to find a direct effect of the investments in physical improvements and population changes on the estates. The variable investments per square metre is significant, but the effect is small and the sign is wrong. Besides the above-mentioned inaccuracy of the investment variable, this could also be due to some correlation with the strong variable of rent reductions. Moreover, the physical improvements had only recently been completed when the data was collected.

Another statistical analysis (see Table 7.11) has shown that improving the visual appearance of the estates has had a significant effect on the reputation of the estates. We also know from other analyses in our project (Skifter Andersen, 1999b) that a bad reputation has an important influence on mobility rates and the composition of newcomers. The effect on reputation increases over time after renovation work is completed. This was especially the case on estates that had bad reputations before the initiatives started. Considerable improvements were also achieved on estates with bad locations.

As was the case with rent reductions, it can be argued that the physical improvements had an indirect effect on reputation and population changes, as social problems were reduced by improvements made to common facilities and open spaces (Table 7.6). Finally, a direct effect was found for expenses for *social initiatives* on improvements in reputation (Table 7.11) but not on mobility and composition of newcomers.

The reduced segregation strategy This category of initiatives proposed by the Urban Committee proved to be much more difficult to implement than the other strategies because new legislation and new agreements with local governments were required. The main proposals concerned dispersing newly arrived refugees more among municipalities to give local authorities better opportunities to disperse social problems throughout the social and private housing stock, and to make it possible for housing associations to regulate the composition of new occupants. Moreover, a special proposal was made to set up a special institution to coordinate the assignment of dwellings in the capital region of Copenhagen.

Some of these initiatives were never realised and others were implemented several years after the other efforts. From the beginning of 1999, an agreement with local governments has been in place regarding how to disperse refugees among municipalities with few immigrants. Since 1998, exemptions have been given to housing associations on certain approved estates permitting them to deviate from rules stating that newcomers should always be taken from waiting lists. The purpose of this has clearly been to limit the number of immigrants and socially weak persons among new occupants. In addition, local authorities have been allowed to give compensation, paid by the state, to private landlords who place some of their dwellings at the disposal of refugees and other people in need of a dwelling. This last initiative never did work, as very few private landlords have shown any interest.

The dispersal of refugees has been a success. Exemptions given to housing associations have also been used. The problem here is that this has reduced housing possibilities for immigrants and other weak groups in some municipalities without creating alternatives for them. However, some politicians in municipalities that still have a great influx of immigrants because of family reunification believe these initiatives have not been sufficient. As a result of their pressure on the government, a controversial new initiative to limit family reunification has been implemented. New legislation approved by the Danish parliament has raised the age limit for unification through marriage from 18 to 25 years.

What can be Learned from European and Danish Experience of Area-based Initiatives

Research literature on experiences gained from initiatives to revitalise deprived urban neighbourhoods in Europe shows that there is much disagreement on the purpose of these efforts and also on their effects. Some researchers have been quite positive in their judgements. Others have been very negative, saying that regeneration initiatives appear to have made little impact and that they are based on ideas that are questionable. Initiatives that have been too limited in size or time, or too narrow in scope have been especially likely to fail, while more extensive programmes of longer duration that combine physical, organisational, financial and social initiatives have been more positively evaluated.

The discussion of European experiences in the section above highlighted that one of the main reasons for disagreement on the effects of area-based initiatives is the generally inadequate understanding of the nature of deprived urban areas. As described in the introduction, in much of the literature, deprived neighbourhoods have been interpreted as 'pockets of poverty' – a spatial concentration of poor people in parts of cities caused by social inequality and segregation. This kind of understanding has led people to see potential purposes of area-based efforts as limited and the effects of them have to some extent been misinterpreted. The alternative understanding proposed in this book sees segregation as a product of both social and spatial inequality with deprived urban areas understood as 'excluded places', which themselves contribute to spatial inequality and segregation.

Based on this understanding, I have proposed that area-based initiatives could have two different objectives:

1   to stop or reverse the exclusion of neighbourhoods;
2   to combat social exclusion at a neighbourhood level.

The second objective could be motivated by the fact that area deprivation creates special problems for residents and that local resources could be mobilised to supplement public resources. However, the first objective should be the most important.

Danish efforts to revitalise 500 social housing estates suit the understanding described above very well. The Danish initiatives featured four core strategies:

1   to strengthen social networks and reduce social problems in the areas (combat social exclusion);

2   to improve the ability of the estates to compete in the housing market (combat exclusion of place);
3   to reduce segregation in general;
4   to reduce other consequences for local authorities generated by deprived neighbourhoods.

The main instruments for the two first strategies were rent reductions, physical upgrading and social and organisational support.

Unfortunately, the extensive research evaluation of the initiatives was conducted a little too soon after the efforts were implemented. The efficiency of the programme was also weakened by the fact that for political reasons resources have been spread throughout too many estates with smaller problems and limited initiatives.

Having said that, marked positive effects have been achieved through the improved competition strategy, which has stopped the negative development on most of the estates, especially in areas with the largest problems and the strongest initiatives. Rent reductions have proved especially effective. But the problems have not yet been removed and efforts must continue.

The reputations of many estates have been improved, which has had an effect on mobility among tenants and the social composition of newcomers. The moving frequency has fallen – especially among tenants in employment – and more people in employment are being found among newcomers. As a consequence, the earlier strong development in the composition of tenants towards more people on public welfare and less in employment, has come to a halt.

What has not been achieved is a suspension of the growth in the number of immigrants on the estates. The number of immigrants in the period 1996–97 after the measures were implemented therefore rose. This can be explained partly by a general increase in the number of immigrants and refugees seeking somewhere to live during the period. Moreover, the rate of increase for immigrants on the estates was larger in the previous period 1994–95. So some progress has been made.

On many estates, the local network strategy has succeeded in creating cooperation between the estates, local authorities, residents and other local actors and has reduced social problems to some extent – problems involving crime and vandalism have been reduced particularly through efforts targeting young people.

The Danish case therefore confirms the conclusion reached by Power (1997) and others, i.e. that area-based initiatives have a purpose and can be effective. We are, however, 'swimming against the tide' (Power and Tunstal, 1995). Initiatives must be of sufficiently length and scope and must also combine physical, organisational, financial and social aspects. This is costly, but the alternative is to let these urban neighbourhoods spiral into ultimate abandonment and demolition.

Notes

1 France, Germany, Austria, Switzerland, Holland, UK, Denmark, Sweden and Norway.
2 Taylor, 1998, Morrison, 1999, Mumford and Lupton, 1999, Parkinson, 1998, Power, 1997, Kürpick and Weck, 1998, Cameroun, 1998, Evans, 1998, Hall, 1997 and Vestergaard, 1999.
3 The reports from the evaluation are in Danish with an English summary and consist of: Skifter Andersen, 1999a, Skifter Andersen, 1999b, Vestergaard et al., 1997, Vestergaard et al., 1999, Munk, 1999, Varming, 1999.

Bibliography

Adams, C. et al. (1991), *Philadelphia, Neighbourhoods, Division, and Conflict in a Post-industrial City*, Philadelphia: Temple University Press.
Ærø, T. (2001), PhD thesis on choice of dwelling and neighbourhood among moving households, Danish Building Research Institute.
Aitken, S. (1990), 'Local Evaluations of Neighbourhood Change', *Annals, Association of American Geographers*, Vol. 80, pp. 247–67.
Albon, R.P. and Stafford, D.C. (1990), 'Rent Control and Housing Maintenance', *Urban Studies*, Vol. 27, pp. 233–40.
Allen, J. (1998), 'Europe of the Neighbourhoods', in Madanipour, A., Cars, G. and Allen, J. (eds), *Social Exclusion in European Cities, Regional Policy and Development 23*, London: Jessica Kingsley Publishers.
Allen, J. and McDowell, L. (1989), 'Landlords and Property. Social Relations in the Private Rented Sector', *Cambridge Human Geography*, Cambridge University Press.
Alonso, W. (1964), *Location and Land Use*, Cambridge, MA: Harvard University Press.
Andersen, H.T. (1991), 'The Political Urbanisation. Fringe Development in Copenhagen', *Espace. Populations. Societies, 1991-2*, pp. 367–79.
Andersen, H.T. (1999), 'Urban Restructuring – Towards a New Urban Form', paper for ENHR Conference in Balatonfüred, Hungary.
Andersen J. and Elm Larsen, J. (1997), 'From Social Class to Social Exclusion', paper for the 19th Nordic Sociological Congress, København.
Apgar, W.C. (1990), *Preservation of Existing Housing: A Key Element in a Revitalized Housing Policy*, Cambridge, MA: Joint Center for Housing Studies, Harvard University.
Apgar, W.C. (1991), 'Which Housing Policy is Best', *Housing Policy Debate*, Vol. 1, pp. 1–32.
Apgar, W.C. et al. (1987), *The Determinants of Renovation and Repair Activity*, Cambridge, MA: Joint Center for Housing Studies, Harvard University.
Arnell-Gustafsson, U. (1983), *Blanda eller utjämna (Mixing or Smoothing)*, Meddelande M83:33, Statens Institut för Byggnadsforskning, Gävle.
Arnott, R. (1995), 'Time for Revisionism on Rent Control?', *Journal of Economic Perspectives*, Vol. 9, pp. 99–120.
Atkinson, R. and Kintrea, K. (2000), 'Neighbourhood Experiences of Social Exclusion: Evidence from Deprived and Non-deprived Neighbourhoods', paper for ENHR Conference, Gävle, Sweden.
Auletta, K. (1982), *The Underclass*, New York: Random House.
Babcock, F.M. (1932), *The Valuation of Real Estate*, New York: McGraw-Hill.

Bailey, N. and Robertson, D. (1997), 'Housing Renewal, Urban Policy and Gentrification', *Urban Studies*, Vol. 34, pp. 561–78.

Bartelt, D. (1986), 'Abandonment, Economic Change and the System of Cities', paper presented to the Conference on Housing Policy, Gävle, Sweden.

Bell, D. (1994), 'Theories of Post-Industrialism and Post-Modernity', in Grusky, D.B. (ed.), *Social Stratification. Class, Race and Gender in Sociological Perspective*, Boulder, CO: Westview Press.

Berghman, J. (1995), 'Social Exclusion in Europe', in Room, G. (ed.), *Beyond the Threshold. The Measurement and Analysis of Social Exclusion*, Bristol: The Policy Press.

Biterman, D. (1994), *Utvecling i miljonprogrammeområderne i Stockholms län* (*The Development of Regeneration Areas in Stockholm*), Stockholm: Hyresgästernes riksförbund.

Blauw, W. (1996), 'Housing Policy and Segregation in Dutch Cities', paper for ENHR Conference, Helsingør, Denmark.

Boal, F.W. (1997), *From Undivided to Undivided: Assimilation to Ethnic Cleansing*, Belfast, NI: Queens University of Belfast.

Bourdieu, P. (1993), 'Effets de lieu' ('Importance of Place'), in Bourdieu P. et al. (eds), *La misere du monde*, Paris: Seuil.

Bradley, H. (1996), *Fractured Identities*, Cambridge: The Polity Press.

Broadway, M.J. and Jesty, G. (1998), 'Are Canadian Inner Cities Becoming More Dissimilar?', *Urban Studies*, Vol. 35, No. 9, pp. 1423–38.

Burgess, E.W. (1924), 'The Growth of the City', *Publications of the American Sociological Society*, No. 18, pp. 85–97.

Burgess, E.W. (1925), 'The Growth of the City: An Introduction to a Research Project', in Theodorson, G.A. (ed.) (1961), *Studies in Human Ecology*, New York: Harper & Row.

Burrows, R. and Rhodes, D. (1998), *Unpopular Places? Area Disadvantage and the Geography of Misery in England*, Bristol: The Policy Press.

Børresen, S. (2000), 'Fremmedhed og praksis – om tyrkiske og pakistanske indvandreres bosætning og boligvalg' ('Foreignness and Praxis – on Settling and Housing Choice among Turkish and Pakistani Immigrants'), PhD thesis.

Cameron, S. and Davoudi, S. (1998), 'Combating Social Exclusion', in Madanipour, A., Cars, G. and Allen, J. (eds), *Social Exclusion in European Cities, Regional Policy and Development 23*, London: Jessica Kingsley Publishers.

Cars, G. (2000), 'Social Exclusion in European Neighbourhoods – Processes, Experiences and Responses', final report of project financed under the TSER programme, Bruxelles: European Commission.

Cars, G., Madanipour, A. and Allen, J. (1998), 'Social Exclusion in European Cities', in Madanipour, A., Cars, G. and Allen, J. (eds), *Social Exclusion in European Cities, Regional Policy and Development 23*, London: Jessica Kingsley Publishers.

Christensen, G. and Benjaminsen, L. (2000), 'Sammenhængen mellem fysiske og sociale ændringer i boligbebyggelser' ('The Connection between Physical and

Social Problems and Changes on Housing Estates'), SBI-meddelelse 125, Danish Building Research Institute.

Christiansen, U. and Vestergaard, H. a.o. (1993), 'Bedre bebyggelser – bedre liv?' ('Better Estates – Better Lives?'), SBI-byplanlægning 65, Hørsholm, Danish Building Research Institute.

Cole, I. and Shayer, S. (1998), 'Tenure Mix as Social Fix? Community Diversity and Social Networks on Mixed Housing Estates', paper for ENHR Conference, Cardiff 1998.

Costa Pinho, T. (2000), 'Residential Contexts of Social Exclusion: Images and Identities', paper for ENHR Conference, Gävle.

Crook, A.D.H. and Kemp, P.A. (1996), 'The Revival of Private Rented Housing in Britain', *Housing Studies*, Vol. 11, pp. 51–68.

Dangschat, J.S. (1991), 'Residential Desegregation', paper for ENHR Conference, Oslo.

Dangschat, J. (1994), 'Segregation – Lebensstile im Konflikt, soziale Ungleichheiten und räumliche Disåparitäten' ('Segregation – Lifestyles in Conflict'), in Dangschat, J.S. and Blasius, J. (eds), *Lebensstile in den Städten*, Opladen: Konzepte und Methoden.

Danish Government Commission on Rent Legislation (1997), *Lejeforhold*, Copenhagen: Ministry of Housing.

Dean, J. and Hastings, A. (2000), *Challenging Images: Housing Estates, Stigma and Regeneration*, Bristol: The Policy Press.

DiGiovanni, G. (1984), 'An Examination of Selected Consequences of Revitalization in six US Cities', *Urban Studies*, Vol. 2.

Dildine, L. and Massey, F.A. (1974), 'Dynamic Model of Private Incentives to Housing Maintenance', *Southern Economic Journal*, Vol. 40, pp. 631–39.

Downs, A. (1981), *Neighbourhoods and Urban Development*, Washington DC: Brookings Institution.

Downs, A. (1988), *Residential Rent Control: An Evaluation*, Washington DC: The Urban Land Institute.

Duncan, O.D. and Duncan, B. (1955), 'Residential Distribution and Occupational Stratification', *The American Journal of Sociology*, Vol. 60, pp. 493–503.

Ellen, I.G. (2000), 'Race-based Neighbourhood Projection: A Proposed Framework for Understanding New Data on Racial Integration, *Urban Studies*, Vol. 37, No. 9, pp. 1513–33.

Ellen I.G. and Turner, M. (1997), 'Does Neighborhood Matter? Assessing Recent Evidence', *Housing Policy Debate*, Vol. 8, No. 4, pp. 833–66.

Elsinga, M. (1996), 'Home Ownership as a Remedy against Segregation and Deterioration', paper for ENHR Conference, Helsingør.

Erbring, L. and Young, A.A. (1979), 'Individuals and School Structure', *Sociological Methods and Research*, Vol. 7, pp. 396–430.

Esping-Andersen, G. (1993), *Changing Classes*, London: Sage.

European Commission (1997), 'Social Indicators. Problematic Issues', collective paper issued at a seminar, Directorate General XII.
Evans, R. (1998), 'Tackling Deprivation on Social Housing Estates in England', *Housing Studies*, Vol. 13, No. 5, pp. 713–26.
Fossett, J.W. (1987), 'Market Failure and Federal Policy: Low-income Housing in Chicago 1970–83', in Tobin, G.A. (ed.), *Changing Patterns and Racial Segregation*, California: Sage Publications.
Friedrichs, J. (1997), 'Context Effects of Poverty Neighbourhoods on Residents', in Vestergård, H. (ed.), *Housing in Europe*, Danish Building Research Institute.
Friedrichs, J. (1998), 'Do Poor Neighborhoods Make their Residents Poorer? Context Effects of Poverty Neighborhoods on Residents', in Andress, H.J. (ed.), *Empirical Poverty Research in a Comparative Perspective*, Brookfield: Ashgate.
Friedrichs, J. and O'Loughlin, J. (1996), *Social Polarization in Postindustrial Metropolises*, Berlin: Walter de Gruyter.
Galster, G.C. (1992), 'Research on Discrimination in Housing and Mortgage Markets', *Housing Policy Debate*, Vol 3, pp. 639–83.
Galster, G.C. and Zobel, A. (1998), 'Will Dispersed Housing Programmes Reduce Social Problems in the US?', *Housing Studies*, Vol. 13, No. 5, pp. 605–22.
Gibb, K. (1990), 'The Private Renting Problem', Discussion Paper No. 30, Centre for Housing Research, University of Glasgow.
Gibb, K., Kearns, A. and Kintrea, K. (1999), 'Low Demand Housing Preferences and Neighbourhood Choices', paper for ENHR Conference, Balatonfüred, Hungary.
Giffinger, R. and Reeger, R. (1997), 'Changes in Housing Conditions of Selected Immigrant Groups in Vienna', paper for ENHR Conference, Balatonfüred, Hungary.
Gottschalk, G., Engberg L.A. and Pedersen, D.O. (2000), 'Beboersammensætning og tilfredshed i fem boligområder i Odense' ('Composition of Residents and Neighbourhood Satisfaction in Five Housing Estates'), SBI-rapport 325, Danish Building Research Institute.
Goul Andersen, J. (1996), 'Velfærdssystem, marginalisering og medborgerskab' ('Welfare System, Marginalisation and Citizenship'), *Dansk Sociologi*, 1.
Grigsby, W.G. (1963), *Housing Market and Public Policy*, Philadelphia: University of Pennsylvania Press.
Grigsby, W.G. (1990), 'Housing Finance and the Subsidies in the United States', *Urban Studies*, Vol. 27, pp. 831–45.
Grigsby, W.G. and Rosenburg, L. (1975), *Urban Housing Policy*, New York: APS-Publications.
Grigsby, W.G. et al. (eds) (1987), *The Dynamics of Neighbourhood Change and Decline*, New York: Pergamon Press.
Groth, N.B. and Møllgaard, J. (1982), 'Byplanlægning, kulturlandskab og livsform' ('Town Planning, Cultural Landscapes and Lifestyle'), Miljøministeriet.
Haffner, M. (1993), 'Housing Expenses of Tenants and Owner-occupiers in Western Europe', paper for ENHR Housing Conference, Budapest.

Hall, P. (1997), 'Regeneration Policies for Peripheral Housing Estates', *Urban Studies*, Vol. 34, Nos 5–6, pp. 873–90.
Hamnet, C. (1994), 'Social Polarisation in Global Cities', *Urban Studies*, Vol. 31, No. 3, pp. 401–24.
Hansen, K.E. and Ærø, T. (1996), 'Kommunernes organisering af byfornyelsen' ('How Local Authorities Organise Urban Renewal'), SBI-report 266, Danish Building Research Institute.
Hansen, K.E., Skifter Andersen, H. and Foerlev, B. (1990), 'Forvaltning af forbedring og vedligeholdelse i private udlejningsejendomme' ('Administration of Improvement and Maintenance in Private Rental Properties'), SBI-meddelelse 78, Danish Building Research Institute.
Harloe, M. (1985), *Private Rented Housing in the United States and Europe*, London and Sydney: Croom Helm.
Harris, C.D. and Ullman, E.L. (1945), 'The Nature of Cities', *Annals of the American Academy of Political and Social Science*, No. 252.
Helbrecht, I. and Pohl, J. (1995), 'Pluralisierung der Lebensstile: Neue Herausforderungen für die sozialgeographische Stadtforshung' ('Pluralisation of Lifestyles – challenges for Social Geography'), *Geographische Zeitschrift*, Vol. 83, pp. 222–37.
Herbert, D.T. and Johnston, R.J. (1978), *Residential Area Characteristics*, New York: Wiley and Sons.
Hirschfield, A. and Bowers, K.J. (1997), The Effect of Social Cohesion on Levels of Recorded Crime in Disadvantaged Areas, *Urban Studies*, Vol. 34, No. 8, pp. 1275–95.
Hirschl, T.A. and Rank, M.R. (1991), 'The Effect of Population Density on Welfare Participation', *Social Forces*, Vol. 70, pp. 225–35.
Hjärne, L. (1991), *Segregation, en begrebsanalys* (*Segregation, a Conceptual Analysis*), Reprint Series No. 68, Gävle: The National Swedish Institute for Building Research.
Hjarnø, J. (1996), 'Global Cities in Two Ways, a Comment on Saskia Sassens Global City Hypothesis', *Migration*, No. 18, South Jutland University: Danish Centre for Migration and Ethnic Studies.
Hjarnø, J. (1997), 'Copenhagen: On the Housing Battlefield. An Analysis of the Causes of Spatial Segregation in a Multiethnic Metropolis', Danish Centre for Migration and Ethnic Studies, SUC.
Hoyt, H. (1939), *The Structure and Growth of Residential Neighborhoods in American Cities*, Washington DC: Federal Housing Administration.
Hoyt, H. (1939), 'The Pattern of Movement of Residential Rental Neighbourhoods', in Mayer, H.M. and Kohn, C.F. (eds), *Readings in Urban Geography*, Chicago: University of Chicago Press.
Hummelgård, H. et al. (1997), *Udsatte boligområder i Danmark* (*Deprived Housing Areas in Denmark*), Amternes og Kommunernes Forskningsinstitut.

Hurtig, E. (1995), *Hemhörighet och stadsförnyelse (Belonging and Urban Renewal)*, Göteborg: Doktorsavhandling, Chalmers tekniske högskole.
Huttman, E.D. (1992), 'Subsidised Housing Segregation in Western Europe', in Huttman, E., Blauw, W. and Saltman, J. (1992), *Urban Housing Segregation of Minorities in Western Europe and the United States*, Durham and London: Duke University Press.
Huttman E.D., Blauw, W. and Saltman, J. (eds) (1992), *Urban Housing Segregation of Minorities in Western Europe and the United States*, Durham and London: Duke University Press.
Høyrup, T. (1983), *Det glemte folk (The Forgotten People)*, Statens Byggeforskningsinstitut.
Ingram, G. and Oron, Y. (1977), 'The Production of Housing Services from Existing Dwelling Units', in Ingram, G. (ed.), *Residential Location and Urban Housing Markets*, Cambridge, MA: Ballinger.
Jargowsky, P.A. (1997), *Poverty and Place: Ghettos, Barriers and the American City*, New York: Russel Sage Foundation.
Kaplan, M. (1991), 'American Neighbourhood Policies: Mixed Results and Uneven Evaluations', in Altermann, R. and Cars, G. (eds), *Neighbourhood Regeneration*, London and New York: Mansell.
Kearns, A., Atkinson, R. and Parker, A. (2000), 'A Geography of Misery or an Epidemic of Contentment? Understanding Neighbourhood (Dis)Satisfaction in Britain', paper for ENHR Conference, Gävle, Sweden.
Kending, H.L. (1984), 'Housing Careers, Life Cycle and Residential Mobility', *Urban Studies*, Vol. 21, No. 3, pp. 271–84.
Kennedy, R.J.R. (1952), 'Single or Triple Melting Pot?: Intermarriage Trends in New Haven 1870–1950', *American Journal of Sociology*, Vol. 58, pp. 56–9.
Kintrea, K. and Atkinson, R. (1998), 'Reconnecting Excluded Communities?', Scottish Homes Research Reports No. 51, Edinburgh.
Kirkegård, O. (1985), 'Forbedring af nyere etageboligområder – Et litteraturstudium' ('Improvement of Newer Housing Estates'), SBI-meddelelse 55, Hørsholm: Danish Building Research Institute.
Knox, P. (1995), *Urban Social Geography*, London: Longman.
Kortteinen, M. and Vaatovaara, M. (1999), 'Model of Segregation within the Metropolitian Area of Helsinki', paper for ENHR Conference at Balatonfüred, Hungary.
Kürpick, S. and Weck, S. (1998), 'Policies against Social Exclusion in Germany', in Madanipour, A., Cars, G. and Allen, J. (eds), *Social Exclusion in European Cities, Regional Policy and Development 23*, London: Jessica Kingsley Publishers.
Kutty, N. (1996), 'The Impact of Rent Control on Housing Maintenance', *Housing Studies*, Vol. 11, pp. 69–88.
Lee, P. and Murie, A. (1999), 'Spatial and Social Divisions within British Cities: Beyond Residualisation', *Housing Studies*, Vol 14, No. 5, pp. 625–40.

Lee, P., Murie, A. and Gordon, D. (1995), *Area Measures of Deprivation*, Birmingham: University of Birmingham, Centre for Urban and Regional Studies.
Lejelovskommissionen (The Danish Governmental Commission on Rent Legislation) (1997), Lejeforhold.
Leven, C. et al. (1976), *Neighbourhood Change: Lessons in the Dynamics of Urban Decay*, New York: Prager.
Lindberg, G. and Lindèn, A.-L. (1989), *Social segmentation på det svenske bostadsmarknaden (Social Segmentation on the Swedish Housing Market)*, Sociologiske Institutionen, Lunds Universitet.
Lowry, I. (1960), 'Filtering and Housing Standards', *Land Economics*, Vol. 36.
Lundberg, S. and Ström, I. (1979), 'Segregation vid bostandsförnyelse' ('Segregation in connection with Housing Renewal'), Rapport R93:1979, Byggforskningsrådet, Stockholm.
Lundström, S. and Gustafsson, B. (1985), *Privatägda hyresfastigheter. Underhåll och ombygnad vid ägareskiften (Private Rental Properties. Maintenance and Improvement after Purchase)*, Stockholm: The Swedish Council for Building Research.
Madanipour, A. (1998), 'Social Exclusion and Space', in Madanipour, A., Cars, G. and Allen, J. (eds), *Social Exclusion in European Cities, Regional Policy and Development 23*, London: Jessica Kingsley Publishers.
Madanipour, A., Cars, G. and Allen, J. (1998), *Social Exclusion in European Cities, Regional Policy and Development 23*, London: Jessica Kingsley Publishers.
Malpezzi, S. (1990), 'Costs and Benefits of Rent Control', Washington: World Bank Discussion Papers No. 74.
Marcuse, P. (1993), 'Degentrification and Advanced Homelessness: New Patterns, Old Processes', *Netherlands Journal of Housing and the Built Environment*, Vol. 8, No. 2, pp. 177–91.
Margolis, S. (1981), 'Depreciation and Maintenance of Housing', *Land Economics*, Vol. 57, pp. 91–105.
Marsh, A. and Mullins, D. (1998), 'The Social Exclusion Perspective and Housing Studies: Origins, Applications and Limitations', *Housing Studies*, Vol. 13, No. 6, pp. 749–59.
Massey, D. (1994), 'American Apartheid: Housing Segregation and Persistent Urban Poverty', Department of Sociology, University of Chicago (Internet paper).
Mayer, N. (1981), 'Rehabilitation Decisions in Rental Housing', *Journal of Urban Economics*, Vol. 10, pp. 76–94.
Mayer, N.S. (1985), 'The Impact of Lending, Race and Ownership on Rental Housing Rehabilitation', *Journal of Urban Economics*, Vol. 17, pp. 349–74.
Metzger, J.T. (2000), 'Planned Abandonment: Life-cycle Theory and Urban Policy', *Housing Policy Debate*, Vol. 11, No. 1, pp. 7–40.
Mills, E. (1967), 'An Aggregate Model of Resource Allocation in a Metropolitan Area', *American Economic Review*, Vol. 57, pp. 197–210.
Mingione, E. (1996), *Urban Poverty and the Underclass*, Oxford: Blackwell.

Ministry of Housing in Denmark (1997), 'Boligfraflytninger. En analyse af samtlige fraflyttede boliger i perioden 1981–1992'.
Ministry of Housing and Urban Affairs in Denmark (2000), 'Blandede ejerformer' ('Mixed Ownership in Urban Areas').
Modig, A. (1985), 'Grannrelationer i förort. En studie av socialt liv i bostadsområden med mange problemhushåll' ('Neighbour Relations in Suburbs. A Study of Social Life in Housing Areas with Many Problem Households'), Rapport R147:1985, Byggforskningsrådet, Stockholm.
Moorhouse, J.C. (1982), 'Optimal Housing Maintenance under Rent Control', *Southern Economic Journal*, Vol. 39, pp. 93–105.
Morrison, N. (1999), 'Addressing the Difficulties in Letting Social Housing across the UK', paper for ENHR Conference, Balatonfüred, Hungary.
Mumford, K. and Lupton, R. (1999), 'Low Demand for Housing and Area Abandonment, Compounding Effects of Areas on Life Chances', paper for ENHR Conference, Balatonfüred, Hungary.
Munk, A. (1998), 'Forfalds- og fornyelsesprocesser i ældre bykvarterer' ('Processes of Decay and Renewal in Older Neighbourhoods in Copenhagen'), SBI-rapport 305, Danish Building Research Institute.
Munk, A. (1999), 'Byudvalgets boligsociale indsats' ('The Social Inititatives Started by the Danish Urban Committee'), SBI-report 319. Danish Building Research Institute.
Murdie, R. (1976), 'Spatial Form in the Residential Mosaic', in Herbert, D.T and Johnston, R.J. (eds), *Spatial Processes and Form, Vol. I: Social Areas in Cities*, London: John Wiley & Sons.
Murie, A. (1994), *Cities and Housing after the Welfare State*, Amsterdam: Study Centre for the Metropolitan Environment.
Murray, C. (1990), *The Emerging British Underclass*, London: IEA Health and Welfare Unit.
Musterd, S. (1994), 'A Rising European Underclass? Social Polarization and Spatial Segregation in European Cities', *Built Environment*, Vol. 20, No 3.
Musterd, S. and Ostendorf, W. (1998), *Urban Segregation and the Welfare State*, London and New York: Routledge.
Musterd, S., Priemus, H. and van Kempen, R. (1999), 'Towards Undivided Cities: The Potential of Economic Revitalisation and Housing Redifferentiation', *Housing Studies*, Vol. 14, No. 5, pp. 573–84.
Muth, R. (1969), *Cities and Housing*, Chicago: University of Chicago Press.
Møllgaard, J. (1984), 'Byens sociale geografi' ('The Social Geography of Towns'), SBI-byplanlægning 47, Statens Byggeforskningsinstitut.
Nelson, K.P. (1988), *Gentrification and Distressed Cities*, Madison: University of Wisconsin Press.
Nesslein, T. (1988a), 'Housing: The Market Versus the Welfare State Revisited', *Urban Studies*, Vol. 25, pp. 95–108.

Nesslein, T. (1988b), 'Urban Decay and the Premature Obsolescence of Housing: a Cross Country Examination of the Basic Economic Determinants', *Scandinavian Housing and Planning Research*, Vol. 5, pp. 209–23.

Niebank, P.L. (1985), *The Rent Control Debate*, Chapel Hill: University of North Carolina Press.

Norusis, M.J. (1993), *Advanced Statistics*, Chicago: SPSS Inc.

Nørgaard, H. (2000), 'The Global City Thesis: A Study of Social Polarisation and Changes in the Distribution of Wages in the New York Metro Area from 1970 to 1990', PhD thesis, Institute of Geography, University of Copenhagen.

Olsson Hort, S.E. (1992), *Segregation – ett svensk dilemma (Segregation – a Swedish Dilemma)*, Stockholm: Bilaga til Långtidsutredningen.

Pacione, M. (1982), 'Evaluating the Quality of the Residential Environment on Deprived Council Estates', *Geoforum*, Vol. 13, pp. 45–55.

Park, R. (1926), 'The Urban Community as a Spatial Pattern and Moral Order', in Burgess, E.W. (ed.), *The Urban Community*, Chicago: University of Chicago Press.

Park, R. (1952), *Human Communities*, New York: The Free Press.

Parkinson, M. (1998), *Combating Social Exclusion. Lessons from Area-based Programmes in Europe*, Bristol: The Policy Press.

Peach, C. (1996), 'The Meaning of Segregation, Planning', *Practice and Research*, Vol. 11, No. 2, pp. 137–50.

Peach, C. (1997), 'Is All Segregation Bad?', paper for international workshop *The Undivided City*, The Hague, Netherlands, October.

Peterson, G.E. et al. (1973), *Property Taxes and the Cities*, Massachussets: Lexington Books.

Pickwance, C.G. (1973), 'Life-cycle Housing Tenure and Intra-urban Residential Mobility', *Sociological Review*, Vol. 21, pp. 279–97.

Porell, F.W. (1985), 'One Man's Ceiling is Another Man's Floor: Landlord/Manager Residency and Housing Conditions', *Land Economics*, Vol. 61, pp. 106–17.

Power, A.E. (1997), *Estates on the Edge: The Social Consequences of Mass Housing in Europe*, London: Macmillan.

Power, A. and Tunstall, R. (1995), *Swimming against the Tide. Polarisation or Progress on 20 Unpopular Council Estates, 1980–1995*, The Homestead: Joseph Rowntree Foundation.

Priemus, H. and Metselaar, G. (1992)'Urban Renewal Policy in a European Pespective: An International Comparative Analysis', *Housing and Urban Studies*, No. 5, Delft: Delft University Press.

Quigley, J. (1979), 'What Have we Learned about Urban Housing Markets', in Mieszkowski et al. (eds), *Current Issues in Urban Economics*, Baltimore: Johns Hopkins.

Quinn, M.A. et al. (1980), 'Maintenance Effort and the Professional Landlord: An Empirical Critique of Theories of Neighbourhood Decline', *Journal of American Real Estate and Urban Economics*, Vol. 8, pp. 345–69.

Ratcliff, R.U. (1949), *Urban Land Economics*, New York: McGraw Hill.

Rijpers, B. and Smeets, J. (1998), 'Housing Challenge: Managing Neighbourhood Image', paper presented at the ENHR Conference, Cardiff.

Rossi, P.H. (1955), *Why Families Move*, Illinois: The Free Press.

Rothenberg, J. et al. (1991), *The Maze of Urban Housing Markets: Theory, Evidence and Policy*, Chicago: University Press of Chicago.

Rydell, C.P. (1970), 'Factors Affecting Maintenance and Operating Costs in Federal Public Housing Projects', The New York Rand Institute.

Rydell, C.P. (1977), *Effects of Market Conditions on Prices and Profits of Rental Housing*, Santa Monica: Rand Corporation.

Rydell, C.P. and Neel, K. (1982), *Rent Control, Undermaintenance and Housing Deterioration*, Santa Monica: Rand Corporation.

Salins, P.D. (1980), *The Ecology of Housing Destruction*, New York: New York University Press.

Saltman, J. (1992), 'Theoretical Orientation: Residential Segregation', in Huttman E., Blauw, W. and Saltman, J. (eds), *Urban Housing Segregation of Minorities in Western Europe and the United States*, Durham and London: Duke University Press.

Sassen, S. (1991), *The Global City*, New York: Princeton University Press.

Sassen, S. (1994), *Cities in a World Economy*, London: Pine Forge Press.

Schill, P. and Nathan, L. (1983), *Revitalizing America's Cities. Neighbourhood Reinvestment and Displacement*, Albany: SUNY Press.

Schilling, J.D. et al. (1991), 'Measuring Depreciation in Single-Family Rental and Owner-Occupied Housing', *Journal of Housing Economics*, Vol. 1, pp. 368–83.

Schnare, A.B. and Struyk, R. J. (1976), 'Segmentation in Urban Housing Markets', *Journal of Urban Economics*, Vol. 3, pp. 146–66.

Shevky, E. and Bell, W. (1955), *Social Area Analysis*, Stanford, CA: Stanford University Press.

Skifter Andersen, H. (1987), 'Boligmarkedet og kommunernes ulige økonomiske vilkår' ('The Housing Market and the Uneven Economic Conditions for Local Authorities'), *Samfundsøkonomen*, Vol. 4, pp. 25–9.

Skifter Andersen, H. (1990), 'The Welfare State Housing Policy Versus the Unregulated Housing Market – a Comment on Articles by Thomas S. Nesslein', *Scandinavian Housing and Planning Research*, Vol. 7, pp. 45–9.

Skifter Andersen, H. (1992), 'Regulation of Private Rental Housing – Some Danish Experiences', *Scandinavian Housing and Planning Research*, Vol. 9, pp. 41–5.

Skifter Andersen, H. (1993), 'Hvordan fungerer et ureguleret boligmarked – erfaringer fra USA' ('American Experience of How an Unregulated Housing Market Functions'), SBI-meddelelse 103, Statens Byggeforskningsinstitut.

Skifter Andersen, H. (1994), 'The Welfare State Versus the Social Market Economy – A Comparative Study of Housing Policies in Denmark and Germany', *Scandinavian Housing and Planning Research*, Vol. 11, pp. 1–25.

Skifter Andersen, H. (1994), 'Den private boligfornyelse i ældre andelsboliger og private udlejningsejendomme' ('Private Initiated Rehabilitation of Private Rented

Housing and Cooperatives'), SBI-meddelelse 105, Danish Building Research Institute.

Skifter Andersen, H. (1995a), 'Privat byfornyelse – en lov med forhandling mellem udlejere og lejere' ('Evaluation of a Subsidy Programme for Rehabilitation of Private Rented Housing'), SBI-rapport 250, Danish Building Research Institute.

Skifter Andersen, H. (1995b), 'Explanations of Urban Decay and Renewal on the Housing Market – What can Europe Learn from American Research?', *Netherlands Journal of Housing and the Built Environment*, Vol. 10, No. 1, pp. 65–85.

Skifter Andersen, H. (1995c), 'Afkastet af investeringer i private udlejningsejendomme – under huslejeregulering og ved afvikling af reguleringen' ('Profitability from Investments in Private Rental Housing – Under Rent Control and from Lifting Control'), report prepared for the Danish National Commission on Rent Legislation.

Skifter Andersen, H. (1999a), 'Byudvalgets indsats 1993–98. Sammenfattende evaluering' ('The Efforts of the Danish Urban Committee 1993–98'), SBI-report 320. Danish Building Research Institute.

Skifter Andersen, H. (1999b), 'Virkningerne af Byudvalgets indsats i almene boligområder' ('The Effects of Initiatives on Social Housing Estates initiated by the Danish Urban Committee'), SBI-report 321. Danish Building Research Institute.

Skifter Andersen, H. and Ærø, T. (1997), 'Det boligsociale danmarkskort' ('A Map of the Social Composition of Residents in Housing Tenures in Danish Municipalities'), Danish Building Research Institute.

Skifter Andersen H. and Ærø, T. (1998), 'Sociale konsekvenser af byfornyelse' ('Social Consequences of Urban Renewal'), SBI-report 297, Danish Building Research Institute.

Skifter Andersen, H. and Als, J. (1986), 'Boligbyggeriet og kommunernes befolkningsudvikling' ('New Housing in the Municipalities and Trends in Population'), Danish Building Research Institute.

Skifter Andersen, H. and Bonke, J. (1980), *Boligsektorens fordelingsmæssige virkninger I: Bolig-markedet* ('Distributional Effects of the Housing Market'), Copenhagen: Lavindkomstkommisionen.

Skifter Andersen, H. and Foerlev, B. (1996), 'Private udlejeres økonomiske vilkår under den offentlige byfornyelse' ('Economic Conditions for Private Landlords Participating in Public Urban Renewal Schemes'), Danish Building Research Institute.

Skifter Andersen, H. and Leather, P. (ed.) (1999), *Housing Renewal in Europe*, Bristol: The Policy Press.

Skifter Andersen, H., Munk, A. and Hansen, K.E. (1992), 'Boligpolitik, byfornyelse og socialt boligbyggeri i Tyskland' ('Housing Policy, Urban Renewal and Social Housing in Germany'), Danish Building Research Institute.

Skogan, W.G. (1990), *Disorder and Decline. Crime and the Spiral of Decay in American Neighbourhoods*, Berkeley: University of California Press.

Smith, N. (1991), 'On Gaps in our Knowledge of Gentrification', in van Weesep, J. and Musterd, S. (eds), *Urban Housing for the Better-off: Gentrification in Europe*, Utrecht: University of Utrecht.

Smith, N. and Williams, P. (eds.) (1986), *Gentrification of the City*, Boston: Allen and Unwin.

Smith, N. et al. (1989), 'From Disinvestment to Reinvestment – Tax Arrears and Turning Points in the East Village', *Housing Studies*, Vol. 4, pp. 238–52.

Social Exclusion Unit (1998), *Neighbourhood Renewal*, London: Cabinet Office.

Soja, E. (1980), 'The Socio-spatial Dialectic', *Annals, Association of American Geographers*, Vol. 70, pp. 207–25.

Sommerville, Peter (1998), 'Explanations of Social Exclusion: Where does Housing Fit in?', *Housing Studies*, Vol. 13, No. 6, pp. 761–80.

Stegmann, M.A. (1972), *Housing Investments in the Inner City: The Dynamics of Decay*, Cambridge, MA: MIT Press.

Sternlieb, G. (1969), *The Tenement Landlord*, New Brunswick: Centre for Urban Policy Research, Rutgers University.

Sternlieb, G. (1974), *The Realities of Rent Control in the Greater Boston Area*, New Brunswick: Centre for Urban Policy Research, Rutgers University.

Sternlieb, G. and Burchell, R.W. (1973), *Residential Abandonment: The Tenement Landlord Revisited*, New Brunswick: Center for Urban Policy Research, Rutgers University.

Stokes, C.J. and Fischer, R. (1976), *Housing Performance in the US*, New York: Praeger.

Taueber, K.E. and Taueber, A. (1964), 'The Negro as an Immigrant Group', *American Journal of Sociology*, Vol. 69, pp. 374–82.

Taylor, M. (1998), 'Combating the Social Exclusion of Housing Estates', *Housing Studies*, Vol. 13, No. 6, pp. 819–32.

Turner, M. (1990), *Housing Market Impacts of Rent Control*, Washington DC: The Urban Institute.

van der Heijden, H. and Boelhouwer, P. (1996), 'The Private Rental Sector in Western Europe: Development since the Second World War and Prospects for the Future', *Housing Studies*, Vol. 11, pp. 13–34.

van Kempen, E. (1994), 'The Dual City and the Poor: Social Polarisation, Social Segregation and Life Chances', *Urban Studies*, Vol. 31, No. 7, pp. 995–1015.

van Kempen, R. and Özükren, A.S. (1998), 'Ethnic Segregation in Cities', *Urban Studies*, Vol. 35, No. 10, pp. 1631–56.

van Kempen R. and Priemus, H. (1999), 'Undivided Cities in the Netherlands: Present Situation and Political Rhetoric', *Housing Studies*, Vol. 14, No. 5, pp. 641–57.

Varming, M. (1999), 'Virkninger af byudvalgets renovering af bygninger og friarealer' ('Effects of Renovation of Buildings and Open Spaces made by the Urban Committee'), SBI-report 323. Danish Building Research Institute.

Vestergaard, H. (1998), 'Troubled Housing Estates in Denmark' in Madanipour, A., Cars, G. and Allen, J. (eds), *Social Exclusion in European Cities, Regional Policy and Development 23*, London: Jessica Kingsley Publishers.

Vestergaard, H. et al. (1997), 'De otte modelområder' ('Evaluation of Eight Model Areas'), SBI-report 288. Danish Building Research Institute.

Vestergaard, H. et al. (1999), 'Byudvalgets boligsociale aktiviteter' ('The Social Initiatives made by the Urban Committee'), SBI-report 311, Danish Building Research Institute.

Wacquant, L. (1993), 'Urban Outcasts: Stigma and Division in the Black American Ghetto and the French urban Periphery', *International Journal of Urban and Regional Research*, Vol. 17, pp. 366–83.

Wacquant, L. (1996), 'The Rise of Advanced Marginality: Notes on its Nature and Implications', *Acta Sociologica*, Vol. 39, No. 2, pp. 121–39.

Wacquant, L. (1997), *Urban Marginality in the Coming Millennium*, Berkeley: University of California Department of Sociology.

Weesep, J. and Musterd, S. (eds) (1991), *Urban Housing for the Better-off: Gentrification in Europe*, Utrecht: University of Utrecht.

Wheaton, W.C. (1977), 'Income and Urban Residence. An Analysis of Consumer Demand for Location', *American Economic Review*, Vol. 67, pp. 630–51.

Wheaton, W.C. (1978), 'Urban Spatial Development with Durable but Replaceable Capital', *Journal of Urban Economics*, Vol. 12, No. 1, pp. 53–67.

Whitehead, M.E. (1996), 'Private Renting in the 1990s', *Housing Studies*, Vol. 11, pp. 7–12.

Wilson, W.J. (1987), *The Truly Disadvantaged. The Inner City, the Underclass, and Public Policy*, Chicago: The University of Chicago Press.

Yates, J. (1996), 'Towards a Reassessment of the Private Rental Market', *Housing Studies*, Vol. 11, pp. 35–50.

Index

area-based initiatives
  categories 158
  and job creation 160
  lessons 159, 160, 181–3
  objectives 181
  and segregation 159
  and 'social exclusion' 158–9
  strategies 10, 158–9, 181–2
  time dependency 160–61
  UK 157–8, 159, 160
  urban renewal 6, 10–12
  see also urban renewal
Australia, landlords 74
Austria
  social housing 21
  urban renewal 136

bathrooms, dwellings without 50, 155
Bourdieu, Pierre 15
buildings, deterioration 4

cities
  segregation, emergence 17
  social structure, models 14–15
City Challenge Programme, UK 159
Copenhagen
  demography 24
  growth 24
  housing market 36–7
  housing policies, local authorities 36–8
  immigrants
    definition 33
    social housing 33, 42–3
  marginalised groups 29, 31–2, 39–42
  segregation 2–3
    demographic 24, 25–8
    and housing location 38–45
    immigrants 33–4, 42–5
    income-based 28–9, 30
    and the labour market 29, 31–3
    processes 23–5
  service professionals 33
  social geography 44
  social housing 20–21, 24–5, 40
    immigrants 33, 42–3
  see also Denmark
crime, and neighbourhood decay 104–5

Danish Building Research Institute 25, 142, 164
Danish Building and Urban Research 107
Danish Institute of Social Research 164
demography
  and segregation 18–19
  Copenhagen 24, 25–8
Denmark
  ethnic minorities, integration 115–17
  housing deterioration 99–107, 141–2
  housing maintenance 57, 58, 77, 85–6
  housing market 34–5, 112
  housing policies 20–21
    and the housing market 34–5
    local authorities 35–6
  housing rehabilitation
    evaluation 164–80
    programmes 161–4
  incomes, Gini coefficient 28, 161
  landlords 75–96
  problem estates 100–101
  rent control 76–7
    and housing renewal 77
  rental market 75–6
  segregation 6, 15
    and housing policies 24
    reduction 180
  Slum Clearance Act 143
  social housing
    allocation 21
    decay processes 99–124, 157
    and local authorities 35–6
    programme 11–12
  Urban Committee 164
  urban decay 53
    area-based initiatives 11–12
  urban renewal

strategy 136–9, 156
  study 142–56
    lessons 154–6
  Urban Renewal Act 142, 143, 154
  see also Copenhagen
deprivation
  interior processes 101–7
  and mobility 118–19, 120, 168
  model, elements 108–10
  and newcomers 119, 121–2
  and social problems 114–15, 167
  study
    data 110–12
    results 123–4
    statistical methods 112
    variables 112–14
  see also housing deterioration
dwellings
  vacant, and urban decay 168
  value of 61–2
  without bathrooms 50, 155

economic theory
  and landlords' behaviour 72–3
  and segregation 18
employment, and gentrification 66
England
  'Housing Plus' programme 160
  landlords 74
  social housing 53
  urban decay 53
English House Condition Survey 53
estates, problem, Denmark 100–101
ethnic minorities
  Denmark, integration 115–17
  see also immigrants
Europe
  discrimination, housing market 21
    housing policies 21
  housing rehabilitation
    programmes 157–61
    variation 136–9
  neighbourhood decay 104
  segregation 15
  slums
    clearance 9, 132
    research 5
  social geography 19

social housing 47, 68
urban decay 5
  area-based initiatives 10–11
  extent 53
  interventions 68–70
  problems 50–53
  public policies 9, 48–9
  urban renewal, policies 130–9

family life cycle, and mobility 143–5
Finland, segregation 6
France, urban renewal 137, 139

gentrification
  advantages 140, 155
  disadvantages 140, 155
  and employment changes 66
  and expectations 66
  housing rehabilitation 140, 152–4
  meaning 65
  process 65, 66
  research 5
  and segregation 140
  USA 5, 65–7
Germany
  landlords 74
  urban renewal 138, 139
ghettos 14, 15
Gini coefficient, incomes, Denmark 28, 161
globalisation, and urban decay 5, 6
growth, economic and urban decay 7

housing deterioration
  Denmark 99–107, 141–2
  economic explanations 56–61
  and the housing market 55
  and landlords 71–5
  and maintenance costs 56–8, 72–3, 77
  and rent control 49, 71–5
  socioeconomic reasons 57–61
  USA 55–61
  'vicious circles' 7, 98–9, 112–13
  see also deprivation
housing market
  Copenhagen 36–7
  Denmark 34–5, 112
    segmentation 19, 35
  Europe, discrimination 21

and housing deterioration 55
and local authorities 35–8
and rent control 55
USA, discrimination 21
'Housing Plus' programme, England 160
housing policies
  Copenhagen 36–8
  Denmark 20–21, 24, 35–8
  Europe, discrimination 21
  and segregation 19–21, 24–5
  USA, discrimination 21
  see also social housing
housing rehabilitation
  Denmark
    barriers to 91–3
    evaluation 164–80
    expenditure 162
    investment 86–7
    landlords 86–93
    ministries involved 162
    programmes 161–4
    and rent control 77, 165
    segregation 163
    strategies 162–4
      evaluation 170–80
  Europe
    programmes 157–61
    variation 136–9
  and gentrification 140, 152–4
  programmes, efficacy 156–7
  social renewal 140
  see also gentrification

image
  improvement, reasons 179–80
  and neighbourhood decay 5, 53, 105–6, 111, 117–18, 126, 167–8
immigrants
  Copenhagen
    definition 33
    segregation 33–4, 42–5
    social housing 33, 42–3
    and social problems 111, 114, 167, 173
  USA 14–15
  see also ethnic minorities
incomes
  Denmark, Gini coefficient 28, 161

differentiation, and urban decay 48
distribution, USA 47
  and segregation, Copenhagen 28–9, 30
investment, housing rehabilitation 86–7

job creation, and area-based initiatives 160

land use, and local authorities 20
landlords
  Australia 74
  characteristics 74, 75
  Denmark 75–96
    definitions 84
    and housing rehabilitation 86–93
    motives 78–9, 94–6
    private lettings 75–6
    rent control 76–7
    types 79–85
  and economic theory 72–3
  England 74
  Germany 74
  and housing deterioration 71–5
  Sweden 74
  see also rent control
life cycle theory, neighbourhoods 5
lifestyles, and segregation 15
local authorities
  and the housing market 35–8
  and land use 20
  and urban renewal 135

maintenance costs
  housing, Denmark 57, 58, 77, 85–6
  and housing deterioration 56–8, 72–3, 77
  life cycle 57–8
marginalisation, meaning 16
marginalised groups, Copenhagen 29, 31–2, 39–42
mobility
  causes 174–5
  and deprivation 118–19, 120, 168
  and family life cycle 143–5
  and rent control 173, 176–8
  and segregation 18–19
  and urban renewal 146–51

neighbourhoods
  attachment to 19

decay
  and crime 104–105
  Europe 104
  and expectations 64, 68
  and image 5, 53, 105–106, 111, 117–18, 126, 167–8
  and insecurity 105
  Portugal 104
  processes 62–5, 101–107, 128–9
  and resident involvement 106
  school problems 106–7
  and segregation 68, 125–9
  and services reduction 107
  and social activities 113–14
  and social cohesion 106
  and social conflict 103
  Sweden 103
  USA 62–5, 101–102
  and visible quality 102, 114
  life cycle theory 5
  renewal 65–7
  see also urban decay
Netherlands, urban renewal 137
newcomers, and deprivation 119, 121–2
Norway, urban renewal 137, 139

people, and space 3, 22, 23
planning, and segregation 20
Portugal, neighbourhood decay 104
private lettings 75–6
privatisation, UK 71

race relations, and segregation 15
rent control
  Denmark 76–7
  and housing deterioration 49, 71–5
  and the housing market 55
  and housing rehabilitation 77, 165
  and mobility 173, 176–8
  and segregation 68–9
  see also landlords
rental market, Denmark 75–6
research
  slums, Europe 5
  urban decay 1–2

school problems, and neighbourhood decay 106–7

segmentation, housing market, Denmark 19, 35
segregation
  and area-based initiatives 159
  causes 126–8
  cities, emergence 17
  Copenhagen 2–3
    demographic 24, 25–8
    and housing location 38–45
    immigrants 33–4, 42–5
    income-based 28–9, 30
    and the labour market 29, 31–3
    processes 23–5
  demographic theories 18–19
  Denmark 6, 15
    housing policies 24
    housing rehabilitation 163
    reduction 180
  dimensions 22–3
  ecological theories 17–18
  economic theories 18
  Europe 15
  Finland 6
  and gentrification 140
  and housing policies 19–21
  influences 3, 11
  and lifestyles 15
  meaning 2, 13
  and mobility 18–19
  and neighbourhood decay 68, 125–9
  and planning 20
  and race relations 15
  and rent control 68–9
  and social differentiation 14–16
  and social housing 19
  studies 2, 14–16
  Sweden, emergence 17
  and urban decay 3, 7, 49
  USA 15
services reduction, and neighbourhood decay 107
Slum Clearance Act, Denmark 143
slums
  Europe
    clearance 9, 132
    research 5
  USA, growth 7, 46–7
  see also deprivation; urban decay

social activities
  increase 171
  and neighbourhood decay 113–14
social cohesion, and neighbourhood decay 106
social conflict, and neighbourhood decay 103
social consequences, urban renewal 9–10
social differentiation, and segregation 14–16
'social exclusion'
  and area-based initiatives 158–9
  meaning 16
Social Exclusion Unit, UK 159
social geography
  Copenhagen 44
  European cities 19
social groups, and urban renewal 151–2, 155
social housing
  Austria 21
  Copenhagen 20–21, 24–5, 40
    immigrants 33, 42–3
  Denmark 53
    allocation 21, 35–6
    decay processes 99–124, 157
    programme 11–12
  England 53
  Europe 47, 68
  problems 49
  and segregation 19
  USA 47
social problems
  and deprivation 114–15, 167
  and immigrants 111, 114, 167, 173
  reduction 172
  and urban decay 8, 109
social renewal, housing rehabilitation 140
social spatial segregation see segregation
space, and people 3, 22, 23
statistical methods, deprivation study 112
Sweden
  landlords 74
  neighbourhood decay 103
  segregation, emergence 17
  urban renewal 136
Switzerland, urban renewal 138, 139

UK
  area-based initiatives 157–8
  City Challenge Programme 159
  privatisation 71
  Social Exclusion Unit 159
  urban renewal 137, 139
  see also England
'underclass', meaning 16
Urban Committee, Denmark 164
urban decay
  Denmark 53
    area-based initiatives 11–12
    and economic growth 7
  emergence 1
  England 53
  Europe 5
    area-based initiatives 10–11
    extent 53
    interventions 68–70
    problems 50–3
    and public policies 9, 48–9
  Europe/USA, compared 7
  factors 2, 3–4, 7–8, 48, 132
  and globalisation 5, 6
  and income differentiation 48
  research 1–2
  and segregation 3, 7, 49
  and social problems 8, 109
  USA
    factors 4–5, 67–8
    increase 47–8
    processes 62–5
    and public policies 8–9
  and vacant dwellings 168
  variation 7, 131–2
  see also deprivation; housing deterioration; neighbourhoods, decay; slums
urban renewal
  area-based initiatives 6, 10–12
  Austria 136
  Denmark
    lessons 154–6
    social objectives 141–2
    study 142–56
  Europe
    policies 130–39
      successful 9
      variation 131–2, 133–6
    strategies 136–9, 156

France 137, 139
Germany 138, 139
and local authorities 135
meaning 131
and mobility 146–51
Netherlands 137
Norway 137, 139
objectives 10, 140
social consequences 9–10
and social groups 151–2, 155
Sweden 136
Switzerland 138, 139
UK 137, 139
USA, processes 65–7
see also gentrification; housing rehabilitation
Urban Renewal Act, Denmark 141, 142, 143, 154, 155

USA
discrimination, housing market 21
housing policies 21
gentrification 5, 65–7
housing deterioration 55–61
immigrants 14–15
income distribution 47
neighbourhood decay 101–102
processes 62–5
segregation, and race relations 15
slums, growth 7, 46–7
social housing 47
urban decay
factors 4–5, 67–8
increase 47–8
public policies 8–9
urban renewal, processes 65–7

'vicious circles', housing deterioration 7, 98–9, 112–13